Knowledge, Higher Education, and the New Managerialism

Knowledge, Higher Education, and the New Managerialism

The Changing Management of UK Universities

Rosemary Deem, Sam Hillyard, and Mike Reed

OXFORD
UNIVERSITY PRESS

OXFORD

UNIVERSITY PRESS

Great Clarendon Street, Oxford OX2 6DP

Oxford University Press is a department of the University of Oxford.
It furthers the University's objective of excellence in research, scholarship,
and education by publishing worldwide in

Oxford New York

Auckland Cape Town Dar es Salaam Hong Kong Karachi
Kuala Lumpur Madrid Melbourne Mexico City Nairobi
New Delhi Shanghai Taipei Toronto

With offices in

Argentina Austria Brazil Chile Czech Republic France Greece
Guatemala Hungary Italy Japan Poland Portugal Singapore
South Korea Switzerland Thailand Turkey Ukraine Vietnam

Oxford is a registered trademark of Oxford University Press
in the UK and in certain other countries

Published in the United States
by Oxford University Press Inc., New York

British Library Cataloguing in Publication Data

Data available

Library of Congress Cataloging in Publication Data

Deem, Rosemary.
    Knowledge, higher education, and the new managerialism: the changing
management of UK universities/Rosemary Deem, Sam Hillyard, and Mike Reed.
        p. cm.
    Includes bibliographical references and index.
    ISBN 978–0–19–926590–9 (alk. paper)
1. Education, Higher–Great Britain–Administration.   2. Universities and
colleges–Great Britain–Administration.   I. Hillyard, Sam.   II. Reed, Mike.   III. Title.
    LB2341.8.G7D44   2007
    378.1'010941–dc22   2007013669

Typeset by SPI Publisher Services, Pondicherry, India
Printed in Great Britain
on acid-free paper by
Biddles Ltd., King's Lynn, Norfolk

ISBN 978–0–19–926590–9 (Hbk.)
      978–0–19–926591–6 (Pbk.)

1 3 5 7 9 10 8 6 4 2

Preface

This book explores some of the main findings of a piece of research funded by the UK Economic and Social Research Council (award 00 23 7661) that the authors, Rachel Johnson, Oliver Fulton, and Stephen Watson conducted at Lancaster University from 1998 to 2000, on the theme of New Managerialism and the management of UK universities. Our main focus in that research, although academics, career administrators and other university employees were also part of our investigations, centred on the accounts of practice, values, and career development provided by those whom we term manager-academics, that is, academics who, whether temporarily or permanently, have taken on managerial and leadership roles in their university. Although some features of the UK higher education system and higher education policy directions have changed since the study's conclusion in 2000, we believe (and this is borne out by other evidence) that the processes, technologies, and narratives involved in running universities as organizations and the perceptions, motivations, and practices of those engaged in managing UK universities have not substantially changed in the intervening period. In any case, we also place the ESRC research in a broader theoretical and empirical setting, focusing on a conceptual understanding of recent changes to the ways in which public services are managed in Western societies and have grounded this in an analysis of the organizational forms, processes, technologies, narratives, learning, identities, practices, values, and cultures involved in the management of academic knowledge work in publicly funded universities more generally.

Acknowledgements

We should particularly like to thank the other members of our 1998–2000 ESRC project at Lancaster University, namely Oliver Fulton, Rachel Johnson, and Stephen Watson, for all their work on the project and on publications associated with it and also Heidi Edmundson, our project administrator, for her role in organizing the fieldwork and overseeing much of the transcription. We are most grateful to the assorted learned societies and the sixteen UK universities that allowed us access for the purposes of carrying out the research on which this book is based. Thanks should also go to the many conference audiences to whom we have presented papers, particularly at conferences of the Society for Research into Higher Education, the Higher Education Network of the European Educational Research Association, the Consortium of Higher Education Researchers, and the British Sociological Association. We are also indebted to a number of our academic colleagues and friends, notably Lisa Lucas (Bristol), Louise Morley (Sussex), Barbara Zamorksi (East Anglia), Gareth Parry (Sheffield), Jenny Ozga (Edinburgh), Sue Clegg (Leeds Metropolitan), Harry de Boer (Twente), Jurgen Enders (Twente), Liudvika Leisyte (Twente), Heather Eggins (former Director, SRHE), Debbie Epstein (Cardiff), Rebecca Boden (UWIC), Jonathan Morris (Cardiff), Bob Burgess (Leicester), Mike Wallace (Cardiff), Kevin Brehony (Roehampton), Anwar Tlili (Kings College, London), Nick Abercrombie (formerly Lancaster), John Dearlove (Sussex), Paul Trowler (Lancaster), and Henry Miller (Aston), with all of whom we have at times shared ideas about the management and organization of universities. Chapter 2: 'The changing context of university knowledge work: from the 1960s to the twenty-first century' is an updated and adapted version of a previously published article, namely Deem, R. (2004). 'The Knowledge Worker, the Manager-Academic and the Contemporary UK University: New and Old Forms of Public Management'. *Financial Accountability and Management*,

20(2 May): 107–28 and appears by permission of the copyright holders, Blackwells. Chapter 3: 'The knowledge worker in the divided university' is based on an inaugural lecture given by Rosemary Deem at the University of Bristol in October 2001.

Contents

Notes on the Authors

Rosemary Deem is Professor of Education at the University of Bristol where she has worked since 2001. She was Social Sciences and Law Graduate Dean and Joint Education Director from 2004 to 2006 and is currently Director of Research for the Faculty of Social Sciences and Law. She is a sociologist who has also worked at Loughborough, York, the Open and Lancaster Universities, and at the former North Staffordshire Polytechnic. Her academic work spans inequalities and educational organizations; education and public policy; lifestyles, physical activity, and leisure; qualitative methods; educational governance and management, and organizational cultures. She has been a Head of Department, Dean of Social Sciences and University Graduate School Director, a governor of several primary and secondary schools (including Chair of Governors at Stantonbury Campus, Milton Keynes, from 1981 to 1990) and a Senate-elected member of University Council at both Lancaster and Bristol Universities. She was Principal Investigator for the Economic and Social Research Council funded project 'New Managerialism and the Management of UK Universities' (1998–2000) on which this book is based. She was also director of the UK Learning and Teaching Support Network Education Subject Centre, ESCalate, from 2001 to 2004. She has been an Education Research Assessment panellist in the 1996, 2001, and 2008 UK Research Assessment Exercises and was on the Economic and Social Research Council Grants Board from 1999 to 2003 and is a former Chair of the British Sociological Association. She was joint editor of the Blackwell's international journal *The Sociological Review* 2001–5, chaired the Publications Committee of the Society for Research into Higher Education and is on the Editorial Board of *Studies in Higher Education*, *Higher Education Quarterly*, and *Equal Opportunities International*. She is currently co-directing, with Mike Wallace (Principal Investigator), Mike Reed (co-director), and Jonathan Morris (co-director), an ESRC funded project on change agents and leadership development in UK public services, including hospital and primary health care trusts, secondary schools, and higher education. Rosemary is principally responsible for chapters 2, 3, and 6.

Sam Hillyard did her Ph.D. at the University of Warwick and then worked as a Research Associate on the Economic and Social Research Council funded project 'New Managerialism and the Management of UK Universities' at Lancaster University from 1999 to 2000. She moved onto a Lectureship in Sociology at the University of Keele (2000–1) and was a Lecturer in Sociology at the University of Nottingham in the Institute for the Study of Genetics, Bio-risks and Society (IGBiS) from 2001 to 2006. She is currently Senior Lecturer in Research Methods at the University of Durham. Her research interests include theorizing through ethnographic research, sociology of education, the management of higher education, the public understanding of science and rural sociology. Sam is principally responsible for chapters 4 and 5.

Mike Reed is Professor of Organizational Analysis and Associate Dean (Research) at Cardiff Business School, Cardiff University. Previously, he was Professor of Organization Theory, Head of Department and Associate Dean for Research at Lancaster University Management School. He was a member of the Economic and Social Research Council funded project 'New Managerialism and the Management of UK Universities' (1998–2000) on which this book is based. Currently, he is a Council Member of the British Academy of Management, and has responsibility for ensuring effective liaison with the Research Assessment Exercise (RAE) Business and Management sub-panel in the run-up to RAE 2008. He is a founding editor of the journal, *Organization*, and has published extensively in leading journals such as *Organization Studies* and *Journal of Management Studies*. He has conducted empirical research in a range of public service organizations, including the National Health Service and Higher Education, focusing on new forms of expert management and control. He is also a member of the American Academy of Management, the British Sociological Association, and the British Universities Industrial Relations Association. Mike's research interests focus around the new forms of organizing and organization that are emerging in the 'knowledge-based economy' and their implications for the management and control of 'expert labour'. He has a particular interest in the longer-term impact of 'New Managerialism' and New Public Management on the organization and management of public service provision in the UK. He has also played a significant role in the further development of a 'critical realist' perspective on the study of power/control relations and discourses in contemporary organizations and their management systems. Mike is principally responsible for chapter 1.

Rachel Johnson, who contributed to Chapter 5, did her Ph.D. at the Universities of Sheffield and Sheffield Hallam. She was senior Research Associate on the Economic and Social Research Council funded project 'New Managerialism and the Management of UK Universities' at Lancaster University from 1998 to 2000 and then worked as an academic and as a research methods trainer at the Universities of Nottingham and Leicester and also as a field officer for the National Youth Bureau. She is currently pursuing interests outside of academe.

1

New Managerialism and Public Services Reform: From Regulated Autonomy to Institutionalized Distrust

Introduction

New Managerialism (NM) has dominated the academic and policy agendas for public services reform in the UK and other Anglo-American political economies and welfare systems over the last two decades (Hood 1995, 1998; Ferlie et al. 1996; Clarke and Newman 1997; Clarke, Gewirtz, and McLaughlin 2000; Pollitt and Bouckaert 2000; Newman 2001; McLaughlin, Osborne, and Ferlie 2002; Ferlie, Hartley, and Martin 2003; Deem and Brehony 2005). It has generated and sustained a powerful ideological and discursive context within which its more technical and less ideological conceptual relative (Deem and Brehony 2005), New Public Management (NPM), has also flourished as a policy paradigm and control technology. These two 'loosely coupled' innovations in policy discourse and organizational practice have been focused on the detailed restructuring of public services delivery, organization, and management in a way that facilitates a flexible, and changing balance, between 'strategic control' and 'operational control' (Farnham and Horton 1993; Kean and Scase 1998; Exworthy and Halford 1999; Flynn 1999; Farrell and Morris 2003). Higher education institutions in the UK are not constitutionally part of the 'public sector' and enjoy a relatively high degree of strategic and operational autonomy in comparison to, for example, schools and hospitals. But the developmental trajectories and organizational 're-imagining and reshaping' of UK universities over the last two decades or so have been fundamentally directed by the ideological context and organizational strategy set down by NM and NPM, respectively (Reed 2002, 2002a; Reed and Deem 2002; Deem and Brehony 2005). Although formally retaining a significant degree of institutional, managerial, and organizational autonomy in the arena of knowledge work over this period of radical reform, UK universities have discovered that they have become subjects of and targets for the 'audit culture' and related 'transparency regimes' that have come to dominate most aspects of public life and provision in the UK and notably in England (Power 1997; Trowler 1998b; Pollitt 1999; Strathern 2000; Miller 2003; Shattock 2003; Palfreyman and Warner 2004). Universities may still be 'houses of knowledge' (Calás and Smircich 2001) or where they are not merely teaching-only institutions, prototypical 'knowledge-intensive organizations' in which highly specialized experts must be allowed, indeed encouraged, to take risks and to critique existing forms of knowledge if they are to make their proper contribution to intellectual and social innovation (Fuller 2002; Alvesson 2004). But the organizational reality of everyday university life seems to suggest that for many, if not most, academics there has been a fundamental loss of control—over work organization and professional culture—as NM and NPM have transformed universities from 'communities of scholars' into 'workplaces' (Smith and Webster 1997; Deem and Johnson 2000; Trowler 2001; Reed 2002a). Thus, the longer-term implications of NM and NPM for the organizational restructuring and cultural re-engineering of the academic profession within the UK over the coming decade are likely to be profound. They are also likely to generate all sorts of unintended consequences that are only vaguely perceived at the present time (Parker and Jary 1994; Rustin 1994; Prichard and Wilmott 1997; Edwards 1998; Henkel 2000).

This opening chapter has a number of interrelated purposes. First, to provide a general theoretical orientation and framework within which the substantive exposition and analysis of changes in UK higher education at the institutional, organizational and individual academic and manager-academic level can be developed. Second, to provide an analytical narrative about the emergence and subsequent development of 'New Managerialism', in its various forms, as it has influenced the redefinition and restructuring of public service provision and organization. Third, to review the discursive strategies and control technologies embodied in different formulations of NM and NPM as they have achieved enhanced visibility and increased penetration across UK public services in general and higher education in particular. Fourth, to identify and assess the endemic contradictions, tensions, and conflicts within and between these discursive strategies and control technologies, as well as their broader implications for longer-term institutional change and organizational innovation. Fifth, to provide an initial interpretation of the process of 'hybridization' (Ferlie et al. 1996) in public services domains and organizationals and its wider significance for the development of universities as 'knowledge-intensive organizations'.

General Theoretical Orientation/Framework

This chapter draws on a number of analytical perspectives to provide the conceptual raw materials for our general theoretical approach and framework. In particular, neo-institutional/archetype theory and critical realism/morphogenetic theory—as they have been developed and deployed in the study of changing professional and managerial work organization(s) in both the private and public sectors (Newman 2001, 2002; Ferlie, Hartley, and Martin 2003; Kirkpatrick and Ackroyd 2003)— will provide the major sources of conceptual input for the development of our theoretical approach. Selected elements of both of these general analytical schemes will be synthesized to provide an analysis of the complex interplay between the institutional pressures and organizational logics that have informed the redefinition and restructuring of public services, including higher education, in the UK over the last three decades or so.

Neo-institutionalism/archetype theory (Edwards 1998; Dimaggio 2001; Ferlie and Fitzgerald 2002; Kirkpatrick and Ackroyd 2003; Deem and Brehony 2005) focuses on the changing cultural forms and discursive strategies that have played a central role in reshaping our understanding of 'public services' and the most appropriate institutional modes and organizational means for their delivery since the 1970s. Critical realism/morphogenetic theory (Fairclough, Jessop, and Sayer 2002; Kirkpatrick and Ackroyd 2003; Reed 2004, 2005) is more concerned with the material, structural, and political imperatives that have framed the conditions under and within which public services reform has been initiated by successive UK governments during this period. Our analysis will suggest that we can only begin to understand, much less explain, the recent history of public services reform in the UK, if we examine the complex interplay between structural change and collective or corporate agency as it redefines the 'reform agenda' and the new organizational forms most appropriate to its potential realization.

Neo-institutionalism/archetype theory suggests that NM and NPM are most usefully conceptualized as two separate but linked components of a cultural-cum-policy paradigm that provides the overarching ideological framework and more detailed control technology within and through which public services can be reformed and restructured in ways that conform to the underlying normative principles and operational logic that such a paradigm specifies. Thus, the neo-institutional/archetype approach maintains that organizations are highly constrained by the institutional environments and operational fields in which they are embedded and located, such that they tend towards the adoption and retention of very similar forms and practices. Institutional isomorphism—that is the irresistible cultural pressure generated by the dominant cultural values, policy priorities, and structural designs that hold sway over defined historical periods within a particular institutional domains or fields—forces individual organizations to conform to whatever a prevailing archetype demands. Thus, 'organizational archetypes' are reasonably well-integrated and relatively coherent and stable 'deep patterns or structures' that fundamentally define and shape formal structures, decision-making systems and, most crucially, underlying interpretive schemes configured around core values and ideology (Hinings and Greenwood 1988). Institutional reform and organizational change are only likely to occur to any significant scale or degree when a transformation in underlying core ideological commitments and cultural values generates system-wide, and self-reinforcing, transitions in administrative forms and decision-making processes. First and foremost, then, NM and NPM can be understood as entailing a fundamental shift in the underlying cultural values and discursive forms through which 'public services' are conceptualized, represented, and legitimated. The NM and NPM paradigm entails a veritable 'cultural revolution' that initiates a chain of interlocking transitions in the discursive strategies, organizational forms, and control technologies that cumulatively transform the institutional terrain on which 'public services' are defined and justified. In this respect, NM and NPM have played a pivotal role in redefining the nature and legitimacy of certain forms of public services provision and organization at the expense of others. More specifically, it has narrowed the focus and scope of the 'public domain' by justifying the much more extensive use of market-based resource allocation mechanisms and the managerial control regimes that they require to operate effectively within institutional environments in which 'competition', rather than 'collaboration', has become the dominant cultural imperative.

Critical realism/morphogenetic theory accepts much of the analysis that institutional/archetype theory advances. But the former suggests that the transformation of public services organizations that NM and NPM have legitimated and facilitated over the last two decades or so must be explained in terms of the changing material conditions and structural constraints that have radically reshaped Anglo-American welfare state systems during this period (Clarke and Newman 1997; Newman 2001; Jessop 2002; Reed 2002; Farrell and Morris 2003; Deem and Brehony 2005). In particular, the rise of the 'managerial state' and the development and implementation of much more sophisticated 'control-at-a-distance' technologies have facilitated the emergence of forms of 'regulated autonomy' (Hoggett 1996) or 'soft bureaucracy' (Courpasson 2000) that could be only a veritable 'gleam in the eye' for older generations of political and managerial elites. In turn, the historical rise and institutional embedding of the 'managerial state' have to be viewed in the historical and economic context of an intensifying fiscal crisis for Anglo-American welfare states. The latter have struggled, certainly since the early 1970s, to come to terms with the destabilizing impact of economic globalization and financial deregulation, as well as their deleterious consequences for the management and control of public sector spending (Jessop 2002; Harvey 2003). Thus, the steadily deteriorating economic position, cultural legitimacy, and political influence of public service organizations and professionals, under the new audit regimes and control technologies driven by NM and NPM, have to be set in a global ideological arena that is increasingly suspicious of, if not downright hostile to, the 'professional state' and the material and ideological support that it traditionally offered to the public realm (Flynn 2000; Marquand 2004b). Cost reduction, service rationalization, and organizational standardization are as important drivers for state-initiated reforms as are changing 'legitimacy needs' in a political context in which 'market populism' or 'consumer democracy' has become the ideological lodestone against which all new policy changes must be evaluated. Universities are by no means isolated from these underlying structural pressures and the ideological momentum that they generate. Both Thatcherite-style 'market-Managerialism' and Blairist-style 'modernizing-Managerialism' (Flynn 2000) have achieved discursive supremacy and, at least, a substantial degree of ideological legitimacy and organizational control within global and national power structures that have made neoliberal policy the dominant political reality for a generation.

Given this wider theoretical background, we intend to provide a more wide-ranging and inclusive analysis of the longer-term impact of NM and NPM on university organization and management than is usually the case. We will achieve this by analytically combining a neo-institutionalist focus on culturally driven policy and practice change with a neo-realist concern with the material conditions and structural context in which institutional reconfiguration is necessarily embedded. We will also look both at the organizational level and at individuals within institutions. In this way, we intend to avoid the cultural determinism that often underpins neo-institutional/archetype theory by emphasizing the dynamic structural contexts and forms of corporate agency through which institutional reproduction, elaboration, and transformation are achieved (Reed and Anthony 2003).

Varieties of Managerialism

'Managerialism' can be defined as a broad ideological movement that has been highly influential in all modern industrial societies since the late nineteenth/early twentieth century onwards (Enteman 1993; Grey 1999; Parker 2002). Broadly speaking, Managerialism insists that 'managing' and 'management' are, respectively, socio-technical practices and the collective agents and institutions responsible for their enactment that are universally required in a modern, economically and technologically advanced society. These practices, agents, and institutions stand above, indeed 'outside', the wider social, moral, and political struggles that conventionally defined the nature of the 'good life' and the means to its potential attainment. As such, Managerialism is a general ideology or belief system that regards managing and management as being functionally and technically indispensable to the achievement of economic progress, technological development, and social order within any modern political economy. Management is regarded as that generic activity, group, and institution that is necessarily, technically and socially, superior to any other conceivable form of social practice and organization such as craft, profession, or community. It provides the underlying abstract rationale and blueprint for an integrated set of ideas, practices, and mechanisms that can deliver the most efficient and effective forms of planning and organizing work irrespective of time, place, and value. Thus, any variant of Managerialism conceptualizes 'management' and 'managing' as an abstracted social institution and practice that is necessarily better than any other form of organizational governance; that is, as a universal mechanism for *rationally coordinating and controlling* collective action in a modern society (Townley 2002).

Three forms of Managerialism have dominated twentieth–twenty-first-century ideologies of economic and social reform in the UK and other Organization for Economic Co-operation and Development (OECD) countries. First, the gradual emergence of a *'corporatist' form of managerialism* from the First World War period onwards that reached its apogee in the 1960s and 1970s (Middlemass 1979; Williamson 1989; Jessop 2002; Thompson 2003). Neo-corporatist Managerialism was an, inherently unstable and uneasy blend of Keynesian economic policy, state welfarism, political pluralism, industrial tripartism, and Fordist-style management. It was geared to the generation and maintenance of a viable social settlement between the major contending producer/provider classes and interest groups in modern industrial society. This was to be realized through an often subtle blend of interest intermediation and conflict management at the strategic, intermediate, and local levels of collective action. 'Bureau-professionalism' or professional bureaucracy emerged as the dominant organizational form and structure through which this subtle—and sometimes, not-so-subtle—blend of compromise and coercion was to be institutionally and operationally sustained. While a price would have to be paid, in terms of relative market inefficiencies, technological rigidities, and organizational inflexibilities, for this political compromise and cultural trade-off between 'order' and 'progress' to work, most of the elite producer/provider corporate agencies within the UK state and British political economy and their subordinate agencies seemed content to pay that price.

However, from the late 1970s/early 1980s onwards neo-corporatist-style Managerialism began to experience escalating difficulties. It became increasingly difficult to sustain as a viable mode of institutional governance and form of organizational management as a complex interaction between endogenous (such as the breakdown of tripartism and the worsening 'fiscal crisis of the state') and exogenous changes (such as economic and cultural globalization) fundamentally undermined its ideological legitimacy and political cogency (Clarke 2004). Eventually, producer-led, corporatist-style Managerialism seemed to collapse or implode under the weight of its own contradictions and tensions as it struggled to come to terms with the economic, technological, political, and cultural challenges that new forms of international economic competition, cultural individualism, and populist consumerism presented. At the organizational level, the apogee of corporatist-style Managerialism was seen in rapidly escalating political elite disenchantment with, and distancing from, the professional bureaucracies that had dominated strategic policymaking, institutional administrative management and localized operational coordination and control in the UK since the early decades of the twentieth century (Middlemass 1979; Clarke and Newman 1997). The subsequent 'hollowing-out' or 'spatial and organizational dispersal' of the administrative agencies through which the neo-corporatist state had routinely done its business (at macro-, meso- and micro-levels of management)—and the deleterious implications of this radical restructuring for professional power and authority (Farrell and Morris 2003; Deem and Brehony 2005)—further eroded the structural integrity and cultural legitimacy of neo-corporatist Managerialism.

The era of corporatist-led modernization was framed by a service provider-driven ideology and a 'bureau-professionalism' form of governance in which the design, delivery, and development of public services was largely, if not exclusively, in 'the hands' of the professionals (Clarke and Newman 1997). The corporatist managerial state and the professional power structures through which it was served and sustained rested an ideology and practice of governance in which 'service users' were, at best, consulted about their needs and the most appropriate organizational mechanisms required to provide them (Dent and Whitehead 2002). They were not regarded, and did not regard themselves, as proactive agents in a joint process of service design, delivery, and development. The model of the 'service user' most appropriate to corporatist Managerialism was that of a relatively passive and ill-informed client who lacked the knowledge and expertise necessary to develop an informed judgement of what they needed and how they needed it to be provided. This 'knowledge or expertise gap' was to be filled by the professional and/or the manager working under the tight prescriptive guidelines that bureaucratic logic and protocol demanded.

A second form of managerialism, *Neoliberal Managerialism* emerged, from the late 1970s/early 1980s onwards, as a coruscating critique of the endemic weaknesses of neo-corporatist Managerialism. Essentially, it was anti-state/pro-market, anti-provider/pro-consumer, and anti-bureaucracy/pro-network in relation to its underlying ideological principles, allocative norms, and organizational logic. Taken as a loosely coupled political project and discursive strategy, neoliberal Managerialism combined these core ideological principles to generate a powerful cultural critique of corporatist Managerialism as being irrevocably flawed as a governance philosophy and irreparably compromised as a governmental practice. It also promulgated a form of 'market populism' in which free markets and private business enterprise were regarded as universal and infallible solutions to the governmental and organizational problems that continued to beset advanced capitalist societies (Korten 1995; Rose 1999; Frank 2000; Jacques 2002). It was only through the universal imposition of free market forces and private sector market discipline that the public sector would be placed in a position to break free from the power and control of professional 'producer/provider cartels' and sustain a dynamic of entrepreneurial-driven change and transformation. The imposition of market mechanisms and disciplines on the design, delivery, and management of public services would sustain the drive towards strategic effectiveness and operational efficiency so conspicuously lacking in the sclerotic professional monopolies and bloated corporate bureaucracies that continued to dominate public life (Osborne and Gaebler 1993; Du Gay 2000). By rigorously imposing market forces, business discipline, and managerial control across the full range of public sector service provision, neoliberal Managerialism's strategic intention was to weaken, if not destroy, the regulatory ethic and architecture that had protected unaccountable professional and administrative elites under the rule of neo-corporatist Managerialism (Freidson 1994, 2001).

Thus, neoliberal Managerialism provided the ideological underpinnings and strategic political rationale for NPM as it began to make its presence felt as a new policy paradigm or archetype from the mid-1980s onwards (Pollitt 1993; Pollitt, Birchall, and Putman 1998; Clarke, Gewirtz, and McLaughlin 2000; Newman 2001; McLaughlin, Osborne, and Ferlie 2002; Ferlie, Hartley, and Martin 2003). Of course, the 'on-the-ground' practical reform programme that emerged from neoliberal Managerialism/NPM fell significantly short of the 'revolution' in public services provision, organization, and management that its most ardent and committed ideological advocates had anticipated. As Foucault suggests (Foucault 1991), and many others have argued since (Reed 1995; Rose 1999) the practical conduct of government is a 'perpetually failing' activity that has achieved much less than its more grandiose ideologues and theorists consistently envisage. In practice, the implementation of the NM and NPM reform programme consisted of a series of minimally coordinated policy initiatives and organizational experiments—such as 'internal quasi-markets', 'quality management', 'devolved agencies', 'contracting out/competitive tendering', 'best value audits', 'beacon exemplars', 'self-managed trusts', and 'customer satisfaction surveys'—that oscillated between centralized strategic direction and devolved local control.

Nevertheless, neoliberal Managerialism/NPM provided the ideological vision and organizational mechanisms through which the political and administrative agenda for public services reform was radically transformed from the early 1980s onwards. This agenda was transformed in a way that directly challenged the established power structures and control relations that had emerged from the neo-corporatist Managerialism that had been the dominant form of societal, institutional, and organizational governance from the end of the Second World War. Consequently, this neoliberal challenge necessarily entailed a dismantling of the failed governmental and managerial structures that had politically directed and administratively steered economic, political, and social life in the UK since the early decades of the twentieth century—and with even greater force from the 1940s onwards. Over this extended historical period, advocates of neo-Managerialism insisted, the national economy and its core cultural underpinnings had all but been destroyed by an ideology of corporatist compromise and a practice of bureaucratic collectivism that had fundamentally weakened Britain's institutional capacity to compete effectively in an increasingly competitive and unforgiving global market.

Finally, a third form of managerialism, *neo-technocratic managerialism*, began to emerge. A number of commentators (Fergusson 2000; Newman 2001, 2002) have suggested that the coming to power of 'New Labour' in the late 1990s has produced another ideological shift and discursive realignment that moves the debate over public services provision and management away from some of the core elements of neoliberal Managerialism/NPM. Thus, the move towards 'neo-technocratic Managerialism' has begun to redefine the policy priorities, organizational forms, and managerial practices through which public services modernization and rationalization might be progressed. 'Personalization', 'customization', 'localization', 'co-production', and 'empowerment' are emerging as the new discursive genres or mantras through which the modernization of public services is to be discursively re-imagined and reconfigured as an exercise in collective learning and development through self-organization and management (Leadbeater 2004). The professional service provider and manager are still there, just about, but now very much as 'reflexive practitioners' operating in an advisory, technical, and counselling role rather than through a more directive and controlling modus operandi. The experts, or at least those who remain after successive waves of organizational downsizing and restructuring, are very definitely 'on tap' rather than 'on top'. Policy change and organizational experimentation are to be 'bottom-up driven'—that is, by the consumers of public services themselves rather than by over-weaning providers and managers—and legitimated as vital mechanisms directly contributing to effective community participation in service planning, design, and delivery. Professionals and managers are redefined as agents for delivering the aspirations and wishes of citizens and customers rather than as the, rather remote and abstract, 'experts' who previously defined the 'limits of the possible' and the organizational means to their realization (Horlick-Jones 2004). But this, still emergent and inherently unstable, discourse of modernization (Newman 2002) depends on complex power structures and intractable control relations that constrain and shape the struggle for legitimacy between 'policy elites', 'technical experts' and 'citizens/customers' at all levels of institutional and organizational governance (Fischer 2004). It is these endemic power and control struggles, crystallizing as much around mundane practical detail as around 'high policy' and its strategic implications, that will ultimately shape the trajectory of institutional change and determine the complex pattern of organizational outcomes that it generates.

Nevertheless, the New Labour 'Blairite spin' on NM introduces a much stronger technocratic orientation into the ideological and policy equation. By imposing market forces and business discipline right across the full range of public services provision, neoliberal Managerialism intended to weaken, if not destroy, the regulatory ethic and machinery that had protected unaccountable professional and administrative elites under the rule of neo-corporatist Managerialism (Freidson 1994, 2001). But the technocratic Managerialism that has come to define successive New Labour administrations since the late 1990s places rather greater faith in 'metrics' than it does in 'markets'. A series of more sophisticated and integrated performance measurement regimes have been progressively introduced with the aim of realizing the benefits of customer-driven competition between service providers without reproducing the extreme unit-level 'dysfunctionalities' and system-level 'perversities' resulting from unregulated market-based reforms. Thus, Blairite technocratic Managerialism has been much more concerned to enhance performance and accountability in public services delivery, while avoiding the extreme spatial and social inequalities in the scope and quality of service delivery that unregulated market competition inevitably generates over time and place (Walsh 1995; Thrift 2005). Underlying the various 'comparative metrics' that now drive the delivery, organization, management, and governance of public services providers in the UK—such as hospitals, schools, universities, local authorities, social service departments, housing associations, and libraries—is a 'modernizing' policy paradigm and agenda. The latter strives to integrate the rationality of strategic managerial direction and

11

localized managerial control with the reality of, national and international, competition within a globalized market for public service provision in health, education, and anything else you might care to think of as previously being largely the preserve of the UK 'public sector' (Llewellyn 2001; Llewellyn and Northcott 2002). This has led to a very definite blurring of the distinctions, never mind the boundaries, between 'public' and 'private' forms of service provision and the competing moral orders on which they depend for their legitimacy—what one might identify, following Weber, as a fundamental ideological contradiction between an 'ethic of civic responsibility' as opposed to an 'ethic of private accumulation'. It has also raised fundamental questions about the extent to which the wide-ranging expansion of market-based service provision necessarily entails a diminution, not to say terminal decline, of the scope, significance and status of the 'public domain' in UK social, economic, and political life (Marquand 2004b). In turn, this also seems to be an *ideological and structural precondition* for the organizational insertion of radically different modes of institutional governance and managerial control into public service provision that were previously regarded as alien to the 'professional society' (Perkin 1989).

New Control Technologies

Previous discussion has suggested that UK public services have been undergoing a prolonged 'institutional identity crisis' since the middle of the 1970s. Over this period, new managerialist ideology and NPM practice have generated a, loosely coupled but politically powerful, set of 'change discourses, programmes, and techniques' that have cumulatively challenged and progressively undermined the cultural foundations and institutional status quo on which the post-1945 consensus over the identity, role, and operation of the 'public sector' was constructed and reproduced. This underlying trajectory of macro-level ideological reinvention and cultural re-imaging has been reinforced by the fabrication and insertion of new meso-level and micro-level 'control technologies' that hold out the promise of innovative governance structures and delivery systems that will make the 'brave new world' of NM and NPM a practical organizational reality. These control technologies have begun to exert a pervasive influence over the everyday routines through which public service staff go about their business (and, increasingly, 'business' is the operative word in this context) and over the broader framework of institutionalized relations in which these practices are embedded and legitimated. The incremental organizational internalization of the 'audit culture' and the grudging acceptance of the monitoring systems and control technologies associated with it (Power 1997) by managerial, professional, and operational staff have radically called into question the established occupational and organizational identities that once defined 'public sector work' (Clarke, Gewirtz, and McLaughlin 2000; Dent and Whitehead 2002; McLaughlin, Osborne, and Ferlie 2002; Farrell and Morris 2003).

The subsequent reform programmes and policy initiatives generated by successive waves of new managerialist ideology (from the late 1970s/early 1980s onwards) were directed at producing multi-sector, multilevel, systemic transformational change (Ferlie et al. 1996) that would, given time, eradicate any residues of neo-corporatist theory and practice. They were intended to marginalize the producer-dominated bureau-professional ideology that had shaped public service provision and, eventually, to replace it with a customer-focused and performance-driven culture supporting a much 'leaner and fitter' organizational delivery system fully responsive to the threats and opportunities presented by revitalized market competition—for patients, students, passengers, tenants, clients, etc. (Pollitt 1993, 2003; Pollitt, Birchall, and Putman 1998). In addition, they were directed towards an overall strengthening of and tighter integration between strategic corporate control and forms of devolved autonomy encouraging more entrepreneurial and risk-taking behaviour on the part of local professional, managerial, and political elites acting as independent representatives of their respective communities' long-term collective interests. This simultaneous drive to focus centralized strategic development and to build localized managerial capacity was seen to demand much more 'flexible' and 'accountable' forms of service delivery combined with streamlined but robust forms of strategic steering and review (Hoggett 1996, 2005). At one level, policymaking and policy-implementation were to be more transparently and consistently separated through organizational and managerial reforms that simultaneously enhanced 'monitoring' and 'directing' capability at the centre, while encouraging more risk-taking, innovation, and diversity at the level of service delivery. However, the increased strategic complexity and intensified operational fragmentation that this series of reforms released, and their accompanying 'unstable oscillations' between a succession of conflicting policy prescriptions and organizational restructurings (Clarke and Newman 1997), generated a growing demand for the design and implementation of more detailed control technologies that would introduce some degree of coherence and continuity, if not stability, into the planning, organization, and management of service provision.

In broad terms, a 'control technology' consists of an interrelated set of plans, recipes, rules, and instruments for the governing of behaviour through the inculcation of certain 'understandings' of how the world is and how it should be worked on (Rose 1999). It provides a framework of governance mechanisms and practices through which the wider ideological vision and political drive generated by NM and NPM can be translated into flexible operational rules and practical techniques that can be adapted to the complex 'situational contingencies' faced by actors. Any control technology will carry within itself various 'dynamic tensions' (Newman 2001) that are likely to provide a source of continuous change and innovation in relation to the various ways in which it is designed, operated, and represented. These dynamic tensions are likely to become more acute, and consequently generate more complex and ambiguous streams of interactive change and innovation, in a context where micro-level audit and surveillance practices become more intensive and intrusive.

Neo-corporatist Managerialism was dominated by a negotiated compromise between bureaucratic and professional modes of *administrative control* (Child 2005). The latter was embedded within an institutional archetype in which inter-organizational coordination and intra-organizational collaboration were the key mechanisms through which effective conflict regulation and long-term socio-economic stability were to be achieved. Neoliberal Managerialism entailed a substantial move away from a 'bureau-professional' mode of administrative control towards a much more complex combination of market-based and managerial-based regimes of *cultural control* (Child 2005). Neo-technocratic Managerialism generates a move towards a more detailed, intrusive, and continuous regime of micro-level *work control* (Child 2005) in which eclectic combinations of audit, performance, and accountability technologies are constructed and implemented.

Each of these control logics and forms had, radically contrasting, implications for the occupational ideologies and identities of professional service provider groups (Dent and Whitehead 2002). Neo-corporatist Managerialism, and the mode of administrative coordination and control that it facilitated and legitimated, reconfirmed and reinforced the professional identity of service providers as 'technical experts' who developed and applied their knowledge and skill in an objective and value-free manner.

As disinterested and disengaged 'technical experts' professional service providers were seen, and saw themselves, as being independent practitioners who did whatever 'practical deals' they needed to do with political and administrative managers so that they could then 'get on with the job' unencumbered by wider economic and political constraints.

Neoliberalism, and the cultural control regime that it engendered, attempted to transform this pre-existing ideological and discursive regime by radically reconstructing professional service provider identities in a way that made market-based conceptions of enterprise, entrepreneurialism, and innovation the dominant values and symbols (Alvesson and Wilmott 2002). No longer an independent and autonomous 'technical expert', the professional service provider became the conduit for and servant of the external competitive forces and imperatives that would transform the public sector into a set of loosely linked dynamic and efficient businesses set-free from the restraints of centralized political administration and control. Neo-technocratic Managerialism, and the much more intrusive and detailed regime of work-based performance management and control that it instigated, completes this underlying transformation in formally institutionalized professional occupational ideologies and identities. The professional service provider is now, literally, the servant of consumer needs and priorities as these are articulated and mediated through various mechanisms and media that have been specifically put in place, usually by government or one of its agencies, to ensure that 'the user' becomes the dominant partner in the service relationship. As Miller argues, under this ideological and administrative regime, central government insists that service performance be judged and evaluated from a consumerist perspective (Miller 2005). But real consumers are too broad and amorphous a body to perform the task of performance review and assessment. Consequently, a new apparatus of inspection, monitoring, and evaluation has to be constructed and legitimated in a way that seriously downgrades the power and status of professional service providers as independent and autonomous 'experts' and ostensibly ensures that the needs and values of 'the consumer' are the dominant consideration in policy formulation and implementation.

As Newman argues, the control discourses and practices associated with the project of 'modernization' that underpinned New Labour's neo-technocratic Managerialism have the capacity to constitute 'self-regulating' organizations and actors in which particular forms of calculation and power become more legitimate and useable (Newman 2001: 168). Within this policy context, self-governing and self-managing 'networks', rather than hierarchical 'command and control' systems, are identified as the most appropriate organizational means to the effective decentralization of power and the realization of effective 'consumer empowerment'. Within these self-governing and self-managing networks, professional service providers are expected to internalize new modes of control and forms of identity in which consumerism, localism, and populism replace professionalism, centralism, and elitism as the dominant values driving service organization and delivery (Clarke 2005).

But, as with all types of control technologies, there is no guarantee that they will be mobilized and utilized in ways that are consistent with the larger ideological vision and policy objectives that drive the New Labour variant of Managerialism. Indeed, there is every chance, because of its underlying policy rationale and operational logic, that the much more intrusive and intensive regime of work control associated with neo-technocratic Managerialism will generate forms of workplace avoidance and resistance (Bolton 2005; McLaughlin, Badham, and Palmer 2005) that undermine the *organizational practicality* of the 'political project' that New Labour called into existence. The informal logics of action and everyday situated practices that operate within public service workplaces are likely to continue, in however an attenuated form, whatever the ideological imperatives and performance targets that drive New Labour policy. The former will play an important role in meditating between the relatively abstract and remote policy pronouncements of politicians, civil servants and senior managers/professionals and the organizational realities of orchestrated compromise involving substantial trade-offs between competing policy objectives at the level of service delivery (Wallace and Pocklington 2002).

Thus, the development of a hybridized set of governance arrangements at the macro-level, resting on a, complex and inherently unstable, mix of competing organizational logics associated with 'market', 'network' and 'hierarchy', has generated a corresponding hybridization of control mechanisms and practices at the meso-level and micro-level. Hybridization has been both consequence and cause of growing complexity, diversity, and fragmentation in policy objectives, organizational forms, and working practices. By attempting to combine competing, if not conflicting, logics of action and governance in the same institutional fields and forms (Richards and Smith 2004), New Labour has intensified the *inherent diversity and complexity* of policymaking and implementation (Davis 2000) to such an extent that the mediating and interpreting role of various occupational interest groups and organizational factions becomes even more critical to service outcomes. Nonetheless, the ideological context, institutional setting and organizational situation in which public service professionals are now embedded and within which they have to act has been radically transformed from the relatively stable and coherent political consensus and administrative compromise that emerged out of the post–Second World War settlement over the 'welfare state'. This is definitely a 'world that has been lost' to contemporary public service professionals and the competing political demands and managerial imperatives that they now have to meet—or at least placate!

Control/Trust Dynamics

As Ferlie et al.'s analysis of organizational restructuring in the UK health care system (1996) reveals, 'organizational hybridization' is a process by which different, and often competing, logics of action are combined an recombined within the same institutional form in a way that prevents any one logic—say, of market choice or administrative allocation or professional expertise—from becoming dominant. The organizational hybrids that this process of hybridization produces—such as foundation hospitals or city academies or independent treatment centres—may be inherently unstable, fragmented, and ambiguous but they (re)combine material resources, technical skills, and political legitimacy in a way that is consistent with network-based forms of governance consistently favoured by New Labour. They provide, an admittedly complex and often contradictory, organizational logic and form whereby New Labour can respond to increasing demands for efficiency, inclusiveness, diversity, localism, consumerism, and personalization, while ensuring that central government remains the most powerful corporate agency within an increasingly diverse and contested policy field.

Organizational hybrids combine and recombine competing logics of action within more or less stable institutional forms that tend to favour 'horizontal' or 'capillary', over 'hierarchical', modes of decision-making because they have to absorb and respond to relatively high levels of contradiction and conflict. As an organizational response to increased levels of complexity, ambiguity, and uncertainty in the policymaking and implementing context, hybrids are geared to providing a more flexible balance between centralized strategic direction and devolved operational management and control than would normally be the case in more conventional forms. However, hybridization *reinforces the underlying dynamic* of increasing complexity, uncertainty, and fragmentation to the extent that it responds to cross-cutting forces and pressures without allowing any one principle of organizational design or logic of collective action to dominate any other. Organizational hybrids are, necessarily, *inherently unstable and fragmented forms of organizing* in that they operate on the basis of multiple logics pushing in the direction of enhanced specialization, segmentation, and decentralization. Within this kind of organizational locale, 'boundary spanning roles' or 'border work practices' (Horlick-Jones and Sime 2004), usually occupied and performed by 'professionals' or 'experts' of some sort or another, become even more critical for the successful, if temporary, resolution of the messy detail of collective decision-making and action in which multiple and conflicting stakeholder interests are continually in play.

In this respect, organizational hybrids are not simply forms of collective or corporate action; they are also modes or mechanisms of institutional governance entailing the authorization and legitimation of power relationships that endure, in however a schematic form, over extended temporal and spatial locales. They also generate and sustain control technologies, deployed and managed by elite groups, geared to the regulation of social interaction on a detailed and continuous basis. Both on theoretical and empirical grounds, organizational hybridization is most closely associated with the network-based form of institutional governance in that the latter is seen to possess the inherent flexibility, adaptability, and spontaneity required by the former (Child and McGrath 2001; Thompson 2003; Child 2005). As Thompson suggests (2003: 175–8), network-based forms of governance are based on an 'informal or bargained rationality' that contrasts with the 'formal or procedural rationality' associated with hierarchically based governance systems. While the latter is universally open, explicit, and rule-driven in its theory, if not always in its empirical operation, the former tends to be characterized by its opacity, complexity, and pragmatism—even if this is legitimated by its receptiveness and inclusiveness in relation to a much wider range of, usually conflicting, stakeholder interests and values. Consequently, the network-based forms of governance that organizational hybrids seem to require inevitably involves a political and administrative trade-off between increasing complexity, interdependence, and flexibility, at the level of both intra-organizational and inter-organizational relations (Child 2005) on the one hand and enhanced secrecy, fragmentation, and politicization on the other. As Child and McGrath indicate, there is a growing awareness of the contrast, not to say contradiction, between a rhetoric of 'new

organizational forms' generating enhanced decentralization, empowerment and involvement and the reality of opaque mechanisms of institutional governance and organizational control in which power becomes
less transparent, more remote, and lacking in formal accountability (Child
and McGrath 2001).

In this respect, organizational hybrids—and the network-based form
of governance and more detailed and intrusive systems of work control that they seem to generate—present particular problems and tensions for public service professionals as they struggle to come to terms
with the radically changed political and organizational context in which
they have to operate. While putatively offering them certain opportunities for enhanced professional influence and status, hybridized organizational forms (and the network systems of governance and detailed
work control on which they rely) also pose a series of overlapping,
and potentially escalating, threats to professional power and control.
At the core of the professional labour process lies the inherent 'indeterminacy' that highly specialist and esoteric forms of knowledge and
skill, mobilized by various expert groups, must preserve as a basis for
their self-control over what they do, how they do it and how the
results of their work are to be judged. This 'primary indeterminacy' in
work design, performance, and evaluation establishes the material and
practical foundation for professional autonomy and control. It is subsequently elaborated, through a range of political mechanisms and ideological justifications, into various 'secondary indeterminacies' through
which the quasi-monopolistic 'jurisdictional domains' and 'labour market shelters' fabricated and maintained by professional associations
and groups can be protected from external incursion (Larson 1977,
1990; Boreham 1983; Freidson 1994, 2001; Reed 1996, 2001; Ackroyd,
Kirkpatrick, and Walker 2007). These primary and secondary indeterminacies are highly interdependent; they form an interlocking system
of socio-economic, political, and cultural exclusion through which professional groups can mount various 'mobility projects' to enhance and
stabilize their power, control, and status within an increasingly contested and complex matrix of overlapping 'jurisdictional domains' constructed and policed by an ever-growing number of expert groups vying
for a place in the 'professional sun'. They also entail a complex and
changing balance between 'trust' and 'control' in the organization and
management of professional work and the wider governance structures
within which it is embedded (Reed 2001, 2002; Reed and Anthony
2003).

19

Indeed, the underlying trajectory of political, institutional, and organizational change within UK public services, certainly since the second half of the 1990s, has been towards a governance regime in which the complex balance between 'trust' and 'control' has moved decisively in favour of the latter. This is so in a number of respects. First, much of the administrative apparatus of audit and accountability that has been constructed and deployed in recent years has been driven by the strategic political objective of making the professional labour process much more visible, transparent, open, and assessable (Power 1997; Exworthy and Halford 1999; Clarke, Gewirtz, and McLaughlin 2000; Llewellyn 2001; Broadbent and Laughlin 2002; Llewellyn and Northcott 2002; Reed 2002; Rosenthal 2002; Clarke 2004; Pollock 2004a; Ackroyd, Kirkpatrick, and Walker 2007). Second, new forms of 'expert power' have been interpolated into the organizational and management of public services delivery, as a result of this bourgeoning audit and accountability apparatus, that, at the very least, establish alternative sources and centres of specialist knowledge and skill to those conventionally provided by the established professional groups and associations (Shore and Roberts 1995; Laffin 1998; Flynn 1999; Shore and Wright 1999; Strathern 2000; Farrell and Morris 2003; Pollock 2004a; Miller 2005). In turn, these new sources and centres of specialist knowledge and skill have generated their own extensive bureaucratic control systems that have been legitimated by reference to the new policy priorities of market competition, consumer need, and performance quality. Third, very distinctive 'discursive shifts' in the cultural and linguistic milieu in which public services professionals operate have occurred that further embed and empower the ideology of neo-technocratic Managerialism at the expense of the traditional values and icons associated with professional indeterminacy, autonomy, and control. More often than not, these new discursive formations and genres powerfully resonate with the dominant values and icons of neo-technocratic Managerialism and its unrelenting focus on 'performance', 'accountability', and 'control' (Gane and Johnson 1993; Newman 2001; Fairclough 2005). Fourth, the network-based governance regimes that have emerged from, and simultaneously reinforce, these structural and discursive changes incrementally build towards more stable and predictable systems of self-surveillance and self-discipline. Within the latter, established professional groups 'voluntarily' subordinate themselves to the cognitive, linguistic, cultural, and organizational requirements of the new regime, in an attempt to appease their new political and administrative masters, while striving to maintain jurisdictional control over an ever-shrinking primary and secondary configuration of 'professional indeterminacies'.

The cumulative, interactive, effect of these changes has been to pose a direct and continuing threat to established professional autonomy and control within public services institutions and organizations by weakening, and ideally eradicating, both the core/primary and infrastructural/secondary components of professional power and authority. Beginning with externally imposed restrictions and limitations on 'secondary indeterminacies', and then incrementally moving on to the, far more difficult, task of detailed and intrusive interventions in 'primary indeterminacies' crystallizing around micro-level work practices and relations, the interlocking changes generated by neo-technocratic Managerialism have penetrated 'the hidden abode' of the professional labour process. They have laid it bear to external scrutiny and surveillance and, in so doing, they have managed to demystify, at least incrementally and partially, the claims to esoteric, abstract, universal and rational specialist knowledge and skill that have legitimated and protected established professional autonomy, power, and control.

Of course, public services professionals can, and will, engage in various macro-level political strategies and micro-level negotiating tactics through which they attempt to avoid, subvert, and resist the 'transparency regimes' that have been designed and implemented under the auspices of NPM in all its ideological and structural variants (Levay and Waks 2005). These, well researched and well documented, forms of professional avoidance, subversion, and resistance (Kitchener 1999, 2002; Kitchener, Kirkpatrick, and Whipp 2000; Llewellyn 2001; McNulty and Ferlie 2004; Ogbonna and Harris 2004) document the substantial structural, political, and cultural obstacles that still obstinately stand in the way of the radical transformations envisaged by successive generations of managerialists. As McNulty and Ferlie's research (2004) indicates, managerial fragmentation and inertia, professional indifference and avoidance, entrenched clinical control and symbolic power, and local political resistance can often come together to frustrate, and even defeat, radical organizational restructuring programmes promoted by advocates and activists for NPM. But, even here, the hybridized and incremental, rather than single-stranded and transformational, change that actually occurred diluted the established power base, organizational status, and institutional profile of medical professionals. It placed them in a structural position where they were defensively reacting to a 'change agenda' driven by other interest groups and corporate agencies. Indeed, as Townley et al. (2002) contend, the practical operationalization of the discursive, technical, and administrative control systems linked to neo-technocratic Managerialism release powerful cultural, material and political forces and dynamics that, at the very least, present public services professionals with major problems that they simply cannot afford to ignore and which they often have major difficulty in confronting (Townley, Cooper, and Oakes 2002).

In so far as 'New Managerialism', in both its neoliberal and neo-technocratic variants, necessarily entails the progressive and intensifying expansion of market forces, performance measurement and control, and consumer populism into the public sphere, then it inevitably involves the enhanced cultural power and increasing political reach of an instrumental/market rationality that 'gnaws away' at professional autonomy and control. In short, it involves an ideological, political, and organizational 'paradigm shift' that sets the new discursive, institutional, and administrative terrain on which current and future 'professional mobility struggles', of both a defensive and expansionist kind, will be fought out. This is complemented by a series of meso-level and micro-level initiatives in overarching regulative mechanisms and detailed surveillance technologies that incrementally transforms the institutional contexts and organizational settings in which most public service professionals now find themselves.

It also signifies a very significant movement in the 'trust/control nexus' that has shaped the historical development and practical operation of the governance regimes and control technologies through which public service professionals are organized and managed. By striving to transform the public service professional into 'the servant of the customer/user'—rather than an autonomous and high status 'technical expert' who controls the process through which user needs are defined, articulated, and served—both neoliberal and neo-technocratic variants of Managerialism have progressively reasserted the ideological dominance of an instrumental/market-based rationality and the political dominance of the managerial cadres who operate and police its practical functioning. Public services professionals can no longer be trusted, if they ever could, to speak for 'the customer' in an era when market competition becomes the universal principle and mechanism through which resource allocation and utilization are to be organized, evaluated, and justified. Much more powerful governance regimes and intrusive control technologies have to be developed and constructed around the various norms and indicators that stand proxy for 'the consumer' of public services (Smith and May 1993; Miller 2005). The 'modernization' of these services, through the increasing power of market incentives and the various performance management and control systems through which they will be operationalized, will fundamentally change the balance of power within and between professional groups and the various political elites and managerial cadres to which they are formally and substantively accountable. Pre-existing professional and regulative barriers to the further extension of market incentives, network governance, and intrusive work control technologies have been consistently breached by successive waves of modernizing reforms that seem to cause as many problems as they solve. These professional and regulative constraints on the further extension of market competition, consumer choice, and micro-level performance management are likely to become progressively weaker and the 'advocacy role' traditionally played by public service professionals will also be even more diluted and restricted (Pollock 2004*a*).

But the underlying contradictions, conflicts and tensions endemic to the 'New Labour project', and to the neo-technocratic managerialist strategy and forms through which it is to enacted and legitimated, remain a potent structural and ideological source for future phases of dynamic change that cannot be contained within the boundaries that the project and strategy struggle to impose and police. As Clarke summaries the current situation:

> It is not clear that the current evaluation/performance nexus has provided an effective or compelling solution to the governmental or political problems that I identified earlier. As a *governmental project* for enhancing control at a distance, it has been structured around a centralising, consumerist and objectivist model of organizational control. These characteristics generate several distinctive instabilities. Its centralism produces tensions around local responsiveness and innovation. It consumerism produces difficulties from its antagonism towards 'producer interests'.
>
> Clarke 2005: 227

This perceived hostility brings to the fore issues of professional autonomy and judgement, and contributes to wider problems about the recruitment, retention, and motivation of staff in public services. Its objectivism runs into organizational and public scepticism about the construction of evidence and judgements. Finally, its organization-centredness creates tension around the promotion and evaluation of collaboration and partnership working. In the rise of the performance/evaluation nexus, we may be seeing the generic crisis of modern governmentality, but it is profoundly mediated through the instabilities of a particular strategy of governing, in this specific political–cultural conjuncture. These instabilities—forged at the intersection of governmental and political projects—have inhibited the construction of a new settlement of relationships between the public, the state, and public services. Such a settlement is a primary objective of New Labour politics—and is embodied in the performance/evaluation nexus.

This 'new settlement' may be impossible to develop and sustain when the form of neo-corporatist Managerialism that once provided the governance structures and ideological supports for a 'social democratic welfare state settlement' have been largely dismantled. All that neoliberal Managerialism and neo-technocratic Managerialism have put in their place is a blind faith in the power of quasi-market competition and managed consumer choice to produce individual and collective distributional outcomes that makes 'everyone a winner'. The operation of these new allocative and authoritative mechanisms (i.e. the triptych of 'markets', 'metrics', and 'management') have generated a configuration of increasingly complex governance regimes and pervasive control technologies that have institutionalized distrust in the capacity of public service professionals to articulate and defend a robust conception of the 'public interest'. The 'umbilical cord' that Marquand (2004) sees between professional autonomy, authority and ethics and public service within a public domain that is institutionally distinctive, indeed separate from, the private domain of the market, private business and the pursuit of profit, has been severed (Marquand 2004b). However much public service professionals may have contributed to their own downfall, through excessive material self-centredness, ideological myopia and political acquiescence (Reed 2005), they have consistently underestimated the threat that neoliberal and neo-technocratic Managerialism had posed to the material and moral foundations on which their autonomy and authority has depended.

New Managerialism and the University

Previous analysis and discussion have identified a series of linked changes in the regulative frameworks and control technologies within and through which the work of public service professionals is now organized and managed (Kirkpatrick, Ackroyd, and Walker 2005; Ackroyd, Kirkpatrick, and Walker 2007). It has further been suggested that the cumulative effect of these interrelated changes has been one in which public service professionals now operate within, multilevel and highly complex, 'transparency regimes' that much more tightly and intensively monitor and control their work performance. In addition, it has been argued that the role of public service professionals in policy advocacy and formulation has been substantially weakened. This has been seen as the longer-term outcome of a process in which they have been caught between a 'pincer movement' from above, in the form of more intrusive state-centred intervention (such as much more detailed surveillance of professional training and accreditation), and from below, in the shape of external political initiatives aimed at diluting the material and status advantages derived from 'labour market shelters' (Freidson 2001). As 'institutionalized distrust', rather than 'regulated autonomy', has come to define the contemporary condition and practice of public service professionals, so the latter have experienced a sustained ideological, political, and cultural challenge to their occupational identity and status as independent, disinterested, and self-managing experts enjoying the widespread trust and confidence of political elites and general public alike (Dent and Whitehead 2002). Established institutional structures and cultural practices may have somewhat blunted the sharper edges of these challenges to the 'public sector professional state'. There may also be a case to be made in support of the longer-term significance of the 'defensive professionalism' now in evidence right across the latter (Ackroyd, Kirkpatrick, and Walker 2007). But the underlying dynamic and trajectory of change is clear and neither of these will favour the preservation of established professional quasi-monopolies, hierarchies, or identities in their conventional forms. Indeed, as Freidson (2001) contends, the former are likely to generate an underlying dynamic of inter-professional fragmentation and intra-professional polarization in which the material, political and cultural divisions and inequalities within and between professional associations and groups becomes more institutionally pronounced and embedded (Freidson 2001).

'The university' has not remained untouched by these momentous developments. While formally outside the direct or 'unmediated' strategic control and micromanagement of central government agencies, institutions of higher education (as chartered institutions) have found themselves far from immune to the bracing ideological winds of Managerialism and the distinctive political, organizational, and discursive innovations that it has generated and mobilized. Indeed, UK universities and the higher education system in which they are historically and institutionally embedded have been presented with an escalating series of challenges by the wider ideological, political, and discursive landscape that NM has indelibly shaped and sculpted. In turn, the various ways in which the former have responded to the complex range of threats and opportunities presented by the new 'welfare settlement' and 'policy paradigm' that NM and NPM have conjointly mobilized has transformed the institutionalized myths through which the system of higher education has been traditionally legitimated and the material conditions under which its constituent institutions have operated.

More specifically, the fragmenting and hybridizing dynamic that NM and NPM have generated within the UK 'public sector' as a whole has permeated the higher education system and has exerted a major impact on the trajectory of institutional restructuring and organizational change within universities (Parker and Jary 1994; Slaughter and Leslie 1997; Smith and Webster 1997; Amaral, Jones, and Karseth 2002; Dewatripont, Thys-Clement, and Wilkin 2002). In turn, these NM and NPM-inspired institutional and organizational changes have produced a very different sort of work culture and workplace environment for the majority of UK-based academics to that which was evident between the mid-1940s and the early 1980s (Halsey 1992; Dearlove 1997; Prichard and Wilmott 1997; Deem 1998; Trowler 1998; Scott 1999; Taylor 1999; Henkel 2000; Trowler 2001; Reed 2002, 2002a; Reed and Deem 2002).

Many of these developments and discontinuities are discussed and analysed in greater detail in subsequent chapters of this book. However, three of these are worth signalling as a prelude to more substantive exposition and analysis in subsequent chapters. First of all, the impact of NM and NPM on internal management structures, systems, and practices. Second, the longer-term implications of these organizational and managerial changes for professional academic cultures and identities need to be highlighted. Third, the significance of the complex interaction between these two sets of changes, between structural change and cultural change, for the 're-imagining and re-imaging' of the university as a prototypical 'knowledge intensive organization' requires initial consideration.

As indicated in previous discussion, the ideological drive and political logic underpinning NM and NPM were motivated by a consistent aspiration to legitimate and integrate a meta-narrative of strategic change, a programme of organizational reform, and a political technology of workplace control. Previous analysis has also suggested this aspiration 'to legitimate and integrate'—while often frustrated, blocked, and deflected in terms of realized practical outcomes—has generated a dynamic of change in policy discourses, institutional agendas, and workplace cultures that has correspondingly transformed the 'organizational habitus' of public service professional workers and managers. This has produced a number of longer-term effects in relation to university management, professional academic cultures, and the status of the university as a 'house of knowledge' (Calâas and Smircich 2001) that continue to shape the core institutional forms and organizational practices through which 'higher education gets done'.

NM and NPM have ensured that however 'postmodern', 'entrepreneurial', or 'marketized' that contemporary universities have become, the power, status, and role of academics in university governance and management have declined as a long-term consequence of 'the rise of Managerialism' as an ideological movement, policy paradigm, and organizational practice (Amaral, Jones, and Karseth 2002). The latter has come to permeate the institutional fabric, occupational culture, and organizational life of contemporary universities to such an extent that it is often regarded as a 'taken-for-granted' and ubiquitous precondition of everyday talk and action. Of course, it is routinely resisted, avoided, and adapted in all sorts of ways by all sorts of individuals and groups trying to get the day-to-day business of higher education done. However not every academic has resisted it. As we see from our own data, it seems likely that a small minority of academics in management and leadership positions have embraced managerialism in its neo-technocratic form and seized the career opportunities made available to them by managerialism's permeation of higher education. Meanwhile, the beliefs, discourses, and practices promoted by NM and NPM have seeped into every 'nook and cranny' of the organizational cultures and structures through which 'university work' is performed, coordinated, and controlled. In turn, these beliefs, discourses, and practices have come to exercise a 'restraining and restrictive' influence on the 'modes of engagement' through which academic staff come to relate to and identify with their employing institution. The primary allegiance of the 'academic tribes' may have always been to their discipline rather than their institution (Trow 1994; Becher and Trowler 2001; Shattock 2003). But NM and NPM have ensured that a further academic retreat from engagement in institutional management, and with the contemporary structures, beliefs and practices through which that engagement is practised and legitimated, has occurred and is unlikely to be reversed on terms radically different from those imposed by contemporary managerialist doctrine and discourse.

Where does this leave the university and its core workers—the academics? On a pessimistic reading, it leaves 'the university in ruins'

(Readings 1996) and academics as 'merely technical experts in the service of the political and cultural economy' (Freidson 2001: 212). In a more optimistic scenario, it opens up much more promising possibilities for the evolution of more complex and robust governance and management structures in which hybrid forms of collegiality and management emerge to take the university forward in the twenty-first century (Shattock 2003). Within the latter, the distinct possibility, if not probability, of universities taking their rightful place on the leading edge of a new generation of 'knowledge intensive organizations' that come to dominate advanced economies and societies, with professional academics taking their rightful place as 'knowledge workers' critical to their organizations' continued survival and success, becomes something more than a pipe dream. Yet it would be misguided, not to say foolish, to forget the underlying dynamic that drove the emergence and trajectory of NM and NPM from the late 1970s/early 1980s onwards. While it would be wrong to ignore the fact that universities are always 'a mix of organizing practices, which are historically resilient to being wholeheartedly overthrown by the 'new managers' (Prichard and Wilmott 1997), it is also the case that NM and NPM have dominated the ideological context, policy agenda, and organizational technology through and on which universities have been transformed in the course of the last two decades.

The book now moves onto examine some of the recent history of the external and systemic environment for managerial work in UK universities, followed by a discussion of the nature of the contemporary university as an organization. After that comes an exploration of the filtration of manager-academic identities into more traditional research and teaching identities, an analysis of the ways in which managerial activities, skills, and values are acquired (both formally and informally) by academics and finally an examination of the extent of the relationship between public service values and manager-academics who work in publicly funded universities. This concluding discussion is situated within current developments concerning European universities.

2

The Changing Context of University Knowledge Work: The UK Higher Education Systems from the 1960s to the Twenty-First Century

Introduction

In Chapter 1, we considered some of the theoretical debates surrounding the concepts of NM and NPM and how these might be applied to higher educational organizations. The chapter included examining the theorization of NM and NPM (and particularly the differences between neo-institutional archetype theory and critical realist morphogenic theory), the history of the introduction of NM and NPM into public services in western countries, the kinds of strategies and control technologies embedded in different forms of NM and the associated contradictions of these, as well as their implications for organizational change. Finally, consideration was given to the process of hybridization of old and new forms of Managerialism and the linkages and discontinuities between professionalism and bureaucracy in public service organizations in Western countries. This chapter will explore the ramifications of these wider debates in the systemic context of the UK knowledge-intensive university (that is, universities which are concerned with both research and teaching, rather than teaching-only universities), particularly in respect of attempts at higher education reform, changing organizational and cultural forms and the material and political imperatives encouraging universities to organize their activities in particular ways. The chapter includes an analysis of the recent history of the UK higher education systems since the 1970s, in order to consider how far the context of and the actual practices and technologies used to 'manage' academic knowledge work in organizations at the beginning of the twenty-first century appear to differ from the context and oversight of academic knowledge work in UK universities in the 1960s, 1970s, and 1980s. The HE systems of each of the four countries in the UK each have some distinctive features. Until very recently, the most striking differences were those between Scotland and the rest of the UK but following the extension of devolved governmental powers to Wales and Northern Ireland[1] as well as Scotland in 1999, differences are now appearing in all four countries. The chapter also considers, drawing on recent research data, how UK academics in management roles and career managers today, appear to interpret the recent systemic, organizational and other changes that have recently occurred in the academy. Finally, consideration is given to changes in expectations about the roles of academics holding leadership and management roles (hereafter referred to as manager-academics) at different points in this forty-five-year period. Both discontinuities and similarities between the past few decades and the present day are considered, underlining the point made in the preface that although our fieldwork was completed some six years ago, that processes, narratives and technologies of management change much more slowly than that and always have one foot in the past.

The discussion utilises concepts about the management and modernization of publicly funded and partially public-funded organizations, the phenomenon of 'New Managerialism' and the idea of academic knowledge work. The latter term describes what UK universities have increasingly become in the twenty-first century, as research and consultancy funds, international student income, entrepreneurial activity and (in England) variable undergraduate fees, have begun to represent a significant proportion of higher education's funding base alongside money from the public purse. Two particular concepts employed in the chapter, 'old' and 'new' forms of Managerialism, are worth mentioning here. As the previous chapter noted, Managerialism is not in itself a novel concept. Here, notions of 'old' forms of Managerialism are used to refer to those elements in the administration and management of academic work that appear to have remained constant, such as the leadership of research and teaching and the motivation of academic and other departmental staff. In relation to the discussion in Chapter 1 about three variants of recent conceptions of Managerialism, these 'old' forms of Managerialism are

---

[1] This is despite the fact that because of the aftermath of the sectarian troubles, the Northern Ireland Assembly has only been in session for a relatively short period.

largely pre-corporatist, although pressures towards corporatism in public services in general and in universities in particular were present in the UK from the late 1970s onwards. Other elements of Managerialism in its neoliberal marketized form from the mid-1980s and more recently (after New Labour's election in 1997) neo-technocratic Managerialism, have their roots in the period from the early 1980s onwards as Conservative Prime Minister Thatcher's reforms of public service organizations and service, from producer-dominated to more consumer-led organizations, began to take place. The roots also included the effects on the organization and management of academic work of what Slaughter and Leslie call the enhanced resource-dependency of universities in receipt of public funding (Slaughter and Leslie 1997). This dependency has brought greater emphasis on market factors, considerable effort devoted to extra income-generation and devolution of costs to academic units. Further 'new' elements include greater accountability of academics to their public paymasters (including performance management, teaching and research quality inspection, performance indicators and target setting), under the influence of neoliberal regimes and alongside declining funding from the public purse. The general periodization of the three forms of managerialism (corporatist, neoliberal, and neo-technocratic) in public services described in Chapter 1 is not an exact fit with higher education, which has tended to be more resistant to reforms than some other UK public services but has clearly had an impact on the broader landscape of public policy.

There are three further elements relevant to the growth of new forms of Managerialism in higher education. Firstly, one arose from the growth of corporate governance and management. This came about from the 1985 Jarratt Report which examined lay influence in universities vis-à-vis academics on decisions about finance, purchasing and estates/buildings (Jarratt 1985), the establishment of the polytechnics as independent corporations (rather than institutions under the control of local government) in the late 1980s and finally, following the 1997 Dearing Report (National Committee of Inquiry into Higher Education 1997), moves to streamline the governance structure of the chartered universities. Secondly, there were pressures to develop mass higher education in such a way that recipients received the individualized (or perhaps 'personalized') service now so beloved of public policy think tanks (Leadbeater 2003) and which had been so characteristic of the rather de-luxe UK model of higher education expansion since the 1960s (Anderson 2006). Finally there were attempts in the first decade of the twenty-first century at the regionalization of higher education in England, through somewhat contrived regional collaborations of higher education institutions, building on the work of the recently established regional development agencies, but with limited success so far, as shown by a study of the East Anglia region (Brown 2004). Political devolution in the UK and the European Union regionalization agenda has, as already noted, led to significant country by country differences in UK higher education (Universities UK 2004). Regionalization of HE within England has been one attempt at responding to regional differences in higher education, although so far with relatively little effect.

The chapter also draws on examples from research and insider accounts of the management of UK universities from the late 1960s onwards until the present day. Recent perceived changes to the management of academic knowledge work are demonstrated by extracts from accounts of this work and its context given by manager-academics in the ESRC project on 'NM and the Management of UK Universities' on which much of the book is based.

The ESRC New Managerialism Project

The conceptual framework having been established in Chapter 1, it now remains to describe the empirical base of the book. This draws upon a detailed study of manager-academics (defined as academics who have temporarily or permanently taken on management roles) in sixteen UK universities. The project was funded by the UK Economic and Social Research Council (award number R00 23 7661) and conducted between 1998 and 2000 by a team of researchers including the authors, Oliver Fulton, Rachel Johnson, and Stephen Watson. The research examined the extent to which 'New Managerialism', defined as an ideologically driven set of reforms in the management of publicly funded services popular with many western governments (Deem and Brehony 2005), was perceived to have permeated the management of UK universities. The study also explored the roles, practices, selection, learning, and support of manager-academics. The main objectives of the research were:

- The acquisition of new knowledge about how university academic managers perceive and give accounts about current and recent university management and the development of theory about 'New Managerialism' consistent with these perceptions and accounts;

- The illustration of management practices and mechanisms currently found in different UK higher education institutions;

- The description and explanation of current organizational forms in four case-study HE institutions; and

- Using analysis of the data collected to improve our understanding of the ways in which universities and their core activities may best be organized and managed and making a contribution to future policy on the selection and training of academic managers.

Project Methodology, Data Analysis, and Ethics

The research utilized qualitative methods and data-generation. A quantitative survey was considered as a further method of generating data but rejected both on grounds of the likelihood of a poor response from busy manager-academics and also because it would provide only superficial data. Using qualitative methods ensured a good response from participants and also provided in-depth data. The first phase of the study comprized twelve focus group discussions with academics, manager-academics, and administrators who belonged to learned societies from a cross-section of disciplines and professional academic bodies, with focus group participants drawn from a wide range of UK universities. The second phase involved interviews with 137 manager-academics (Head of Departments, Deans, Pro and Deputy Vice Chancellors/Principals, and Vice-Chancellors/Principals) and 29 senior administrators in 16 purposively selected pre- and post-1992 universities. Pre-1992 universities have a charter to award degrees and are often highly research-intensive, although they are all also substantially involved in teaching. They vary from ancient foundations to former colleges of advanced technology and university colleges, civic universities, and new institutions founded in the 1960s on green field campuses. Post-1992 universities are independent corporations that were formerly polytechnics or colleges of advanced technology, which focused mainly on teaching a range of academic, semi-vocational, and vocational programmes to undergraduate students. The post-1992 institutions did not receive core funding for research until after they became universities, although considerable research is conducted in the post-1992 sector, particularly applied research for industry and commerce. In phase 3 of the project, detailed case studies of the cultures and management of 4 of the 16 universities, enabled comparison of the views of manager-academics and 'managed staff'.

Learned societies and professional bodies were approached in the first instance through their Chair, President, or Senior Administrator. We tried to run most of the focus groups at existing meetings or conferences of the bodies concerned, which meant no one travelled especially for us. We also took care to seek permission from each individual participant. Discussions were taped, we also took notes and then the notes and tapes were transcribed and anonymized. In phase 2 and 3, after making decisions on possible institutions representing a cross section of universities (based on location, institutional type, size, mission, and curriculum mix) universities were approached initially through Vice Chancellors or Principals. With initial access secured, we then used a combination of data from personnel or human resource units, website information, and personal contacts to construct a theoretical sample of manager-academics at different levels and senior administrators/career managers. Next permission was sought to conduct interviews with manager-academics (in phase 2) in all institutions, and focus groups and interviews in four phase 3 case study institutions (with employees), all of which were taped and then transcribed. We were extremely conscious of ethical issues throughout the project, particularly the need for utmost confidentiality during the research process itself and the need for individuals to be confident that they would not be identifiable in any research outputs. We ensured that there was anonymization of individuals (and any other individuals mentioned by name) and institutions in the End of Award Report, conference papers and articles. In all three phases of the research, we also took great care not to unintentionally communicate anything confidential learnt in the fieldwork from one individual participant to another, whether in the same institution or not. This was particularly important in phase 3 where we were asking employees of four universities, from manual staff to academics, what they thought about how their institutions were managed.

In terms of data analysis, all tapes were listened to carefully by the research team, who also read through the transcripts several times. We then identified themes and issues arising from the transcripts and agreed on these before using a combination of a database (Filemaker-Pro) which allowed us to organize and store extracts of data from focus groups, interviews, case study interviews/observation and documentary analysis, and the qualitative software Nud*ist (which was used for phase 2 interviews). We aimed for maximum discussion of categorization and organization of data and constantly reviewed contrasting interpretations of our material at research team meetings. We also exposed our findings to regular peer comment, presented papers at major conferences and towards the end of the study organized a two-day project seminar with invited academic experts when we were in the crucial stages of our data interpretation process.

Our Findings

Though our research predates the book's appearance by several years, the depth of our analysis and data-sets and the concentration on organizational process (as well as on current policy-pre-occupations and individual views) mean that our data are still as applicable now as in 2000. Here, we summarize some of our main findings which later form the basis of a more detailed examination of the views and accounts of manager-academics in particular.

The focus group data suggested that the UK higher education system was now highly managerial and bureaucratic, with declining trust and discretion. Higher workloads and long hours, finance-driven decisions, remote senior management teams, and greater pressure for internal and external accountability were all mentioned. Phase 2 interviewees noted changes to the environment (such as reduced funding, massification of student-intake and the rise of research and teaching quality assessment) but were often more positive about the effects than focus group participants. Respondents discussed their routes to management, emphasizing personal biographies, gender processes and identities defined by teaching, disciplinary commitment, and research. We identified three typical routes into management. Career track managers had often experienced early and full acceptance of a management and leadership role and were most often found (below Pro-Vice Chancellor level) in the post-1992 former polytechnics. This group constituted a tiny minority of interviewees at Head of Department and Dean level in pre-1992 universities. Clearly at Pro-Vice Chancellor level more of our respondents were focused on a career path around management and leadership, although even at this level we found some in the pre-1992 sector who did not wish to be a manager on a permanent basis. Career managers were often in pursuit of higher salaries and a career in administration to the virtual exclusion of teaching and research. The 'reluctant manager' was typically found amongst fixed-term Heads of Department in pre-1992 institutions, most of whom rejected the label manager and saw themselves as academic leaders and almost all of whom at the time we interviewed them were planning to return to research and teaching at the conclusion of their term of office. Motivations included fear of incompetence of others as manager-academics in their department and a desire to protect their subject or discipline. Finally there was the 'good citizen' route, often identified at a late-career stage and found in both pre- and post-1992 institutions, motivated by repaying a perceived debt to the institution by 'giving something back'.

The project drew on models of 'New Managerialism' derived from research on the late 1980s reforms to the UK National Health Service (NHS) done by Ferlie et al. (1996). The efficiency model, 'doing more with less', backed up by funding policies and league tables, was perceived as having significantly permeated higher education. We found no evidence of the downsizing model but there was some evidence of decentralization in the form of partially devolved budgets and internal markets. The learning organization model was perceived to have some permeation, for example attempts at cultural change, teamwork, and strategic activity but not empowerment. Elements of Ferlie et al.'s model four, comprising a new value-base for public services, with genuine user involvement in the design and provision of services, were not mentioned by any respondent. UK Higher education, as noted in Chapter 1, appears to display *hybridized* forms of NM. Unlike in the UK NHS, where big organizational changes were introduced in the late 1980s and where the pace of organizational change has continued since universities have tended to develop within existing organizational structures. However, as Reed noted in Chapter 1, the narratives and technologies used in universities have shifted considerably, as have some elements of academic cultures, whilst the external environment for universities has become much more hostile than in the period up to the end of the 1970s, when the state and universities still tended to hold each other in mutual respect (Kogan and Hanney 2000). Most internal change mechanisms have been subtle (self-regulation of research and teaching performance) rather than overt. A few manager-academics we interviewed had fully adopted 'New Managerialism' practices and had exploited the career opportunities available to them, but most in our sample had not done this. However, not fully embracing management as an activity also has implications for manager-academics' appreciation of the idea of the virtual and new technology-informed university (Reed and Deem 2002) and their capacity to assess risk-taking (Deem and Johnson 2003). Manager-academics' lives were described by respondents as involving long hours packed with meetings, mountains of paperwork and email and the search for additional resources, with research marginalized and little time for reflection. Academic autonomy, the absence of proper reward-structures, long-hours cultures and lack of adequate administrative support for HoDs and Deans all contributed to heavy workloads. Appraisal, target-setting, peer-scrutiny, and mentoring were used in negotiating with academic staff. HoDs had to manage increasing tensions between different good performance requirements in teaching and research. We used data from phases 2 and 3 to explore forms and cultures. We found no clear evidence for the merits of particular organizational types, but de-layering seemed popular (e.g. merging departments into schools or removing faculties). All the institutions studied had devolved resource models but often new appointments were decided centrally. Cultural variations between institutions were strong, based on institutional history, location, niche, and size. We did not find the organizational isomorphism which neo-institutional archetype theory suggested might exist. There were also sharp contrasts between stories told by senior manager-academics and the accounts given by other staff. Managed staff claimed high loyalty to their institutions but alleged poor communication, failure to listen, slow decision-making, absence of clear policies, and a growing gap between senior management and others. Although the book is far more than simply an analysis of the NM project, the data from it are drawn upon extensively in the subsequent chapters. A full report of the project can be found elsewhere (Deem et al. 2001).

The only previous empirically-based comprehensive study of UK university management (as distinct from analyses of governance or analyses of particular categories of manager-academics such as Vice Chancellors or Heads of Department) is that undertaken by Middlehurst in 1986–8 and 1989–91. However, that study focuses more on leadership than management or governance and because it predated the giving of university status to polytechnics, it included only respondents from the chartered universities (Middlehurst 1993). Hence our study broke new ground in terms of its empirical focus on both chartered and incorporated universities, its particular emphasis on making heard the voices of manager-academics and its theoretical perspectives linking the management of higher education to the management of public service organizations more widely. Attention now turns to an examination of the main characteristics of UK universities from the 1960s onwards before returning to look at some of the ESRC project data in more detail, particularly focusing on our respondents' perceptions of the changes to university management in recent years.

The UK Systems of Higher Education: 1960 to the Present

The UK systems of higher education in 1960 were stable, state-funded and elite in character. During the 1960s and 1970s, UK universities were in expansionist mode. In the 1960s, the number of universities almost doubled (from 25 to 45 by 1969) and in addition, in England in 1970, thirty polytechnics, offering degree-level work but run by local government, were formed from former technical colleges (comparable institutions were also developed in Scotland and Wales). Some £168,312,322 was spent on universities by the main funding body, the University Grants Committee (UGC), in 1965–6. By 1970–1 this expenditure had risen to £268,736,365, whilst substantial sums of public money were also spent on other post-school education and teacher training colleges run by local government, amounting to £436,400,000. The role of universities was not significantly questioned by government, perhaps because it was still very much an elite system, with the percentage of 18- to 20-year olds going into higher education increasing only slowly, from 8.9 per cent in 1965 to 13.8 per cent in 1972 (Kogan and Hanney 2000: 51). Furthermore, in the 1960s and early 1970s a stable UK HE funding regime existed, so that university planning officers could assume little change from year to year (Shattock 2003). UK-domiciled undergraduate students were eligible for means-tested maintenance grants and did not pay any tuition fees. Academic knowledge work was largely unregulated except internally by universities themselves, and decision-making involving collegial committees or groups of academics, notably through departments and Senates, was widespread. The academic heads of universities (mostly called Vice-Chancellors or, notably in Scotland, Principals) regarded themselves as academic leaders, not as Chief Executives. However, significant links to business interests and the generation of large sums of money outside of public funding were already evident at some universities in the early 1970s, notably at the greenfield, campus-based, University of Warwick established in the 1960s (Thompson 1970). Furthermore, in the late 1960s, a series of student protests about the state of higher education and the lack of involvement of students in the governance and decision-making of universities (Crouch 1970), began to change the shape of university governance and management of universities so as to incorporate students. Research on twentieth-century higher education in the Netherlands has attributed much subsequent change in the HE sector there to the catalyst of student protest movements and a more sceptical public view of science and technology dating from the 1960s onwards (Veld 1981), although the analysis perhaps fits the UK rather less well than the Netherlands.

The expansionist and 'laissez-faire' phase of higher education expansion of the 1960s and 1970s did not remain so. It went into decline from 1979 onwards with the election of a Conservative government concerned to cut public expenditure and expose public services and professionals working in them to the discipline of quasi-markets and the regimes of the private-for-profit sector (based on a neoliberal managerialist ideology). Subsequently, UK higher education has been the subject of a series of direct and indirect modernization endeavours by government and university funding bodies. Such an approach to higher education has, since the 1980s, placed considerable emphasis on cultural change and the need to overtly manage academics and academic work in the context of marketization and gradual privatization of publicly funded education, using explicit performance and quality indicators for teaching and research and at times introducing considerable restrictions on units of funding per student and capital expenditure. Corporatism and then neo-corporatism, passing more centralized decision-making powers to administrators and lay members of governing bodies, began to enter the system from the mid-1980s onwards following the Jarratt report (Jarratt 1985) on how universities might best manage their non-academic responsibilities (such as finance and buildings). This more regulated autonomy and neo-corporatizm helped ease the introduction of NM into universities and began to build the foundations of the institutionalized distrust of which Reed spoke in Chapter 1.

There has been considerable expansion of the system from the 1990s onwards. By 2006 there were 89 universities (which counts the Federal universities of Wales and London as one institution each, or 114 if each federal member institution is counted separately), and 168 higher education institutions in total (which includes small specialist institutions). Also in 2006, the median income per institution was £80m and the median institution size by student enrollment, 12,280. In the same year, there were 109,625 full-time academic staff, 51,030 part-time academic staff, and 160,655 academics in total across the whole of the UK higher education sector. The information on students always lags behind other data so the most recent available at the time of writing was for 2004–5. In that year the sector had 1,151,215 full-time students and 817,925 part time students (1,969,140 in total), a participation rate of 42 per cent of 17–30-year olds in England and 49 per cent in Scotland and an income of £17.9 billion and expenditure of £17.7 billion (Universities UK 2006).

This expansion of UK HE from the 1990s onwards came at a price for both students and academics. One of the costs has been the virtual loss of free higher education for students. Since 1998, undergraduate students in England (and initially, until some time after political devolution in 1999, in Wales and Scotland too) have been liable to pay standard tuition fees (remitted for those from low-income households) at the same time that means-tested maintenance grants for accommodation and subsistence were discontinued, replaced by low-interest loans whose repayment depends on the amount earned by former students once in employment. In Scotland after devolution, the requirement to pay upfront fees was then removed (for Scottish students), although it has been replaced by a graduate endowment which is paid after graduation, either in a lump sum (£2,289 for 2006–7 entrants) or by instalments. However, English students studying in Scotland have to pay more than Scottish students (although still less than they would pay in England, £1,700 per year for 2006–7 with a higher fee of £2,700 for medical courses, all of which can be deferred and paid after graduation). From autumn 2006, undergraduates in England and Northern Ireland are liable to pay variable tuition fees (though in most cases these will be paid only after graduating by those earning above a certain salary ceiling), with an initial upper limit of £3,000 (this will also be so in Wales from 2007). Most institutions will charge the full amount. However, overall, most students in all four countries will pay their fee or endowment only after graduating, subject to how much they are earning. Students who come from low-income households will get some fee remittance and under the provisions of the Higher Education Act 2004 and the work of the newly established Office for Fair Access, all HEIs in England will also be required to offer some bursaries to undergraduate students.

Other costs of expansion have affected institutional funding, not least because as Anderson has pointed out, the system of higher education adopted in the UK in the 1960s, with an emphasis on study away from home at an institution of the student's choice, subject only to to their academic qualifications (and for several decades this was accompanied by a right to a maintenance grant subject to household means testing), was an expensive one (Anderson 2006). From the 1980s onwards, universities encountered big reductions in the unit of public resource per student (e.g. a 36% fall in funding per student between 1989 and 1997) and increased funding differentials in favour of the teaching of science and technology subjects at the expense of arts, humanities and social sciences. In 2003 there was also an estimated £8 billion backlog in investment in teaching and research facilities in English higher education institutions (Department for Education and Skills 2003*b*). The salaries and status of academics have declined considerably in relation to other professions (Halsey 1992; Bett Report 1999) and pay levels, as we shall see in the next chapter, are also significantly affected by gender and ethnicity (Association of

University Teachers 2004). At professorial level, salaries are also affected by subject specialisms (in the sciences, medicine, engineering and management/business studies, salaries tend to be higher than other subjects) and the market scarcity of high-earning and world-famous research stars. The management of academic work has also, as noted in Chapter 1, become much more overt, so that there is no longer any attempt to disguise it as collegial self-governance.

As we have seen from the introductory chapter, NM has been through various stages of its development but is best understood in general terms as a set of ideologies about organizational practices and values used to bring about radical shifts in the organization, finances and cultures of public services such as local government, health or education. These ideologies are sometimes referred to, particularly by politicians, as an important part of the processes of 'modernizing' or reforming public services (Hood 1991; Clarke and Newman 1997; Exworthy and Halford 1999). The use of the concept of ideology does not necessarily imply that there is a close connection between approaches to public service management and particular political groups. Indeed, NM has been adopted by those from a variety of political persuasions (Pollitt 2003). Nevertheless, part of what makes the approaches ideological is a common view that public services, which are seen to have been self-serving, producer-dominated and over-staffed, would benefit from practices developed in the private sector, including the devolution of financial and other responsibilities to lower organizational levels (Deem and Brehony 2005). The alternative conception of NPM, also introduced in Chapter 1, is derived from public choice theory and is best regarded as a new technocratic orthodoxy argued by its proponents to be the only way in which public services in contemporary societies can now be run (Deem and Brehony 2005). The shift to NM in public services is as noted in the previous chapter, frequently coupled with greater centralized regulation (often operating in spite of devolved resource systems), which may restrict the capacity of professionals to provide services (Farrell and Morris 2003). In addition, the strong value-basis of public service work, which differs significantly from that of the for-profit sector (Sennett 1998, 2002) in being more enduring and not oriented towards rapid product/service innovation or pleasing stockholders, is often ignored or downplayed in attempts at reform. This issue of the value-base of higher education work in general and managerial work in particular is returned to in Chapter 6. We now turn to examine briefly what the management of academic knowledge work in the UK involves and how and why it may have changed from the 1960s until the present time. This theme is then taken up again in greater depth in Chapter 3 with a greater focus on its contemporary organizational manifestations.

From Academics as Equals to Academic Performance Management?

Contemporary UK academics are in many respects different from other public-service professionals. They retain a good deal of autonomy over what they do, despite some inroads into this in recent years, are significantly engaged in creative knowledge work through research and teaching, and can be particularly challenging to manage. As a number of commentators have noted, both in the 1970s (Moodie and Eustace 1974) and more recently (Henkel 2000), academic loyalty tends to be oriented towards the basic academic unit and subject or discipline, not the university at which they happen to work. In addition, much academic work, especially research, is individual rather than collective, especially outside the laboratory sciences. Furthermore, academics are trained as critical thinkers and can and do apply this to anyone attempting to manage them.

Of course, academics have always worked with knowledge, both creating and transmitting it (Newman 1976; Von Humboldt 1976; Trow 1993). Clearly many other groups of professional workers do so too, especially in the context of the development of new technologies dealing with rapid transfer of information (Castells 1997). But the context of such work in the UK has shifted radically in recent decades. Managing knowledge work in the context of a contemporary audit culture (Power 1997; Strathern 2000) particularly concerned with how well academics and universities are performing on short-term outcome-based measures such as research publications or student evaluation of teaching, is a radically different vision of academic work from that prevalent in the 1960s and 1970s. In that period, UK universities were autonomous, collegially-managed institutions where decision-making was shared by academic equals, with management roles taken on only temporarily by academics (Simmonds 1976; Startup 1976). Teaching was mainly regulated internally and research was regarded as largely a private activity, of interest only to other academics. Now that both research and teaching quality/academic standards are regularly assessed in the UK, and following considerable growth in the HE sector as it has become more of a mass system, many more academics have become involved in management roles, some of them on a permanent rather than a rotating basis as was common in the past. Those holding such management positions are required to monitor income generation and expenditure as well as academic performance in general and indeed often to raise additional funds. In the past, many academics involved in the oversight of teaching and research saw themselves as exercising academic leadership but such identities, whilst still firmly held by many (Henkel 2000) are now in some cases overlain by management identities, even if these are still resisted by others (Deem and Johnson 2003).

The Changing Policy Context of UK Universities

New Managerialism' can be seen as an alternative model of governmental and institutional order for higher education in the UK to that existing under the previous compromise between corporate bureaucracy and professional self-government from the late 1940s onwards (Smith and Webster 1997; Jary and Parker 1998). For several decades of the twentieth century after the Second World War in UK universities, this compromise facilitated a trade-off between managerial control and professional autonomy, as Reed noted in Chapter 1 in his analysis of pre-corporatist and corporatist management. Sometimes called 'professional bureaucracy' and sometimes 'collegiality', it involved consultation of academics by other academics both informally and through committees, with bureaucratic procedures kept to a minimum (Mintzberg 1979, 1983). Up to the 1980s, the UGC, the main funding body for UK universities in the 1960s and 1970s, acted as a buffer between the autonomous universities and the state (Trow 1993). Academics had a great deal of autonomy, low teaching loads and time for research, in return for reasonable salaries and collegial governance. In the 1960s and 1970s, following the Robbins Report that recommended expansion of universities and student numbers (Committee on Higher Education 1963), the system underwent considerable expansion and growth in institutions and subject departments. Thereafter, a period of considerable change and reform began.

Parry, in an excellent analysis of the trajectory of UK higher education systems reform from the 1980s onwards, divides the key periods of significant change into three (Parry 2001). His first period runs from the early to mid 1980s and covers the early stages of education reform, under the aegis of a Conservative government elected in 1979 with a mandate to cut public expenditure and raise the prominence of markets in public services.

This period saw an end to the HE expansion of the 1960s and 1970s, with a 15 per cent cut in university public spending on universities in 1981, and restrictions on introducing new courses. There was pressure to make universities more efficient and accountable to government and the public. To counteract the threat of rigorous outside scrutiny that had occurred in the Civil Service under Derek Rayner, special adviser to Prime Minister Margaret Thatcher and with a background in retailing, the universities set up a committee chaired by an industrialist who was also Chancellor (an honorary position) of Birmingham University. The Report (subsequently known as the Jarratt Report after its chair) led to budget devolution from the centre of universities to smaller units, a greater emphasis on corporate governance (involving lay governors as well as academics and administrators) rather than decisions by academics alone and a reconstruction of Vice Chancellors as Chief Executives rather than leading academics (Jarratt 1985). It can thus be argued that 1981–5 laid the foundations for the overtly managerial university (Scott 1995). The period also saw early attempts to get universities to supplement their government grant with money from industry, and also witnessed rationalization of higher education provision by subject area. These latter changes were carried out by the UGC for universities and for polytechnics in England by the National Advisory Board (NAB). The rationalization exercises resulted in many actual or attempted closures and mergers of departments (Deem 1984; Walford 1987). Under pressure from the Conservative Government to make research funding more competitive, the first Research Selectivity Exercise for universities took place in 1986. This exercise used academic peer review to assess the quality of research (including publications and funding) of academics in different subjects. Departments that entered were awarded a grade based on the perceived quality of their research and obtained funding on the basis of these grades. This 1980s period laid the foundations for the period of neo-corporatist Managerialism in universities.

Parry's second period runs from 1987 to 1993 and equates to a period of neo-liberal Managerialism under a Conservative government. The period saw the resumption of some expansion in student numbers (Department of Education and Science 1987). But there were also efficiency cuts in university public funding (an efficiency gain was assumed each year so there was no inflation-proofing of grants to institutions) and the beginnings of the development of quality assurance systems for teaching. In 1988, following an Education Reform Act, which included radical changes to the school curriculum, assessment and funding, as well as changes in post-compulsory education (Flude and Hammer 1990), the polytechnics, colleges of education and further education colleges in England left local government control and became independent corporations. The NAB for the Polytechnics, which had advised local authorities on their higher education institutions, was replaced by a new body called the Polytechnics and Colleges Funding Council (PCFC). The new polytechnics were encouraged to set up streamlined, powerful governing bodies, although academic boards (the equivalent of a Senate, the highest committee of academics in the pre-1992 universities) were retained. The Education Reform Act 1988 also replaced the UGC with the UFC and ended tenure (a guaranteed job until retirement) for new academic staff entering universities and any existing academic who accepted promotion or a new post.

By the early 1990s, both the UGC and the PCFC had introduced a system of competitive bidding for extra undergraduate places by individual universities, instead of the previous system based on historical enrolments and block grants. However, the additional numbers were confined to a small percentage of total student in-take. Low-interest loans were introduced to supplement student maintenance grants. An Enterprise in Higher Education Scheme encouraged higher education institutions to bid for money to develop degree curricula in collaboration with businesses and develop teaching units that encouraged an entrepreneurial outlook in students. In 1989 a second UK-wide Research Selectivity Exercise was held for all universities but the polytechnics, despite their recent incorporation and removal from the control of local government, were still excluded. A further Research Quality Exercise was held in 1992 but this time it was actually termed, for the first time, a Research Assessment Exercise (RAE).

In 1992, a Further and Higher Education Act established a single framework of higher education with separate funding bodies for England, Scotland and Wales. Making the polytechnics universities was seen as a mechanism that would 'recognize the achievement of the polytechnics in pursuit of 'cost-efficient expansion' (Parry 2001: 125) and expose the established universities to greater competition in respect of their recruitment, research and teaching activities. As a result of the Act 1992, all higher education institutions receiving public funding had to agree to submit to regulatory mechanisms. An audit of the arrangements in each university for maintaining academic standards was introduced by the Higher Education Quality Council (HEQC), which was 'owned' (that is, paid for) by the universities. A periodic assessment of higher education teaching and learning (by subject area) had already been introduced by the Higher Education Funding Councils in the early 1990s. This time from the mid 1980s to the early 1990s saw the establishment of neoliberal managerial approaches in the universities. Something not discussed by Parry is that 1993 also saw a Government White Paper *Realizing Our Potential* which established a future strategy for publicly funded research and emphasized a new technology foresight programme and the importance of higher education establishing links with industry and other non-academic research-users (Great Britain: Chancellor of the Duchy of Lancaster 1993). This in itself was a strong signal that universities were no longer to see their research as purely an ivory tower, curiosity-driven activity unaligned to the economic prosperity of the UK as a whole.

Parry's third period runs from 1994 onwards. Growing financial problems in the sector, as student participation targets were met much earlier than anticipated, alarmed the Treasury and further expansion was quickly halted. Targets were set for full-time undergraduate numbers by institution, with financial penalties for over or undershooting these. The Funding Councils returned to a system of nationally-planned student numbers, as in the 1980s. In 1994 there was also another significant development in England, which Parry does not mention. This was the establishment of the Teacher Training Agency (TTA), which took away from the University Funding Council for England the responsibility for all initial school-teacher training courses (and subsequently also began to fund some in-service courses run by universities, as well as Masters degrees for teachers). As Shattock notes, the TTA development was significant because it introduced 'detailed national prescription of teacher training syllabuses and the opening of university education departments to the Office for Standards in Education (OFSTED) inspections (which) represents an extreme example of the exercise of state power over an area of academic work' (Shattock 1999: 278). OFSTED is an independent body that inspects the standards of teaching and management in schools using contracts with teams of inspectors. OFSTED's wholly public predecessor, Her Majesty's Inspectorate (HMI), did inspect the former polytechnics but the activities and procedures of OFSTED in schools and in teacher education (where severe inspection regimes and penalties for poor outcomes were now established) were regarded with grave concern by many academics. Increased selectivity in research funding followed the fourth RAE in 1996, so that higher grades than in the 1992 Exercise were needed to retain similar levels of research funding. There was also a new focus on subject-teaching quality inspection and assessment grades, linked to five-yearly assessment of subject departments in each university. In 1997, the Quality Assurance Agency (QAA) was established to do this work as a quasi-independent body more distanced from universities than its predecessor, the HEQC. This more distanced teaching-quality inspection regime led to fresh pressures for academics (Brennan and Shah 2000; Morley 2003) who now found themselves enmeshed in a new and highly bureaucratic regime related to teaching, as part of what Reed in Chapter 1 calls neo-technocratic Managerialism. This was one of the aspects of reform that led to the kinds of notions of institutionalized distrust that Reed writes about in Chapter 1.

With the higher education funding crisis deepening, a national review of higher education (known as the Dearing Review, after its Chair Sir Ron Dearing) was set up in England, which reported in summer 1997 (National Committee of Inquiry into Higher Education 1997); there was also a separate but related report for Scotland, the Garrick Report (Scottish Standing Committee 2007). The Dearing Report led to the introduction of tuition fees paid by students themselves, more emphasis on the quality of teaching and learning and a particular stress on the need for stronger governance in universities by lay members of governing bodies. A number of writers suggest that at this stage both the pre- and post-1992 universities began moving towards greater corporatism (Henkel 1997; Tapper and Salter 1998) in response to uncertainty about the external funding and regulatory environment, involving lay governors more and committees of academics less. But as we have seen from the previous chapter, corporatism was by now, overlain by neoliberal and highly marketized forms of Managerialism. Academic salaries began to deteriorate relative to other public service professionals and as class sizes rose rapidly following student expansion, more staff on short-term contracts were employed to teach them. The 1997 Dearing Review was meant to help solve the university funding crisis, yet it did little to resolve this and also said very little about university management (Trow 1997; Jary and Parker 1998; Parry 1999). As Parry notes 'academic institutions have clearly become sites of more directive management and governance... (there is)... little real indication that individual institutions might re-invent themselves as organizations with a distinct public service mission, except some establishments had re-asserted their access-led purposes' (Parry 1999: 131).

Subsequently, with a newly elected Labour Government from 1997 onwards, a fresh diet of HE policies was introduced, including those on widening participation for 18–30-year olds from under-represented

social groups (Brown 2002; Brehony and Deem 2003). Somewhat para-
doxically, another new policy included the abolition of maintenance
grants for such students. Funding of HE, both research and teaching
(and the estate infrastructure) continued to be a problem. The year 2003
saw the publication of the Lambert Review of Higher Education/Industry
links (Lambert Committee on Business-University Collaboration 2003),
a development extending the concern evident under the previous Conservative government in the White Paper *Realizing Our Potential* 1993
about how more university research could be paid for by private rather
than public sources and become more useful to industry. Funding of
teaching also remained under review. In January 2003, a new Government
White Paper on Higher Education in England was produced (Department
for Education and Skills 2003*b*). Amongst its recommendations were a
greater separation between teaching and research (an issue already raised
by the 1999 Transparency Review which had examined the extent to
which teaching and research subsidized each other in universities), with
institutions deciding which best reflected their mission, new rules for
acquiring university status (with the previous requirement for postgraduate research degree awarding powers removed), and extra funding for
the highest quality research departments. It was recommended that an
independent Regulator should be established to ensure fair access to
higher education by disadvantaged groups (Layer 2005) and to make
sure that additional funding was provided to assist such groups. Other
recommendations included the introduction of a graduate contribution
payment, the so-called variable or top-up fee, the level of which could
vary by institution up to a given level, to replace upfront tuition fees.
Controversies about these recommendations continued well beyond the
White Paper (Deem 2003) even after the Higher Education Act 2004,
which focused on student fees and fair access, student support and complaints as well as establishing a Research Council for the Arts and Humanities (Her Majesty's Government 2004) and an easier route to university
status.

The 2003 White Paper, although principally concerned with England,
also had implications for the other three UK countries, all of which now
all display distinctive patterns of higher education (Universities UK and
Standing Conference of Principals 2004). In the case of Scotland, which
has always had a different approach to HE compared with England (e.g.
in respect of age of entry, local recruitment of students, length of first
degree, and so on), a quite different future direction for higher education
has been envisaged, both in relation to the permeability of research across

all institutions (Gani 2002; Deem 2006b) and in connection with the decision not to introduce variable tuition fees. The future of the RAE itself, now in its sixth incarnation (due to take place in 2008), as an extremely expensive and elongated system of peer review of research quality, has begun to be questioned at the time of writing (summer 2006), with proposals from the UK government for a more metrics-based exercise in which any peer review element for some subjects (e.g. laboratory-based science and technology) might be excluded altogether, although perhaps with elements retained for some social sciences and arts/humanities. The merits of a metrics based system (which still rests on peer review of funding applications, journal papers and use of peer citations) and its effects on different universities are the subject of considerable debate at the time of writing (McKay 2003; Weingart 2005; Sastry and Bekhradnia 2006).

We can see in this final period since 1997 that the grip of Managerialism has hardened and became taken-for-granted, effectively being regarded as a form of technocratic rationalism about how services in receipt of public money should be funded (Pollitt 2003), whilst still actually retaining its ideological roots (Deem and Brehony 2005). Universities still retain some autonomy but as the proportion of public funding declines, so the desire of government to micro-manage institutions and their work seems to have increased and trust decreased.

The focus now turns to an illustration of changing expectations and current pre-occupations of those involved with managing academics and knowledge work at the turn of the twenty-first century, drawing on the ESRC 'New Managerialism' project (Deem et al. 2001)

Contemporary Perceptions of University Management: A Cross-Institutional View

In focus groups discussions with academics, managers, and administrators from different institutions who were attending meetings of learned societies, many participants suggested that, under the influence of changing government funding and policy, universities had recently become much more overtly 'managed'. This was felt to be in a manner much more akin to a business than an educational institution, with traditional methods of departmental and academic committee decision-making becoming marginalized. Such views are consistent with much of the contemporary literature (Cowen 1996; Dearlove 1997; Prichard 2000) on what has happened to UK higher education. A typical focus group response outlining some of the key changes identified was as follows:

> (several participants) Centralisation of decision-making! A much sharper sense of accountability and much sharper sets of objectives! The issue of language and vocabulary has changed very much...the use of acronyms! Today, it's all about planning and strategy...it's a sea change in culture from the collegiate to the corporate. It's not just the vocabulary, it's been forced through the whole thing....There's devolution of resources but centralisation of decision-making.
>
> Humanities Learned Society

Yet despite the perceived and actual changes in the last three decades or so, it is likely that most contemporary holders of head of academic department posts in the UK would still recognize elements of Startup's 1970s sociological analysis of HoD challenges and dilemmas arising from dealing with staff, teaching and research, and representing the department at Senate (Startup 1976). Startup points out that beyond the minimum structural requirements of the role (e.g. attending Senate, the main academic decision making body, and writing promotion reports on colleagues) and the conventional aspects (e.g. facilitating research), HoDs could interpret their task in a number of different ways. It was this discretionary element that some respondents in the ESRC study perceived as now being most at risk. Furthermore, it was widely believed that the HoD role had become intimately connected with resource issues, sometimes to the exclusion, or marginalization of the academic leadership function itself. A number of scientists encountered by the research team felt that the actual *tasks* of HoDs had not changed much, perhaps because laboratory science research has long involved getting large research grants and supervising big teams of researchers:

> I was Head of Department ten years ago at X {UK university} when there were real problems and I don't see my role...in that respect, any different {some nods of agreement}.
>
> Science Learned Society

However, social scientists were particularly inclined to think that the financial roles now expected of HoDs did make the job very different now:

> one of the changes that's come, that's been implemented across the public sector...is the idea of the internal market which of course has led to devolved budgeting in most universities...devolved budgeting has actually changed enormously the culture of the universities....The people who like me {ie HoDs}

are now starting to feel that they...made the wrong job decision because here they are at the end of the day 25 years later, being accountants and not academics....

Social Science Learned Society

There was general agreement in almost all the focus group discussions that external audit of teaching and research had significantly changed the climate in higher education and the way academics were managed. This is consistent with other contemporary analyses of UK higher education (Brennan and Shah 2000; Lucas 2001; Harley 2002; Morley 2003).

> Respondent 1: there are national constraints now which didn't exist say ten years ago...{research assessment, teaching quality assessment }...
>
> Respondent 2: There has to be much more team spirit now...ten years ago you could get person 'x', who could be essentially a 'loose cannon', now that person maybe does his lectures badly or turns up late or he doesn't do so well in the labs or even says 'I don't believe in questionnaires, I don't believe in giving tutorials etc, etc'. If you have such a person now...you are looking at potential disaster.

Science Learned Society

> the biggest change is the RAE and the shift that that has made from research as essentially a private, individual trajectory career decision into a public matter...the complete difference from the time when there were people who didn't do any and, you know, they didn't get promoted, but that was about all...you no longer can carry anyone like that....

Social Sciences Learned Society

There was a prevailing view in almost all the focus groups that money rather than academic factors was driving many decisions, especially with the introduction of cost centres to most universities. This was seen as linked to a lack of trust in HoDs over the use of budgets. But what perceptions about management were presented in interviews with manager-academic and senior administrators themselves?

Contemporary Perceptions of University Management: Vice Chancellors

A key feature of senior manager-academic interviews in sixteen universities was their analysis of what had changed. For Vice Chancellors, the rhetoric of corporateness, but also accountability and the idea of their role as Chief Executives, as advocated in the mid-1980s (Jarratt 1985) was evident in what most of them said:

> I think the biggest constraints are external. That I am accountable to governors, to the funding council, to the government for the finances and the success of this organization and like any other chief executive that's my central point, my focus, my anchor. I've got to get it right, I've got to leave this university healthier and happier than when I took it over. Every Vice Chancellor has to do that.
>
> VC, post-1992

It may be that this enhanced accountability and financial pressure has also encouraged VCs to emphasize strategic activities, when much of their actual work is more mundane and reactive (Bargh et al. 2000). VCs as a group may have moved from being the leading academic to something more akin to company Chief Executives (Middlehurst 1993) and also tended to adopt an approach which is both highly managerial and exclusive, not necessarily intentionally so, of many other staff (Deem and Johnson 2000; Deem 2003). If these shifts have occurred there are likely to be related organizational changes. For example, it is claimed that one facet of entrepreneurial approaches to management in Australian universities is the growth of senior management teams (Marginson and Considine 2000) which are not part of the formal governance structure of institutions. All the VCs we interviewed said they had some kind of senior management team, typically a mix of manager-academics (deans, pro-vice-chancellors) and senior administrators (typically registrars and finance directors), which met very regularly, often weekly. Indeed Shattock (2003) seems to take the existence of such a team for granted. A typical response on senior management teams was as follows:

> I don't have a head of administration. . . . I have a registrar, but . . . he doesn't line manage the four other senior administrators. They all report direct to me . . . then they plus the four deans, plus the deputy vice-chancellor, form the senior management team in effect.
>
> VC, pre-1992

The centrality of finance to the work of VCs and the need to develop a business approach to higher education, whether through attracting more money, reducing staff and resources to match funding, target-setting ordevising new devolved resource models, was emphasized by all the VCs interviewed:

I like least the fact that I have to worry about money for a lot of the time and that that distracts me from playing the sort of leadership role that I would really like to play.

VC, pre-1992

modern universities, whether we like it or not, are businesses where you have to make the bottom line of every year and you have to have some profit at the bottom line because otherwise you're utterly insecure as an institution, you can't do things you want to do.

VC, post-1992

If the VCs we interviewed indicated that they were feeling the pressure of some recent changes, when they had at least some control over the narratives, organizational forms and technologies of management, the challenges of managing in the contemporary UK university were experienced even more acutely by Heads of Department who lacked the high salaries of the senior team members and who on the whole had not yet fully committed themselves to a management career.

Contemporary Perceptions of University Management: Heads of Department

As Knight and Trowler note, HoDs must find a way of balancing conflicting priorities (Knight and Trowler 2001) from managing teaching and assessment through encouraging research to dealing with difficult people and balancing their budgets. Such tensions were reflected in almost all the HoD interviews we conducted:

with it being a very, very, competitive university for survival of departments, for getting research funds, keeping up your FTEs {student full-time equivalents} if the department's not run properly then you're all in serious trouble . . . we are very much governed by league tables, by assessment exercises . . . in research or teaching.

HoD, Science, pre-1992

Unlike VCs, HoDs are not always recruited through external advertisement. In the pre-1992 sector, they are often elected by their peers and hold the post only temporarily. Only in the post-1992 universities is it common to appoint HoDs permanently or via external recruitment. Thus HoDs may have quite different degrees of investment in their roles. However, what they do is likely to be fairly similar across both sectors, although there are differences in the extent to which research is emphasized vis-à-vis students and teaching, in the research intensive pre-1992 and the more teaching-oriented post-1992 institutions as in the extracts below:

{there's} a terrific pressure on ensuring that staff do enough research. . . . I've got very good, young staff, but of course they need time to produce, you know, really good, substantial research, but it's very much coming on stream and we got a grade 3 rating in the last Research Assessment Exercise and I'm hoping that it will go up to a 4 this time. . . . So, it's a question of trying to ensure that they get study leave and that we keep the rest of the show balanced as far as the students are concerned.

HoD, Humanities, pre-1992

The danger is always if we lose sight of students and we lose sight of the world of work and where our students go and who our students are, where they come from, how we recruit them, how we do all these different things, if we lose sight of that for one minute, we are dead.

(HoD, Social Science, post-1992)

The HoDs interviewed in our study were almost all working with devolved budgets (either at the department or faculty level) but often found that the crucial decisions about staffing were not devolved and even outside of that, there was little scope for spending on anything but essentials; a typical response emphasized the limitations of devolved budgets:

there is a budget that is devolved to the School but it only covers the current costs. There is a capital budget but largely by the time it comes to the School there are so many things that must be bought like furniture, up-grading computers, there's not a great deal left to be creative with.

HoD, Medicine, pre-1992

Not only budgetary constraints but also the requirements for departments to do well in internal and external audits of research and teaching may present HoDs with problems concerning staff who appear to have lost their motivation. A substantial minority of HoD respondents had needed to encourage such staff to leave:

I've dislodged numbers of people who we didn't wish to continue in our employment. . . . I've given them responsibilities that they weren't ready to take. They've got into a position where they were not contributing and I've said, "Here's your great chance to contribute" and they've discovered that taking the pension was better.

HoD, Humanities, pre-1992

Many HoDs in our sample also recognized that there was also a wider general problem about managing academic knowledge work at the present time:

> I think there's a general tension in terms of academic salaries as against academic workload. A lot of people came into this, particularly into this institution...not being researchers,...having either industrial expertise {or}...educational expertise and coming to teach...{with} what were then termed...reasonable contracts with substantial holidays, and that was instead of a substantial salary. Now, the salaries have fallen behind, and the workload has gone up exponentially.

HoD, Science, post-1992

The overall picture painted by our HoD respondents concerning the main features of the management of UK universities, included the arrival of the audit culture, rising student numbers, the tensions between teaching and research, high workloads for all staff, shortage of resources and the challenges of devolved budgets. Many of these characteristics feature in discussions of NM in other public services too (Clarke and Newman 1994, 1997; Power 1997; Exworthy and Halford 1999). More than half of our HoD respondents claimed that they did not really accept the rhetoric of NM, but felt obliged by their roles and institutional pressures to use the technologies of Managerialism such as devolved budgets and performance management. They also experienced considerable tensions between their role as managers and their academic work and colleagues, tensions also found elsewhere in middle management positions in universities (Santiago et al. 2006).

The Views of Senior Administrators

The ESRC study included interviews with a much smaller number of senior administrators and career-managers, such as Finance Director, Heads of Human Resources, Registrars, University Secretaries, and so on, in each of the sixteen institutions researched. Most such respondents were either part of a senior management team or worked very closely with it. Interestingly, very little critical social science research has been done on UK university administrators *qua* administrators, although interestingly this is not so for the USA (Trow 1998). What UK research has been done on this topic tends to concentrate on the growth and future of the administrative arm of higher education institutions (Allen and Newcomb

1999; Lauwerys 2002) or on how administrators are regarded by service users (Shanahan and Gerber 2004). These are not insignificant themes but they are a long way from our focus on Managerialism. Interestingly, since devolved budgeting is such a central feature of the 'new' aspects of Managerialism introduced to UK universities from the late 1980s onwards, the disciplines of neoliberal and neo-technocratic marketization seem to have been relatively little applied to administrative units as compared with academic departments (Wood 2002). By contrast with the vast majority of manager-academics, not all the administrators we interviewed had spent long periods in academe, although a minority had been in university administration for many years. This feature of administrator respondents means that relatively few of them could look back at the past decades in higher education and give some kind of personally informed view of what changes they thought had occurred over that period. For the minority who could do this, the experiences of those of working in the pre-1992 chartered universities seemed to be very different from those of respondents employed in the post-1992 former polytechnic sector, run by local education authorities until the late 1980s:

> in 1988 the University Grants Committee cut the university's funding rather radically and so, from . . . an institution that was financially quite well off . . . into an institution that had to have radical financial surgery. So, instead of going in to develop, as I thought, management communication systems, which was my interest at the time, I ended up getting involved in strategic financial management and the restructuring of the institution and the effective introduction of a line management . . . methodology's not the right word, but ethos, in the university, which was restructured accordingly, you know, with the {VC and Deputy} and the Management Team driving down to managerial units.
>
> Finance Director, pre-1992

> I think one of the issues there is how you might move away from what I would call the Local Authority culture into a different employment arrangement, which is what we're trying. So there's a, I think, we're sort of burdened with the legacy of the past really in terms of support staff as well. So those are significant factors I think and they weren't ones which I was sort of anticipating, I suppose, when I took the job.
>
> HR Director, post 1992

Many of the administrators interviewed talked of the challenges of working with academics, particularly in respect of the latter's critical capacities and their lack of corporate identity:

they do not have a sense of corporateness, they just happen to be a particular university, they are wedded to their subject matter, they are not wedded to the institution. People will have come here to do medical sciences and research and that because they love medical sciences. The fact that is the University of B or C is neither here nor there. They would not get overly concerned I think... about whether the university has £2,000,000 in the bank or £50,000,000 as long as 'there's enough money for my research budget, that is where I want to be, if I can teach my students'.

HR Director, pre-1992

Other administrator interviews included references to 'herding cats' and concerns about the privileging of academic skills over management ones:

{the} HE sector is perceived as a 'challenge' in which it would be difficult to effect change.... There is a 'laid-back' ethos and a tendency to reject the changes taking place in the real world, particularly in relation to financial changes.... Conventional academic skills {academic pedigree & track record} are not necessarily the skills necessary for good academic management. Presently the latter is not valued.... We've gone some way to achieve this, but it has taken three years to achieve what would have taken six months in industry... time is spent in committees, paperwork, litigious, rendering 'clear and crisp'. Instituting change is more about persuasion here.

Human Resources Director, pre-1992

This respondent was one of several to refer to the slow pace of change in academe and the difficulty of having to wait a long time for decisions to be mulled over by committees, something which caused considerable anguish amongst a good number of administrator respondents:

{I} think I'm struggling with the whole methodology of university workings, I mean, when people sit there and say 'well we'll set up a committee to report in the autumn term and then we'll take a decision in spring term' {laugh} it's a whole new ball game for me and I find great difficulty with that {laugh} and also when I say 'well you know, why can't we insist that they buy from here?' And they say 'well that's academic freedom and autonomy'... one of the things is, I have great difficulty at the moment... understanding what powers I do have, what powers I don't have, because everything seems to be that I can recommend things to go to committees and lay people along with other members of the Schools who are on that committee will actually approve it. Where in industry I would have sat round the Board we would have agreed what to do and we would have done it. Now the time scale involved is just horrendous as far as I'm concerned, coming from industry.

Director of Finance, pre-1992

There was a real sense of frustration evident in the comments of this respondent and in similar views expressed by others, particularly those who had come to HE from the private sector. Whether this apparent trend towards appointing university administrators from outside higher education and the appointees' desire to speed things up in university decision-making was a result of the impact of neo-technocratic Managerialism or just bringing in private sector experience, as was done in the late 1980s UK health services reforms (Ferlie et al. 1996), is hard to assess. Certainly those who had been longer in academe were able to review the changes to the HE context that had taken place since the early 1980s. In a number of such instances, administrator respondents questioned what was happening to higher education in the new audit culture as compared with earlier periods.

> I worry about the number of... areas of activity that are growing up which are very consuming of resources and time and are only ancillary to or associated with the main business of academic teaching and research, which if you look across the system as a whole, consumes a huge amount of resource. Quality is obviously one, Student Support, Access and Widening Participation, all very worthy things in their own senses but they're... It's a bit of research I'd like to do one day, to find out how much more of a portion of the total cake is being used on those things than it was say twenty years ago. Maybe it's right that it should, but when I feel, when I see the main academic posts and money for research for instance being squeezed so hard and you just have a feeling that some of the other things that are being done are not quite as justified, you know, that's a tension which I'm conscious of.
>
> Registrar, pre-1992 University

> there were fewer resource constraints and therefore more flexibility because people tended to have a bit more time, there was more ability to take your job in the direction that you wanted rather than having to take it in the direction that somebody else wanted. And that actually lasted for quite a few years. Well I'm not saying there weren't, there's always constraints. But they were less and therefore there was more flexibility. And there was significant public accountability. So there was a lot less concern about having to justify things, having to know exactly what was going on, having to take account of political... external, political agendas, all those kind of things have really come in, you know, in the context of my working life, which isn't that long ago.
>
> Registrar, post-1992

Some of the discussion of change involved reflecting on the developments that had taken place in the last decade and their likely consequences for the sector. Unlike most of the manager-academic respondents below Vice-Chancellor/Principal level, administrators were more likely to reflect on organizational effects as a whole, not just those affecting a particular sub-unit, as was more common for Heads of Department and Dean whose identities were rooted in disciplinary categories (Becher and Trowler 2001) and the basic academic unit (Henkel 2000). The view expressed below was atypical in that it directly criticized widening participation initiatives but the general message was not much different from that conveyed in other interviews with long-standing career administrators from pre-1992 universities:

> I think what we're going to see over the next few years is a lot of institutions in financial crisis, in academic crisis for that matter. And I think it all stems back to the incorporation {of the former polytechnics as universities) in 1992 because I think since that point, I mean, I've talked about vision and priorities here but I'm sure there are lots of other institutions which would say exactly the same thing simply because now we are all being expected to do everything very well. And I still think that by far the best structure was when the universities did what they did well. The polytechnics, many of them were excellent at what they did and had a specific market for what they did. Um, and whilst I don't question the fact that universities should teach better than they did, I think there are problems about expecting people to suddenly become super researchers in the polytechnics. You know, for all of us to be rushing towards widening participation, for all of us to be looking at making arrangements for special needs students and things of that type. I mean, to a certain extent of course, we can all do that, but it seems to me that to give widening participation as an example, which is probably not politically correct but I just think that, I mean the short answer for us is that we don't want widening participation. The only way that we would widen the participation is if we creamed off the absolutely top of that group of people.
>
> Academic Registrar, pre-1992

A key aspect of the contemporary climate in higher education for the administrators we interviewed was that the distinction once made between administrators and academics (Dobson 2000; Morey 2003; Christiansen, Stombler, and Thaxton 2004) was not as sharp as it had been in the past, an observation perhaps confirmed by the indication that fewer of our sample of manager-academics than in Middlehurst's (1992) study a decade earlier totally, distanced themselves from the label of 'manager', even though not many embraced it as their main identity:

> I think certainly at Y the distinction between administrators and academics has very much been eroded over the last say 10 years since, I mean incorporation {in 1989} is the major threshold for us rather than university status.

> > Secretary-Registrar, post-1992

In all of the accounts from the research reviewed in this chapter, from the mixed participant focus groups through to the views of HoDs, Vice Chancellors and administrators, there is a strong emphasis on the recency of changes to the management of higher education and on the turbulent external funding and policy environment which is thought to have brought some of these changes about. How does this sit with an analysis of old and new forms of management of higher education?

New and Old Forms of Managerialism

Estimates of the time-scale of changes to UK higher education by respondents in the ESRC study varied from vague statements about 'recent' or 'new' changes to estimates of a time-span ten or more years. Indeed it was quite often perceived that the current era was the only one in which universities had experienced a number of specific challenges to their autonomy. Only a tiny minority of interviewees mentioned significant details of the history of UK higher education policy before the early 1980s, even though probably over half of our sample had been working in higher education before that time.

One of the difficulties encountered in trying to work out what is new and what is old about forms of Managerialism in UK universities between the 1970s and the present time is that there are no definitive research data on expectations of manager-academics earlier than Middlehurst's (1993) book. Middlehurst's data suggested mixed views amongst manager-academics and administrators about the desirability of organizational and management changes, with administrators more broadly favourable to committee-streamlining than academics (Middlehurst 1993).

There are, however, a number of pieces that do offer some clues about earlier decades. The phenomenon most often credited with changing the management, planning and governance of UK universities by making it more corporate (institutional rather than academic-committee or department focused) and more tightly organized (Middlehurst 1993) was the

1985 Jarratt Report on University Efficiency (Jarratt 1985). Interestingly though, Jarratt looked mainly at financial management, purchasing and estate and buildings, not at academic management *per se*. Nevertheless, the recommendations of Jarratt can be seen to be the forerunner in UK universities of key changes associated with NM. These included streamlining of committee systems, the use of performance indicators and budget devolution to cost centres at department or faculty level. However, the latter two changes were not specific to the late 1980s. Both were advocated in the early 1970s in a book on university planning (Fielden and Lockwood 1973) albeit, so far as devolved resources were concerned, in an attempt to create innovation. Devolved resources were not seen by Fielden either as a system of departmental accountability using performance controls and target-setting or as a means by which senior managers could distance themselves from the effects of cuts in resources and staffing (Shattock 1999), both of which are commonplace views of such mechanisms now.

The Jarratt Report in the mid 1980s certainly helped to shift strategic decision-making relating to finance, long-term planning, purchasing and estates, into the hands of administrators and Councils (or Courts in Scotland, both are names for the governing bodies of universities, composed mainly of lay people from business and commerce and local politicians, with limited staff representation), rather than relying mainly on academic committees. This was a significant shift. In the 1970s, Moodie and Eustace had noted that although in theory, Councils had overall responsibility for university management, this was in practice rarely exercised

> in the nineteenth century the internal powers of court and council were virtually unqualified. In this century, however, Councils' powers have been steadily reduced by insistence on the need to consult senate and by the grant of specific powers to the latter.
>
> Moodie and Eustace 1974: 34

The authors go on to say, 'the secular trend ... is towards increasing academic self government especially, but by no means only ... on academic issues' (Moodie and Eustace 1974: 58).

The Jarratt Report also recommended that HoDs should have clearly specified duties and be fully supported in their management roles, including being paid an allowance. VCs, it suggested, should begin to see themselves as chief executives, not just academic leaders. Some writers argue that this was initially strongly resisted by academics and some VCs. However, the entry of the former polytechnics into the university sector in 1992 may have brought about a sea change. The 'VC as Chief Executive' approach was much more compatible with the polytechnics, who were given freedom from local government control as independent corporations in the late 1980s, though remaining publicly funded and gained university status in 1992. The polytechnics came to incorporated status from a local government tradition of hierarchical line-management of all staff, considerable bureaucracy, no research funding as of right (although some staff did conduct research) and regular inspection of teaching by the Council for National Academic Awards, which validated polytechnic and college degree programmes (Shattock 1999). Furthermore, whereas Pro-Vice Chancellors in the pre-1992 Universities were mainly academics undertaking the role temporarily, the equivalent, the former Assistant Directors of the ex-polytechnics, were already full-time career managers. As Shattock notes, when in 1988 the former polytechnics left local government, they were reconstituted with small governing bodies, sometimes with very little staff representation (this was only changed after the 1997 Dearing Report on Higher Education), whose powers were much wider than those of the universities.

Much of what we have come to think of as new in the management of UK universities in the late 1990s goes back at least to the early 1980s, if not earlier. This is undoubtedly due in no small part to the election of a Conservative Government in 1979, which introduced large public expenditure cuts and emphasized management practices from the private sector for public services (Shattock 1999; Parry 2001b). The impact of such changes (both positive and negative) were described in a detailed personal account by an academic who experienced these cuts at first hand when his university, Aston, suffered a dramatic decline in funding, losing half its staff and departments over a four-year period (Walford 1987).

Many of the dramatic changes introduced were nevertheless assimilated into the existing structures of Departments, Faculties, Senates (the major decision-making committee of academics), and governing Councils/Courts. HoDs, Deans, and VCs remained in place, although subtle changes to their roles began to occur. The differences today as compared with the 1980s are mostly attributable to four factors. These are firstly, the size of the system today as compared with the 1970s (Shattock 1999), secondly, the reform of the relationship between universities and the state so that the state now has the upper hand (Kogan and Hanney 2000; Parry 2001b), thirdly, declining public funding, and fourthly, the introduction of external audits of teaching, research, and academic standards. These four developments, and especially the last-named, changed many practices previously dear to academics. Universities (unlike the polytechnics) had not been used to external interference in their work or any kind of inspection regime other than external examining, which itself has been subject to critique (Piper 1994; Silver 1996; Hannan and Silver 2004, 2006) as a flawed practice. Thus, the extent of academic autonomy over research and teaching had been high. Robert Aitken, then VC of Birmingham, wrote in 1966.

> The teaching activities of a department must be co-ordinated by a higher authority (the Faculty) for the obvious reason that a given student is often taught in more departments than one; similarly the examining activities of a department must be regulated by the Faculty and Senate in order that reasonably uniform standards may be maintained... By contrast, the research activities of a department are almost entirely its own affair.
>
> Aitken 1966: 14

The activities themselves can still be recognized as being at the heart of academic departments, but few academics in UK universities now can conceive of teaching being regulated only within their institutions or research being simply left to departments. Both are now heavily externally audited and monitored. In the 1970s, Livingstone suggested that the organizational features of UK universities included:

> a complete absence of hierarchy. Moreover the orientation of most staff is 'professional' which implicitly rejects hierarchical organization as relevant for their work. In common with most 'professional' organizations there is an absence of sanctions ...once given a permanent appointment...a teacher has almost total job security...university authorities have very little formal control over the activities of individual members of staff.
>
> Livingstone 1974: 109–11

He would surely hardly recognize the complex array of Deputy and Pro-Vice Chancellors, Deans, associate Deans, Heads of Schools, Directors of Teaching Quality, Directors of Educational Development, Widening Participation Officers, Directors of Research and Enterprise, and other senior administrators who now hold sway in many UK universities.

The UK government (especially in England) has become much more interventionist in higher education and the power of audit has been extended to almost every university activity, except perhaps administration (Wood 2002). Academic work has also lost much of its security. Academic tenure (whereby an academic is appointed to a post until retirement and cannot be removed except for acts of gross moral turpitude) was abolished in 1987 for new appointments. Tenure never existed in the polytechnics. Contemporary HoDs do not have full hiring and firing powers but can 'encourage' early retirement of staff perceived as performing poorly; indeed the desire to do such 'encouragement' may be partially driven by the existence of devolved budgets. More senior manager-academics may, if they follow agreed procedures, offer voluntary redundancy or early retirement to individual staff and Vice-Chancellors now can and do close departments (notably expensive science departments) that cost too much to run or which have done badly in external audits of research or fail to recruit sufficient students. We have come a long way from Aitken's autonomous academics (1966) and Livingstone's lack of hierarchy (1974), even though academic leadership still survives in the form of motivation of staff and representing the university. One analysis assesses the extent to which Fielden and Lockwood's (1973) ideas for planning and management in universities have been implemented (Watson 2000). Certainly devolved resources have been realized and performance indicators (in league tables) are everywhere, even if the values and philosophies promoted by Fielden and Lockwood (1973) do not match those of Managerialism. The recommendation of the 1985 Jarratt Report, that Vice Chancellors should henceforth think of themselves as Chief Executives (thus contrasting with the view of their role as the leading academic in their institution) is also well and truly with us, even though other aspects of more conventional academic leadership still survive intact.

Conclusion

The period in UK universities since the mid-1960s has witnessed many changes, both to the higher education systems it encompasses and also to the number of institutions, how the system is funded, forms of public accountability of academics, management and governance and who aspires to (and gets access to) a university education. It is evident that the blending of new and old forms of Managerialism in UK universities has involved a complex process of internal developments and reforms in universities in response to a more hostile external environment. Amongst these have been changing expectations about how academic knowledge work should be led and managed. The election of a Conservative government in 1979 heralded an end to the previous fairly amicable relationship between the state and universities (Taggart 2003) and saw the first attempts to reduce units of funding per student, shrink academic autonomy and subject higher education to management and governance regimes derived from the private for-profit sector. Though academics in management and leadership roles retained their previous job titles and long-established responsibilities for over-seeing research, teaching and staff morale (the 'older' forms of Managerialism), other expectations related to finance, individual academic performance and enhanced public accountability began to be added (the 'new' elements of Managerialism). The changes were initially resisted but hastened by the gradual transformation of the polytechnics, initially as independent corporations and then as fully fledged universities. They brought with them a more bureaucratic and managerial history as formerly local-government regulated institutions and a different tradition of governance involving more lay people and fewer academics, as well as a much more teaching-focused orientation. At the same time, UK higher education moved from being an elite to a mass system, experienced considerable resource-dependency problems, and faced varying attempts to measure the quality of research and teaching.

Awareness of this relatively recent history of UK HE is not necessarily widespread amongst manager-academics. A considerable number of respondents in the ESRC project at the end of the 1990s thought of changes to what was expected of university managers and leaders (for example dealing with devolved budgets and performance indicators) as very recent. Yet this is not borne out by other evidence of changes to UK higher education over the last two or so decades. The current system of managing universities in the UK is one that has been in train for more than twenty years, since the first cuts in university spending were introduced in the early 1980s, when new expectations about how academic knowledge work should be managed began to surface. Furthermore, although specific policies, reports, and changes to funding arrangements contributed to some of the developments such as devolved budgets, VCs as Chief Executives, the endeavour to remove academic autonomy, the introduction of efficiency savings and new forms of institutional management and governance in the 1980s, a number of such ideas had already begun to surface in the 1970s.

Since then, the purposes of higher education have also been held up to detailed public and political scrutiny (Readings 1996; Barnett 1999;

Delanty 2001) for all sorts of reasons, from post-modern ideas about the end of universal knowledge to the diversity of students, presumed effects of globalization (Etzkowitz and Leydesdorff 1997; Gibbons 1998; Scott 1998; Enders and Fulton 2002; King 2004), new technologies of knowledge management (Fuller 2002) and the view that higher education is central to sustained economic growth (Wolf 2002). New and old forms of Managerialism have indeed been blended together but it is now the (relatively) new that predominate in expectations about how academic knowledge work should be managed and led. Whether the contemporary UK university can survive the domination of management above all else, is something we shall return to in subsequent chapters.

3

The Knowledge Worker and the Divided University

Introduction

In the previous chapter the focus was on the changes that have taken place in the UK higher education systems since the 1960s and 1970s. This chapter examines the contemporary conditions of academic work and management in UK universities as organizations (the level which was the focus of much of Reed's theoretical analysis in Chapter 1). In so doing, it also raises questions about the wider purposes of universities in the modern world. Whilst academics are often now described as expert knowledge workers engaged in teaching and research, as part of the knowledge economy and the knowledge society, the typical organizational and management arrangements of universities and the challenges of higher education policy are seen by many critics to reflect neither the trust and autonomy needed to undertake creative work nor the appropriate strategic direction required of a twenty-first century higher education institution (Trow 1997; Jary and Parker 1998; Delanty 2001; Fuller 2002). Although universities have long been infused by the different subject and disciplinary interests of scholars, both in the UK and elsewhere, these divisions in the UK are now supplemented by further divisions based on academics' contractual position, the institutions they work in, pay differentials unrelated to differences in qualifications, workload, experience and responsibilities, tensions between research and teaching, gender/ethnicity, and a widening gap between managers/leaders and 'managed staff'. Employees and managers of higher education institutions that are both internally divided and also divided from each other in competing for resources and students, despite various attempts at collaboration, have to deal with many contradictory demands and pressures. Indeed, a number of writers have pointed to the challenges that contemporary universities face as their traditional role disappears in the face of technological change, intellectual uncertainty, increased state regulation, and competition from corporate universities (Readings 1996; Smith and Webster 1997; Barnett 1999, 2003).

In the UK, the response to these challenges by government has been to increase the degree of regulation and monitoring of academic work and universities, whilst decreasing the amount of public funding. This is not an uncommon response in countries where spending on a previously well-developed welfare state is now increasingly scrutinized by government (Kwiek 2005, 2006). The UK government has, since 1997, with the election of the New Labour administration, particularly emphasized the key part played by the participation of previously under-represented social groups in higher education in fostering economic growth, even though the basis for this link is highly contentious (Wolf 2002). This has created many constraints as well as opportunities for UK universities, as we saw in some of the comments from HoDs and VCs in the last chapter. In particular, the ways in which knowledge work is managed in universities have begun to change, as we also saw in the last chapter, and there are now active managerial strategies rather than collegial approaches in place to do this.

Knowledge Work and Knowledge Management

The terms 'knowledge economy', 'knowledge society' and even 'knowledge management' are ones that are now very familiar not only to social scientists but to almost everyone in the Western world who reads a daily paper or watches TV news. It follows from this that since 'everyone' is part of the knowledge society then, ergo, everyone in any kind of professional or managerial employment, including academics, must therefore be a knowledge worker. However, rather like the way in which the word globalization is used to refer to every phenomenon which takes place beyond or across the boundaries of a single country, the precise meaning of the various terms related to knowledge work and societies is not always readily apparent. Knowledge is almost certainly as old as civilization and human life themselves and although the so-called information technology revolution does indeed throw into sharp relief the relationship between knowledge and information, this is not the first time the importance of this relationship has been questioned. Furthermore, technological determinism is still as alive and well in the twenty-first century as it was in the twentieth century. In the 1950s and 1960s there was a magazine called *Mechanics Illustrated* which earnestly propagated the view that by the end of the twentieth century robots would carry out almost all paid and domestic work, whilst humans would travel everywhere by monorail, accompanied by sightings of flying saucers. Unfortunately, few of the magazine's predictions have come to pass, nicely demonstrating the problems of predicting future change on the basis of technology alone. A number of the discussions and explanations of 'knowledge societies' and the so-called 'information age', though in some cases brilliantly written (Castells 1996, 1997*a*, 1997*b*, 1997*c*), are no less technologically driven than much older debates such as, for example, the explanation of the effects of the invention of the stirrup on change in medieval societies (White 1962). So arguing that changes to communication technologies alone have altered the context and work of academics and universities, as though academics were never previously part of the knowledge or information society, is unhelpful. The argument that contemporary universities no longer have a monopoly of knowledge is also flawed, since it is not evident that they ever had such a monopoly (or if they did, it was many centuries ago). Notwithstanding, ideas about the place of academics and universities in the knowledge society still proliferate. The latter is a fashionable concept, in which as Fuller, slightly tongue in cheek, says ' "knowledge" is the new "capital" and "knowledge management" the science of this revolutionary order' (Fuller 2002: 6).

Some writers have pointed to changes in the conception of knowledge that affect what universities (and by association, academics too) are concerned with. Amongst these is Gibbons's much cited analysis based on two types of knowledge (Gibbons et al. 1994). The first of these, mode 1 knowledge, is seen as being grounded in strong and hierarchically based academic disciplines, where knowledge is transmitted via an apprenticeship model of learning. This is, for example, how anthropologists explain how they teach their research students to carry out fieldwork (Delamont, Atkinson and Parry 1997*a*, 2000; Delamont, Parry, and Atkinson 1997*b*) and art and design academics encourage doctoral students to relate theory to practice (Hockey 2003). The second type of knowledge, mode 2 knowledge, is seen by contrast to be non-hierarchical, interdisciplinary, not focused on a 'knowledge for knowledge's sake' basis, and responsive to a range of social, political, and economic priorities outside the university itself (Gibbons et al. 1994). Gibbons and some other writers (Lyotard 1984) see the development of mode 2 knowledge as a threat to the existence of universities as we have previously known them, since, they contend that there can be no longer be any agreement on the purposes and goals of universities. The argument about the university in crisis will be revisited again later.

In one sense, the importance of knowledge to higher education is self-evident, even though as Delanty notes, the significance of the link between an understanding of the development of universities and the sociologies of knowledge is not widely recognized (Delanty 2001). Academics deal with knowledge in many different ways, and whatever Gibbon et al. (1994) say about new forms of (mode 2) knowledge, many academics still base their identity on their discipline or subject (Benninghof and Sormoni 2005; Musselin and Becquet 2005; Deem and Lucas 2007). Their allegiance is more often to that discipline, either within their own basic unit or in a learned society or with members of the same 'tribe' in different institutions (Henkel 2000; Becher and Trowler 2001) than their university. In the NM research, we found that the non-academic staff we interviewed during our four detailed case studies, comparing manager-academic views with those of other staff, were far more likely to express loyalty to their institution than were academics (Deem 2003). In Chapter 2, it was noted that a number of the administrators we interviewed also raised this point.

Academics both create knowledge and they also make use of and transmit knowledge; in the UK both their knowledge transmission and their knowledge production are assessed and audited. Indeed, as was mentioned in Chapter 2, there has also been an expectation since the 1993 *Realising Our Potential* White Paper onwards (Great Britain: Chancellor of the Duchy of Lancaster 1993), that academics pay attention to the needs of industry in relation to their research. Furthermore, as Fuller notes, in contemporary times, the new organizational imperative is that knowledge must be 'managed' (Fuller 2002), even though many organizational managers are not at all clear what this means. In the context of universities, it has usually meant 'managing' both research and teaching, though whether a rational or a more anarchic approach to research is better for research creativity remains unclear (Deem 1998). In addition, the tensions between teaching and research are now acute in the UK and the relationship between the two is hotly debated (Harley and Lee 1997; Harley 2002; Lindsay, Breen, and Jenkins 2002, 2005; Deem 2006*b*).

The managing of knowledge production through research in UK universities usually involves at least two different sets of activities. The first of these is the managing of the gathering of funds through external grant applications, intellectual property rights, and spin-off companies, a crucial part of what Slaughter and Leslie refer to as academic capitalism (Slaughter and Leslie 1997). In the UK, as elsewhere, this set of activities is often carried out by a discrete organizational unit, with research and enterprise development as its main focus (ironically, these units rarely contain any actual researchers). The second set of activities focuses on the monitoring and regulating of the performance of research, including analysing the gaining of funding by academic staff and the varied forms of output that they produce, such as publications, software, or artefacts. The processes undertaken may also involve identifying underperforming staff, perhaps persuading them to leave or retire early or changing their contracts to focus solely on teaching and administration. A Pro-Vice-Chancellor interviewed in our research talked of a recent exercise in that university to get rid of academics not considered 'research active' (itself a somewhat controversial term):

Last year, a group of a hundred of my colleagues were offered Premature Retirement Compensation; they weren't forced out, they were offered PRC schemes. And the university is going to get a lot tougher about performance. Now obviously that's tough...I would have to say those people have not performed...if you are then going to be absolutely blunt about it, they haven't fully done what they are paid for doing.

PVC, pre-1992

Such management of research knowledge production may also lead to views like those described by Marginson and Considine (2000) in an encounter on a research visit to a medium-sized institution of higher education in Australia, namely Gumtree University:[2]

The first interview was with the university's leading non-academic administrator. He talked fluently and at length about strategic issues facing the institution.... But when he began talking about research, the confident matter of fact tone gave way to a more distancing voice. There was a kind of diffidence, in a tone of respect, as if the world of research with its various secrets was a world that he as a manager could never completely grasp. Yet there was frustration too. How could all that creative energy be harnessed so as to maximise the university's position? The problem—as he unselfconsciously and unforgettably put it—was 'to make the butterflies fly in formation'.

Marginson and Considine 2000: 133

[2] This name is a pseudonymn.

71

As Marginson and Considine go on to say, universities locked in competition with others for resources are constantly looking for institutional advantage: 'research is a primary source of institutional prestige and income...research is the pre-eminent 'numbers game' in the Enterprise University.... By externalising a university's research, it can be imagined as a single quantifiable system. Managers can count it, control it and give it shape' (Marginson and Considine 2000: 133). This kind of pressure for status and institutional positioning has also increased as league tables of universities have become popular not only within countries but also internationally (Merisotis and Sadlak 2005; Mok 2005), with research indicators a major focus, though teaching indicators are also often included too.

Managing knowledge work in teaching has its own peculiarities and complexities. The conduct and timetabling of teaching are more easily managed than research, as teaching is a much more routinized activity. Its performance can also be monitored via student evaluations, exam results, and external examiners' reports, as well as by external quality inspections. But unlike research, which is valued in all universities albeit to varying degrees, the status of teaching varies enormously in different universities. In some institutions, teaching has high value and status but in others it is held in relatively low regard. It is not unheard of in some research-intensive institutions for teaching to be regarded as a form of punishment for those showing low productivity in research, so that someone who does little or no research (or does not do the 'right kind' of research, that is, grant winning and publications in refereed journals or research-based books or their equivalent) may be given extra teaching. Conversely, those successful in research may have relatively little teaching, and indeed both in the UK and USA, research 'stars', particularly senior members of the professoriate, may negotiate their workload to specifically exclude significant amounts of teaching (Dill 2003). A Head of Department respondent in our NM project said of his workload system:

> I came in idealistically thinking that we could change people, particularly that we could change people who had not been active researchers into active researchers.... I introduced a workload model into the department so people were allocated to bins...low, medium or high research rich and correspondingly low, medium or high teaching rich...we made it very clear that, this was all done in the open so everyone could see what everybody else was teaching and we made it very clear that you can move...if you don't much want to be a high teaching person, then this is what you have to do in order to move into a different category.
>
> HoD, Social Science, pre-1992 University

Other aspects of teaching require more complex treatment in their 'knowledge management'. Although student assessment results and degree classes can be quantified, this has an uncertain relationship to the quality of teaching. Teaching can be managed through such devices as timetabling of lectures, laboratory/practical classes and seminars, monitoring of the staff/student ratio and allocating minimum teaching contact hours to all academics. The curriculum too can be 'knowledge-managed', which is what the UK Quality Assurance Agency for Higher Education tried to do when it introduced the concept of Subject Benchmarking (a kind of national HE curriculum by subject) in the late 1990s (Quality Assurance Agency 2002), although this was highly controversial at the time. Panels of subject teaching specialists tried to decide what the core curricular elements of an undergraduate programme would be in a given discipline, giving rise to interesting debates and processes in some subjects (Wisby 2002). These benchmarks were then to be used by QAA subject assessors when assessing the quality of teaching on inspection team visits to departments in universities. QAA subject review (now replaced by a new system more focused on institutional standards and quality rather than reviewing each subject separately) also provided an opportunity to quantify teaching performance when it moved from its initial post-1997 use of grades such as 'satisfactory' and 'outstanding', to numerical scores on six categories (e.g. quality management and enhancement, student progression and achievement, and so on), with a maximum of four marks for each aspect and a top score of 24 in all. Thus, just as research knowledge managers could talk of a grade 5* (top grade in the UK Research Assessment Exercises of 1996 and 2001, subsequently joined by a grade 6* to reward consistent performance at a high level in the 1996 and 2001 exercises) or a grade 3 (national level) researcher or department, so teaching managers learned to speak of a 24/24 department or a 17/24 department.

But whilst universities like to quantify when they are in control, quantification of QAA scores alongside the proliferation of paperwork involved in assessing teaching quality quickly led to demands for a modified system. Furthermore, analysts of QAA processes and systems like Roger Cook have argued that rising scores in subject review indicated not that standards had risen but that academics and those responsible for teaching quality in higher education institutions had successfully learnt to play the game of teaching quality assessment (Cook 2001; Baty 2002a, 2002b). In England, the modified system of inspection used from 2003 onwards involved institutional visits and more limited investigation of subject departments at the same time, with judgements such as broad confidence or limited confidence in the institution's academic standards, rather than a numerical grade, though at the present time (2006) even the subject trails seem set to disappear. Whether the institutional audits will indeed prove a lighter touch assessment and thus lead to less overt knowledge management in relation to teaching is as yet unknown. External quality assurance mechanisms for teaching have become increasingly central to the activities of many UK academic knowledge workers from the 1990s onwards and are also the source of much anxiety amongst academics (Morley 2003). Whether the elaborate system of UK HE quality assurance has actually made any significant difference to the quality of teaching and learning remains an open question but there is certainly no shortage of critics of the system (Morley 2003; Harvey 2005).

The Contemporary Academic Knowledge Worker: De-Professionalized or Re-Professionalized?

The state of academic knowledge work and the status of academics in the UK has been the subject of considerable investigation and debate in recent years (Halsey 1992; Cuthbert 1996; Fulton 1996a; Henkel 2000; Fulton and Holland 2001). Nor is the debate about the status and pay of academics, the extent of their autonomy, and the conditions under which they work, confined to investigations of academics based in the UK. It is both a European debate (Enders 2001) and a worldwide one (Altbach 1996). There is some agreement that the conditions of academic work, at least for those employed in publicly funded institutions, have changed in recent decades, partly as a result of shifts from elite to mass systems of higher education and cuts in public expenditure (Kwiek 2005, 2006). Systems of external accountability in respect of teaching quality have begun to emerge in many countries (Brennan and Shah 2000; Shah and Brennan 2000). Even the UK emphasis on research assessment (Harley and Lowe 1998; McNay 2003; Lucas 2006) is not entirely unique, with Hong Kong, Australia, and New Zealand now having undertaken somewhat similar exercises (von Tunzelmann and Mbula 2003). As Fuller (2002) and others have noted, the requirements of teaching and research are very different. The tensions between these activities have affected everything from the often low importance attached to teaching innovation (Hannan and Silver 2000) as compared with research innovation, through to the undervaluing of academic staff who are not considered 'research-active' (Elkin 2002; Harley 2002; McNay 2003; Lucas 2006). One of the consequences of activities like research assessment quality exercises is that not all knowledge work is considered of equal value: certain kinds of research, typically blue skies research, may be seen as more valuable than applied research by elite universities. This is despite the fact that the UK government has been trying for some years to emphasize applied research, technology transfer from HE to industry and the importance of higher education/industry links (Lambert Committee on Business-University Collaboration 2003). Teaching as a form of knowledge work may also be devalued by research quality assessment activities. There is, furthermore, a critical question about how research and teaching connect, if at all.

In England, the relative merits and importance of teaching and research in HE have become quite controversial (Deem 2006*b*). In 2002 the then chief executive of the Higher Education Funding Council for England, Professor Sir Howard Newby, suggested that there was too much research in English higher education:

> The volume of research has to reduce. It is the very commitment to research—a professional commitment that often overrides economic considerations—that risks compromising the financial health of universities, the symptom of which is an unsustainable erosion in infrastructure and in staff pay and conditions.
>
> Goddard 2002

This view suggested that future research funding in England was likely to remain highly selective (Newby 2002) whereas in Scotland the Higher Education Funding Council seemed to be working with a somewhat more inclusive agenda for its research (Deem 2006*b*), with a particular emphasis on helping to fund applications of research to arenas outside the university and on increasing the volume of research conducted (Gani 2002) as well as on funding applied research (Scottish Higher Education Funding Council and Scottish Executive Education Department 2002). Thus Scottish universities, which historically have inhabited a differently structured higher education system, look like retaining these differences (Scottish Executive 2003, 2004) and even developing new ones (Deem and Lucas 2007), with the possibility that academics working in Scotland will in future have working lives lived out in institutions which are rather different from those of their English counterparts. Indeed, Scotland has recently moved to a single funding body for all its post-school education (Scottish Parliament 2005), a radical shift not yet replicated elsewhere in the UK.

It is not only the funding and assessment of academics' twin knowledge activities, research and teaching, that have been changing. The kinds of management ideologies and practices used in public service service organizations in the Western world have also changed, as we saw both in Chapter 1 and 2. There has been a shift towards seeing public services as more comparable to private sector organizations, with a move away from ideas and practices developed primarily for use in public service organizations (which recognized the distinctive value basis of those who work in such organizations) and designed for the management of professionals in publicly funded organizations. The latter included what Mintzberg has referred to as bureau-professionalism (Mintzberg 1983), a blend of bureaucracy mediated by the work of quasi-autonomous professionals. Instead, there has been increased adoption of forms of management developed in private sector organizations, moving through neoliberal to neo-technocratic Managerialism from the 1980s through to the present time. Such forms of management have a focus on external markets, internal markets, cost centres, efficiency and value for money, outsourcing, the monitoring of individual and group performances, and emphasis on teamwork and the setting of income and other targets (Ferlie et al. 1996; Clarke and Newman 1997; Exworthy and Halford 1999; Cutler and Waine 2000; Deem 2004). It is not clear that all of these practices have been equally, or (in some cases) at all, successful, either inside or outside the public services. Thus, for instance, some private sector organizations have recognized that outsourcing of their work may bring unanticipated problems. There was discussion in 2004–5 about a wider introduction of performance-related pay (PRP), which already exists for many professorial staff in higher education in England, possibly partially informed by the National Student Satisfaction Surveys (Higher Education Funding Council 2005). These surveys began in 2005 and include all completing undergraduate students in England, Wales, and Northern Ireland categorized by the subjects taken. PRP has largely been rejected by private sector firms (Brehony 2001) as well as proving very challenging to use in public service organizations (Marsden and French 1998; Waine 2000, Cutler and Waine 2001, 2004). Furthermore, for academic staff, any strong emphasis on individual performance, whether in research or teaching, can also lead to what Fuller calls academic bullionism: 'the sheer accumulation in some universities of "big names" or star academics whose enormous salaries and discretionary time allow them to generate a load of publications whilst doing nothing to nurture local talent or even to ensure that the big names productivity has maximum impact' (Fuller 2002: 31). In recent years, public service organizations have also been urged to put more emphasis on things such as teamwork, and indeed the responses of some of our ESRC project interviewees suggested that it was no longer just the laboratory-based sciences which were heavily based on teamwork but that increasingly this had spread to other subjects too, in teaching if not in research. However, Sennett has pointed to the difficulties of translating notions of team-based project work from the private sector, where teams are assembled (and then broken up) for a particular project, often driven by the need for short-term product innovation aimed at company stock-holders, to the public sector where both teams and projects have much greater longevity and quite different aims and values from those found in the private sector (Sennett 1998, 2002, 2006).

The funding basis of UK higher education has also been changing, as the public purse becomes ever less able to keep up with the demands made on it. There are two particularly noteworthy aspects of this. Firstly, public–private finance initiatives (PFI), now quite extensively found in construction projects in public services, are being used in higher education (especially but not exclusively for student residences). PFI is highly controversial and raises many questions about value for money, account-ability to the public, stability of the private sector organizations providing PFI deals and long-term maintenance (Pollock and Price 2004), even if it does provide for the growth needs of cash-strapped public service organizations. In addition, although upfront undergraduate tuition fees introduced into UK HE after the 1997 Dearing and Garrick Reports have now disappeared, new (and more expensive) variable undergraduate fees (with an upper limit which most HEIs intend to charge) have been introduced in England and Northern Ireland from autumn 2006 (and in Wales from 2007), although students from low-income households can get some fee remittance. The fee situation was discussed in more detail in the previous chapter but its consequences are to transfer more of the costs of higher education to individual students or their parents/guardians, thus raising questions about whether UK higher education is still a public service.

Though ideas about new managerial ideologies have permeated UK universities (Reed 2002; Deem and Brehony 2005) and were much to the forefront of discussions in the NM project focus groups, they have arguably had less impact in HE than in the health services or in local government (Ferlie et al. 1996; Exworthy and Halford 1999; Webb 1999). This may be because many academics, with a long tradition of individualistic pursuit of knowledge and senior academics offering or withdrawing academic patronage from those newer to academic life (Bourdieu 1988), have developed a dislike of and resistance to being managed. As we saw in the last chapter, both manager-academics and senior administrators we interviewed referred to the difficulties of managing ever-critical academics and the capacity of the latter for resistance.

There is, however, little agreement on the perceived effects of the many changes to the environment of universities from the outside and inside on academics. Thus there are those who argue that academics have been de-professionalized or proletarianized relative to other professionals, as their work has been increasingly scrutinized, made subject to more routinization (e.g. in undergraduate teaching), and their pay and status have declined (Halsey 1992; Winter 1995). The boundaries between academics and other university staff such as those employed in learning support or administration are also argued to have become more blurred than before, so that academics are now less distinctive (Dobson 2000; Christiansen, Stombler, and Thaxton 2004) as a professional occupation than they once were. Conversely, others have argued that academics are increasingly becoming more differentiated from each other. Some researchers have suggested that a minority of academics, especially in subject areas where applied research is highly marketable to the private sector, have become fully-fledged academic capitalists who are able to supplement their salaries from spin-off companies and consultancy work (Slaughter and Leslie 1997; Clark 1998; Marginson and Considine 2000). It is also claimed that the institutions in which academic capitalists work have become much more enterprise-focused, although some studies of entrepreneurialism and academic capitalism exhibit methodological shortcomings which cast doubt on the veracity of the findings (Deem 2001). Other commentators have noted the wide range of academic responses to change, from those who embrace it wholeheartedly, through those who accommodate to its requirements or adapt it to their own interests to those who ignore or resist it (Trowler 1998; Boxer 2005).

There is also a question mark about who and what constitutes an academic member of staff. Current research by Gallacher[3] and others examines the increased blurring of boundaries between academics and others who support teaching, learning, and research, such as librarians and staff development specialists (Dobson 2000; Christiansen, Stombler, and Thaxton 2004). Furthermore, as we show in this book, academics who take on management roles are another example of such blurring of

---

[3] This research is being carried out by Cathryn Gallacher, Assistant Director of Information Services at Bristol University, for a Ph.D. being supervised in the Graduate School of Education.

boundaries between those who are 'just' academics and those whose work was once the main preserve of career-managers and administrators.

Henkel's work on UK academic identities claims that contemporary academics retain their traditional value adherence to research, teaching, and their discipline or basic unit, whilst also being engaged in a form of communitarian re-professionalization (Henkel 2000). However, such values are severely tested by a system which is constantly trying to prise apart research and teaching and which is also increasing the selectivity of research funding, now with increased emphasis on metrics like grant income and citation indices (Sastry and Bekhradnia 2006) as a possible replacement for the current labour-intensive and peer-review heavy, RAE. In addition, Fulton has drawn attention to the possibility that academics may choose to work in institutions that mirror their own interest in pursuing either a research or teaching-focused career (Fulton 1996a). Strangely though, the debate about academic work seems to have paid relatively little attention to how easy or difficult it is now to establish an academic career and the risks that have to be taken in early career. Generation is also significant in another way too. It seems likely, and Henkel's work (2000) lends some support to this, that early-career academics take for granted a particular set of conditions of academic life, whether research assessment, teaching audits, or high workloads, which some of those in mid-or late-career find more problematic or challenging because it represents a change from when they entered academe. This point is made by Lucas in her study of the UK RAE and staff reactions to it; some more recently appointed academics she interviewed quite explicitly regarded research as game with rules which they needed to learn how to play in order to gain competitive advantage (Lucas 2006), whilst a number of more established academics were much more antagonistic to the notion of assessing research quality. We have already seen how the notion of effective game playing has been applied to the assessment of teaching quality (Cook 2001; Baty 2002a, 2002b). The knowledge worker then has become, or perhaps always was, a knowledgeable player who in turn is knowledge-managed. So much then, for the academics themselves. What of the institutions in which they work? How have these changed in recent decades?

The University in Crisis?

A number of authors in the last few years have pointed to the difficulties faced by contemporary universities (Readings 1996; Barnett 1999, 2003,

2006; Delanty 2001; Kwiek 2006), no longer sure of their role and purpose in a complex, globalized, and uncertain world, with new technologies and modes of communication raising questions about the future of conventional academic teaching and research and fresh priorities for the public purse questioning public expenditure on higher education. In the knowledge society, everyone, not just a few academics and industrial scientists, is engaged in knowledge work. The debate about the role of universities depends partially for its inspiration on what was seen to be the purpose of universities in the past. For many, Cardinal John Henry Newman's book *The Idea of the University*, first published in 1853, provided an important starting point. Newman, as newly installed rector of the new university in Dublin, gave a series of lectures in 1852 in which he set out his vision of the university (Newman 1976). He saw the university as a place where universal knowledge was pursued, though as Delanty (2001) notes, Newman was more concerned with knowledge in a teaching context than in relation to research. University knowledge for Newman made a strong contribution to the public sphere, since he saw the university as an institution for communication and circulation of thought through the personal interaction of students and tutors. Delanty argues that Newman did not pursue the more Germanic vision of a university (Von Humboldt 1976) in which the position of the professor was based on the authority derived from research in a distinct disciplinary field. Rather, Newman drew principally on an English (Oxford) model of university education, where the tutor rather than the professor was the most important person in the university, with a strong emphasis on pastoral care of the student is concerned. Nevertheless, there was some overlap between Humboldt and Newman. Humboldt's vision of a university, manifested in Berlin University founded in 1810, saw Berlin as the mother of all modern universities. His concept of a 'Universitas litteratum' incorporated both research and teaching and was seen to facilitate an all-round humanistic education (Von Humboldt 1976).

Newman's view of the educational process was not one that would be likely to be approved of by the UK Quality Asurance Agency or the UK Higher Education Academy, which combines enhancement of academics' teaching and the student experience with accreditation of HE teaching qualifications. In his speech in Dublin in 1852, Newman explained how he saw the university as engaged in a transmission model of learning where a received body of knowledge was passed from tutor to student, with knowledge as an end in itself.

It is the place to which a thousand schools make contributions; in which the intellect may safely range and speculate, sure to find its equal in some antagonist activity, and its judge in the tribunal of truth. It is a place where inquiry is pushed forward, and discoveries verified and perfected, and rashness rendered innocuous, and error exposed, by the collision of mind with mind, and knowledge with knowledge. It is the place where the professor becomes eloquent, and is a missionary and a preacher, displaying his science in its most complete and most winning form, pouring it forth with the zeal of enthusiasm, and lighting up his own love of it in the breasts of his hearers.

Newman paid much less attention to the creation of new knowledge through research than he did to teaching, a reminder that the current obsession of many academics and university managers with research was not necessarily part of every traditional conception of the university.

Since the idea of universal knowledge is so central to Newman's vision of the university, it might be supposed that if this notion of knowledge is threatened or questioned, then the whole Newmanian conception of a university collapses. As the possibility that knowledge is partial, culturally specific, and relative takes hold (and it is this idea, together with the collapse of the grand theoretical narrative such as that found in Marx or Durkheim, which is at the heart of postmodernism), so anything clinging to universalism is undermined. Yet changes in ideas about knowledge are only one possible source of challenge to the Newman vision of a university. Furthermore, some other challenges may have been around for much longer than we might think.

Thus the German sociologist Max Weber, writing in the second decade of the twentieth century, talked about the potentially deleterious effects of a process of rationalization and Americanization of the German university. He referred in his essay *Science as a Vocation* (Weber 1948), first published in 1919, to the ways in which the American and German systems of higher education differed. In the German system at that time, the new academic was not paid a salary, but received the fees of students taking the courses taught, and it could take many years, if at all, before an academic had established a sufficiently strong academic reputation to make a reasonable living. In the American system, by contrast, new lecturers were salaried from the start but also, according to Weber, over burdened with teaching, and the effects of what he termed 'officials' prescribing the curriculum. So contemporary academics are not the only ones to be concerned about curriculum control, too much teaching, and whether their careers will be sustained. Weber also offered a further critique of the more bureaucratized American university which has much contemporary resonance: 'An extraordinarily wide gulf, externally and internally, exists between the chief of these large capitalist, university enterprises and the usual full professor of the old style' (Weber 1948: 131). The role of the professional university manager-academic may therefore be rather older than some of us imagine. It is certainly much older than some of the respondents from the NM project believed, as we saw in the previous chapter.

So far as the university today is concerned, the only agreement amongst scholars of higher education is that the purposes of higher education are in transition. Delanty, arguing that the history of Western social and political systems of thought are an expression of a conflict between knowledge as science and knowledge as culture, sees the university as a 'key institution of modernity and as the site where knowledge, culture and society interconnect. In essence . . . the modern university . . . {is]} a producer and transformer of knowledge as science and science as culture' (Delanty 2001: vii). He goes on to say: 'The current situation of the university reflects the contemporary condition of knowledge. The most striking aspect of this is the penetration of communications into the heart of the epistemic structure of society precisely as this is also happening to democracy, for both knowledge and democracy are being transformed by communication' (Delanty 2001: 1). Delanty argues that the university could make a fresh contribution to society by becoming the basis for a new form of public sphere and societal communication, not the Enlightenment version (Habermas 1989) of the public sphere (dependent on universal knowledge and free communication) but a new public sphere. This sphere would rescue knowledge from both diffusion and trivialization by re-linking knowledge and human interests and using the potential of new modes of knowledge production to develop cultural models that can exploit the democratic potential of knowledge transformation. 'It is the task of the university to open up sites of communication in society rather than, as it is in danger of doing, becoming a self-referential bureaucratic organization' (Delanty 2001: 7). The theme of the over-bureaucratized university recurs in other critiques too (McNay 1995; Schuller 1995; Smith and Webster 1997), though not all authors offer convincing alternatives.

Delanty goes onto explain why he believes that the university is so challenged in the current conjuncture. For him, social movements such as feminism, gay rights, and movements based on ethnicity began from the 1980s onwards to ensure that the private domain entered into the public domain of the university. He sees this as having major repercussions for academic freedom, which, he claims, is then no longer seen as neutral.

However, it has to be asked whether academic work and freedom ever was neutral, marked as it was for many decades by white male dominance. This is demonstrated in accounts of their experience of studying in a patriarchal department given by women sociology graduates from the Department of Sociology at the University of California Berkeley from the 1950s onwards (Meadow Orlans and Wallace 1994). This was far from an American-only experience; their story echoes the author's experiences as a postgraduate research student in a male-dominated sociology department in Leicester in the early 1970s (Deem 1996). For Delanty, these cultural and social shifts have meant that the university has become entangled with the development of new cultural identities.

At the same time, Delanty notes, there have been three other major changes to both universities and knowledge. Firstly, the role of state, he suggests, has moved from provider to regulator. This view is consistent with other accounts of changes to higher education policy in the UK (Kogan and Hanney 2000; Parry 2001; Taggart 2003), which detail the ways in which the state and university funding bodies have become a much more critical and controlling partner in higher education over the last decades of the twentieth century than previously. Secondly, there is the emergence of new non-university knowledge producers such as think tanks and consultants (Saint-Martin 1998), as well as the growth of the research and development sections of large private sector organizations. Finally, Delanty argues that knowledge is no longer the privilege of elites and that there are now many more people involved in definition of problems and application of solutions than there once were. At the same time, he suggests, the university still provides a base for experts, acts as a dispenser of credentials, and remains a significant arbiter of cultural capital, despite the loss of its monopoly on knowledge. Delanty also contends that the university was never as dominated by Gibbons' et al.'s mode 1 or theoretical knowledge, as is claimed (Gibbons et al. 1994).

Other writers such as Barnett echo Delanty's comments. Barnett refers to the challenge of living with uncertainty in age of chaos and organizational super-complexity as one of the main problems that the contemporary university has to deal with (Barnett 1999). He suggests that the frameworks academics use to think are constantly challenged by cultural, economic, and social political change, which in turn affects the ways in which knowledge work is conducted. In a later book Barnett suggests that universities have also been adversely affected by the presence of ideologies in the university, though managerialism does not seem to be one of these (Barnett 2003). Kwiek has argued that globalizing factors and changes to the welfare state in many Western countries have removed the unique nature of the university (Kwiek 2003, 2005, 2006). Some commentators go even further. Readings, with the US system in mind, argued that the effects of external changes on the university mean that it is now in ruins. The twin effects of globalization and the weakening of the nation state, he claimed, affect the university drastically, so it can no longer transmit and nurture national culture (Readings 1996). For Readings, the academic institution has become a tool of corporate capitalism and its past historical purpose has vanished. However, as others have pointed out, for an institution that is supposedly in ruins, there are still a lot of universities in existence and thus perhaps a role for them remains. But no one can quite agree on what it is. Thus, whereas, Fuller argues that the university can become a site of cultural resistance (Fuller 2002), Delanty suggests that 'The challenge of the university today is to have a critical and hermeneutic role in the orientation of cultural models. The university must be capable of giving society a cultural direction' (Delanty 2001: 155). The only real agreement amongst writers on the purpose of the university is that its role is changing as a result of outside forces and factors. But it is also necessary to pay attention to changes occurring inside the university. If the university is internally divided, as well as in crisis, ruins or transition according to taste, where does that leave the knowledge worker?

The Divided University: Disciplines, Pay, Contracts, and Collegiality

If the university is not in ruins just yet, simply a little confused as to its purpose and role, its internal dynamics are nevertheless contested and its cultures complex. The contemporary organizational heir of Newman and Humboldt's legacy is one in which there is little sign of consensus, common purpose, or universalism, whether this refers to knowledge work, students, or academics. However, as Fuller notes, the origins of some of the divisions in higher education are not new. Fuller uses David Harvey's work to look at different stages of development of the university (Harvey 1990). The first stage is the holistic one, when a small number of students study under an even smaller number of intellectuals in a one-to-one situation. In stage two, divided labour, universities established distinct disciplines, introduced the idea of textbooks, and began to insist that academics had certain qualifications. In the third or mass production stage, classroom attendance became compulsory and degrees become necessary for many kinds of employment. In the final stage of customized consumption, students regain control over their education, using instructional software and reprogramming it as it suits them. Leaving aside the possibility that these stages may not be as linear or as separable as Fuller suggests, the divided labour stage clearly refers to the impact of the separation of the disciplines on the university (Fuller 2002). Of course, disciplinary divides, which despite trends in some fields towards interdisciplinary work remain crucial, as Henkel's study and other work on disciplinary territories demonstrate (Henkel 2000; Becher and Trowler 2001). Henkel emphasizes the communitarian commitment of academics, which usually revolves around subject or discipline-based departments, though of course academics also tend to identify strongly with those in their specialist field in other universities too, both nationally and internationally. The disciplinary divides apply to teaching as well as research. For example, the quality enhancement arm of the UK Higher Education Academy is based on twenty-four Subject Centres on the assumption that academics are more likely to be responsive to teaching enhancement if it is grounded in their subject communities (Deem 2002; Leon 2002). Disciplinary divides are thus both long-established but still thriving.

However, the expansion of the university has also led to other divisions becoming more evident, in what has been termed the 'unequal academy' (Association of University Teachers 2004). These include divisions between different categories of staff and staff on different kinds of contracts (e.g. temporary and permanent, contract researchers vs. permanent academic staff), gender, ethnicity/'race', tensions between those who specialize in teaching, and those who focus mainly on research and a growing chasm between those who manage and those who are managed (Deem and Johnson 2000; Deem 2003). Yet it is also misleading to think that the past history of UK or other Western universities was one in which all who worked in universities were there on equal terms with each other. This was never true of support staff, some of whom (mostly those not on academic-related pay scales) in many UK universities were not even legally considered members of the university in the same manner as academic staff and students. Furthermore, as Bensimon has noted, departmental and university collegiality, even amongst academics, was never as widespread as some of its proponents claim and rarely included women or blacks (Bensimon 1995). The case of Rosalind Franklin in the 1950s well illustrates the partial remit of collegiality in UK universities in the past. Franklin was a scientist at King's College London (where she was not permitted to eat her lunch in the senior common room, which was the sole preserve of male academics), whose research was crucial to the discovery of the structure of DNA, yet she was never properly recognized for her work and the credit went entirely to male scientists Crick and Watson at Cambridge (Watson 1969). The Cambridge scientists learnt of her work through a male colleague at King's who, unbeknown to Franklin, shared her results with them. When Franklin left King's for a new post at Birkbeck, King's let her leave only on the understanding that she would do no more work on DNA (Maddox 2002). Although she did return to DNA-related research at Birkbeck, sadly Franklin died in mid-career in 1958, with her important research contribution still not properly acknowledged.

Collegiality amongst academic staff, in so far as it was ever present, has in any case been considerably undermined in the last decade or so by the growth of a range of types of contracts for academic staff. Contract researchers, part-time teachers, and teachers on fixed-term contracts are not new to universities but their numbers have increased considerably in recent years. Many of those holding such posts feel that they operate at the margins of their institution and are often paid at or near the bottom of the pay scale, whether they are researchers (Hey 2000, 2001; Reay 2000), teachers (Husbands 1998; Watson 2000), or postgraduates (Husbands and Davies 1997). Yet their work is vital to the sustenance of both teaching and research. As Henkel's research (2000) indicates, it is becoming harder for academics in some subjects (clearly not all as there are some like computing, accountancy, and economics where it is very difficult to recruit) to begin their established careers. Thus a series of temporary, low paid, and insecure posts is becoming more common before, if at all, a permanent post is achieved. However, though undoubtedly fixed-term contracts (now challenged in the UK by European legislation on equality in employment) are at least partially related to the financial difficulties of universities and their desire to remain flexible, as well as the scarcity of research funding, the uncertainty of beginning academics is not itself new. Max Weber, writing in 1919, referred to the difficulty and risks involved as those new to academe tried to establish their careers (Weber 1948).

Pay differentials are also a source of divisions in universities. The 1999 Bett Report on UK university pay and conditions pointed to many inequalities not related either to the level of work and responsibility or to qualifications and experience (Bett Report 1999). Some of these inequalities, such as those based on pay discrimination in relation to gender, are now being addressed through the Framework Agreement (Joint Negotiating Committee for Higher Education Staff 2003) which aims to put all university staff (academic and non-academic) on a single pay spine with, as far as possible, equalization of working conditions (such as holiday entitlement) and the Reward programme in England (based on institutional human resource strategies and job evaluation). However, gaps in pay based on ethnicity and gender have persisted for some time (Association of University Teachers 2002, 2004). A 2001 investigation by the Association for University Teachers found that average pay for full-time academics employed in the UK was consistently lower for non-white members of staff. Non-white academics received on average 88% of the pay of their white colleagues. The gap was narrowest in England, and widest in Northern Ireland. For white and non-white staff of UK nationality, the pay gap decreased to 94% (Association of University Teachers 2002). Earlier work on ethnicity and academic pay suggested that pay gaps related to ethnicity is a long-standing problem in HE (Modood and Acland 1996). The available evidence suggests that the challenges posed by the Amendment to the Race Relations Act 2002 Public Bodies (Her Majesty's Government 2002) for higher education are considerable, not to mention other recent legislation such as the Special Educational Needs and Disability Act 2001 (Government 2001), the 2004 Disability Discrimination Act, the disability duty introduced for public bodies in 2006, and recent EU directives on equality in employment bringing into play other forms of potential exclusion such as those based on sexual orientation and religion. The evidence is that not all higher education institutions are responding quickly and positively to employee equality matters (Deem, Morley, and Tlili 2005; Strebler and O'Regan 2005; Deem and Morley 2006).

It is also likely that in future divisions on the basis of pay will increase, for example, those between academics in different subjects. Such differentials arise in relation both to relative market scarcity or surplus but also in connection with the amount of research and entrepreneurial funding that academics in different disciplines can attract. This is particularly likely to affect those working in areas like the humanities (Pan 1998), where there are still plenty of applicants for posts and limited opportunities for external fund generation. However, the most striking gap that exists in salaries is that between Vice-Chancellors and the rest of their staff (Goddard 2002a, 2002b, 2003, 2004, 2005). Whilst the range of salaries for Vice-Chancellors and Principals runs from under £100,000 for a few small specialized colleges, most are well over £100,000. The top pay package for the head of an institution in the academic year 2004/5 was that of the female head of the London Business School, Laura Tyson, £310,000 but those in the management field can earn huge amounts in consultancy and at least two other members of her staff earned more than £30,000 in the same year, so this is perhaps a somewhat unusual case. In the period between 2001/2 and 2004/5, two male Vice-Chancellors (Surrey and Cardiff) received a pay increase of more than 60 per cent, and two incoming male Vice-Chancellors (at Manchester and Oxford) received over 50 per cent more salary than their predecessors over a similar period. Eighteen vice-chancellors earned more than £200,000 in 2004/5 (of which only two were female) and 33 earned more than the UK Prime Minister whose salary in March 2006 was £18,400. Apart from the London Business School, the next highest female salary was sixteenth in the list (at Bath). Between 2003/4 and 2004/5, the average VC salary rise was 8 per cent (Sanders 2006; Times Higher Education Supplement 2006). Meanwhile, in 2005, non-professorial academics earned a mean of £40,657 a year, whilst in May 2006, the starting salary of a new academic lecturer in both the pre- and post-1992 universities was £24,352 (although in some universities the actual salary of a new academic may be nearer to £29,000) and there was evidence that the long-term decline in UK academic salaries relative to other comparable professional groups identified in 1999 by an independent salary review (Bett Report 1999) had continued (Stothart 2006). There is also still a significant gender pay gap in some institutions (Times Higher Education Supplement 2004). However, the position for non-academic staff in universities has slowly improved as recent steps have been taken to improve their conditions of work. As part of a pay settlement for 2003/4 and 2004/5, UK HEI Trade Unions and the Universities and Colleges Employers Association (UCEA) reached an agreement on a set of principles for modernizing pay and conditions (Joint Negotiating Committee for Higher Education Staff 2003). The Framework Agreement aims to put all university staff on a single pay spine and equalize working hours and conditions for those occupations with fixed hours, using systematic job evaluation to determine pay levels for different categories of work. Salaries, contracts, and conditions, however, reflect only some of the differences that exist between academics. Three further examples will be considered—gender, research and teaching tensions, and the gap between managers and managed staff.

The Divided University—Gender, Teaching versus Research and Management

It might be assumed that gender divisions between women and men staff in universities have long since disappeared, given the long-standing legislation on gender in employment dating from the 1970s. Indeed, a predominant contemporary view of equality issues in general is that they are largely now irrelevant, with differences in life styles and chances, with a few exceptions like disability, attributable to individual choice (Howard and Tibballs 2003). A 2004 study examining how equality policies are currently being managed in UK HEIs (Deem, Morley, and Tlili 2005; Deem and Morley 2006) included interviews with thirty-seven senior managers (including Vice-Chancellors). These interviews suggested that gender was a dimension of inequality in higher education largely regarded as being 'solved', with just a few remaining concerns over female representation in senior management teams and amongst academics in science and engineering departments. Certainly overt sex discrimination is probably in decline. However, what remains is probably more difficult to tackle, since it is based on more subtle social and cultural practices and institutional micro-politics (Morley 1999*a*) which are not very visible to outsiders and resistant to change. Women academics (as contrasted with women administrators in higher education) are still not reaching senior posts in large numbers, although they are increasing their presence as academics. The total number of female academics rose by 4.9 per cent from 2003/4 to 2004/5, compared with an increase of only 1.2 per cent in the number of male academics and among full-time staff, the proportion of academics who are women increased at all grades. The biggest move was at senior lecturer and senior researcher level, where women's numbers climbed from 5,815 to 6,480. The number of female professors rose from 1,815 to 2,055 in 2004/5 (Higher Educational Statistical Agency 2006; Tysome 2006), but nevertheless, just 14 per cent of UK professors and 26 per cent of senior lecturers were women in that year (Hill 2004). There are also wide subject variations in professorial posts, so, for instance, in 2004 only 1.2 per cent of professors in electrical, electronic, and computer engineering were women, compared with 64 per cent in nursing and paramedical studies. At the same time, over 50 per cent of undergraduate students are now female (women overtook men in 1996/7 as a proportion of all undergraduate students). Though the number of women managing universities is growing, it is still small. In May 2006, there were 17 women heads out of the 127 member institutions belonging to the Vice-Chancellors and Principals' organization Universities UK. Of these, there were three women principals in Scotland but none in Wales or Northern Ireland. Seven women in 2006 were Vice-chancellors of pre-1992 universities as compared with ten who headed former polytechnics or colleges.

During our ESRC research, we conducted fieldwork in sixteen universities from 1998 to 2000. Though we were able to identify some female heads of department (typically in social sciences or health sciences, and less often in arts/humanities than we had expected) and a rather smaller number of deans, women Pro-vice-Chancellors were very thin on the ground and typically had responsibility for teaching and learning, rather than research or resources. Some of our male respondents were apologetic about the slow progress of women academics into senior positions but felt that this would happen over time, a version of what has been called the pipeline theory (Brooks and Mackinnon 2001), whilst others blamed it either on the fact that academic life does not suit women who are mothers (ironically most such male respondents were fathers) or declared that women in their institution lacked the necessary talent:

> this is a 50 week a year job with long hours, in a lab-based subject...a heavily research-oriented environment, also it's a dangerous subject...a woman with a family could not do the job and bring up children in the traditional way.
>
> Male Head of Science, pre 1992 University

> Interviewee (to male VC): Your group of PVCs is all men. Is this an issue? VC: if there had been a woman, er...who was eligible, they would be there....No I don't think it's an issue at all, I think it's just purely a question of who can do the job best....and um, I don't think it even, I don't think it comes into it at all really.
>
> Male Vice-Chancellor, pre-1992 University

However, some of the women who were beginning to succeed in management roles had some interesting tales to tell about their experiences, which suggested that they had been affected as much by old fashioned sexism as by motherhood or lack of talent (though it is fair to point out that some of these respondents were looking back on their career biographies rather than reflecting on very recent occurrences):

> I had extremely unpleasant reactions from men whom I actually beat for the job {HoD},...reactions that went on for six months...very, very uncomfortable and actually, on two occasions, physically threatening.
>
> Female HoD, Financial Services, post-1992 University

> I was the only woman, senior manager...it took quite a while for the chaps...they didn't like to deal with me....I wasn't part of the job 'cause I didn't go to the toilet with them and things like that.
>
> Female HoS, Management, post-1992 University

Clearly knowledge work and knowledge management have some unexpected dimensions in respect of gender. Some further insights into the gender divide in higher education are provided by Canadian research where women academics said that they felt they were the good citizens of their departments, doing a lot of extra pastoral work with students, low-level administration, and other not very glamorous work such as introductory teaching which male colleagues often preferred not to do (Acker and Feuerverger 1996; Acker 1997). The experiences of these Canadian women academics also appeared to involve a good deal of stress, long working hours, and lack of sleep (Acker and Armenti 2004). Doing low-level pastoral care and a lot of teaching does not very often lead to promotion, as research in Australia on what makes academics successful has noted, since factors like visibility, publication records, and spending a great deal of time on research (rather than teaching) were seen to be key (Harris, Thiele, and Currie 1998; Currie, Harris, and Thiele 2000). This leads us onto the tensions and differential rewards of research and teaching per se, since these tensions and their various resolutions by different academics and via institutional missions also divide higher education.

In visions about the role of traditional universities in the nineteenth century, both research and teaching were seen as important, with the latter sometimes the most prominent. Thus, Cardinal Newman's vision of universities was mostly concerned with teaching and students. Humboldt in Germany, although more research focused, stressed the linkages between research and teaching. In the contemporary period, Henkel's research (2000) on academic identities has also emphasized the extent to which many academics see teaching and research as linked:

> my teaching is only any good when it is connected with research...it is not so much directly drawing on it because that's often very difficult...it is more about shaping the climate of ideas in which the course is being run.

> Humanities lecturer, Henkel 2000: 185

Henkel did find a few academics, mostly in the more teaching-oriented post-1992 universities, for whom teaching was the mainstay of their identity. A recent recruitment and retention study for the UK government (Department for Education and Skills) based on a survey of research students and academics in UK universities suggested that research remains a more important motivating factor for academics and would-be academics than teaching (Metcalf, et al. 2005). Undoubtedly, the pressures of the UK Research Assessment Exercise (where since the mid-1980s, high grades have accompanied by substantial sums of money for successful departments) have made many academics acutely aware of the tensions between teaching and research (Lucas 2006), particularly those in early- and mid-careers. Hannan and Silver's research (2000) on teaching innovation found that whilst some, mostly post-1992, universities did reward and encourage teaching innovation, others were not so welcoming

> The general staff response to teaching and learning is 'We've got the RAE to think about!' People are not being rewarded for teaching in a real sense.'
>
> Academic involved in teaching innovation, Hannan and Silver 2000: 120

Some academics are also concerned that only certain kinds of research count, as Harley found in her research on the RAE on four disciplines (Harley 2002, 2003), namely psychology, sociology, accounting and finance, and marketing:

> I am concerned about the move away from meaningful research and toward short term publications as a measure of worth . . . I refuse to have my life's work dictated by the fads and fashions of journals . . . this is not a RAE. It is a research *control* exercise.
>
> Social Scientist, New University, Harley 2002: 199

Institutional priorities on the balance to be struck between research and teaching also vary considerably, as these two contrasting views demonstrate

> we define ourselves by the research that we do . . . actually we don't want to grow as an institution and student numbers. It's not something we'd be good at. We want to emphasise quality and a shift towards postgraduates and probably a shift away from conventional undergraduate/postgraduate teaching.
>
> PVC, pre-1992 University

> Very first thing I ever said . . . first speech . . . what I said was 'students come first'. . . . I would say 80% of the organization breathed a sigh of relief . . . well I believe in that, but I also believe it's right for this organization at this time in its history.
>
> VC, post-1992 University

In the 1990s, there have been attempts to review how the UK Research Assessment Exercise is carried out (Roberts 2003) or to end it in its current form altogether and replace it with a metrics-based review (Sastry and Bekhradnia 2006). There have also been endeavours to reward good teaching more fully, such as (in England) the seventy-four well-funded Centres for Excellence in Teaching and Learning (Higher Education

Funding Council for England 2005) and also (for 2006/7), money for special teaching and learning initiatives (in all four UK countries) and (in England) money for non-research-intensive institutions to allow staff to keep up to date in their subjects. Nevertheless, there is a strong possibility that all these moves will achieve is a greater separation between those academics who primarily think of themselves as teachers and those who regard themselves as researchers, despite a growing literature on research and teaching connections (Jenkins 2005). Knowledge work as teaching is becoming increasingly cut off from knowledge work as research in much of the UK higher education system (Deem 2006b). This is not the only divide amongst academics however. For the ambitious knowledge worker, there is also another career route available, the management track. As we saw in Chapter 2, since the mid-1980s, the importance of management and leadership to UK universities has been growing in importance, alongside the various shifts in managerial ideologies from neoliberal to neo-technocratic. Taking the management track, for those academics who choose to do so, may be opening up yet another divide in the contemporary university.

The management/academic divide is not new to UK higher education, as we saw in Chapter 2 but with the growth of mass higher education, trends in public spending moving expenditure away from higher education, global competition for research funding, the search for world-class excellence through rankings and league tables of universities (Jarrar and Mohamed 2001; Liu and Cheng 2005; Mok 2005) and an international market for students, as well as the emphasis in the UK since the 1980s on seeking new approaches to the management of public services, that divide has undoubtedly become more pronounced. We have already seen that the manager-academic route can lead to very high salaries if it culminates in appointment as a Vice-Chancellor. But salaries are not the only factor that separates manager-academics from their staff. Although it could be argued that every academic is now involved in management of teaching and research, and that at department level, in practice (in all but very small departments), a number of people in addition to the Head of Department (e.g. those who take on the role of director of research or undergraduate studies) are likely to be engaged in distributed management (Gronn 2000; Woods, Bennett, Harvey, and Wise 2004), this is a quite different kind of managing and leading from that encountered at senior levels of universities. Heads of department, as we shall see in the next chapter, are still very much embedded in their discipline or subject and even Faculty Deans tend to be responsible for a cognate group of disciplines/subjects. Both of these roles focus principally on personnel and budget management, performance and target management and academic leadership, with some emphasis on future planning. Above the level of Dean however, discipline or subject lose their significance as roles become university-wide, and activities become much more specialized (e.g Research and Enterprise, Teaching and Learning, or Resources), with a high emphasis on strategic planning and project management but seldom involving direct responsibility for staff. Senior management, whether involving manager-academics or senior administrators, is fast becoming a community of practice quite detached from other parts of the university (Deem and Johnson 2000). Research in Australia on entrepreneurial universities has identified the growth of senior management teams in many universities (Marginson and Considine 2000) and others have noted a strengthened steering core at the centre of universities as a characteristic of enterprising universities (Clark 1998). Of course, senior management teams may be entirely necessary in order to manage complex institutions. But they seldom appear in diagrams of how universities structures work. In the NM research, we found that senior management teams consisting of VCs, pro-VCs and a small number of senior administrators were commonplace (Deem 2003). These were usually informal groupings (and hence unaccountable to other members of the university) apparently without full decision-making powers, so that ideas and strategies generated in such teams generally still need to be passed on to committees or working groups for processing. It was confirmed by most of our interviewees who were members of senior management teams that ideas for future directions did tend to emerge from team meetings and that on occasions ways were found of 'fast-tracking' these so that they entirely or largely bypassed the institutional committee structure. The volume of work undertaken by senior manager-academics and also the need to significantly engage with non-academic stakeholders and rest of the world outside the university, mean that there may be relatively little contact between senior manager-academics and even their former academic peers, never mind other staff. Often the geographical site location of senior manager-academics and their team of administrators is, for reasons including security, in a place which is difficult for other staff or students to access except by invitation. This tends to reinforce the view that senior managers are a group apart. Senior managers do not often go out of their offices to meet staff and students except for committee meetings—rather anyone needing to see a senior manager goes to them. A considerable number of academic and support staff in our four case study universities in the ESRC study told us that they felt very remote from senior management (Deem 2003) and the existence of senior management teams, although a somewhat tautologous response, was one of the reasons given for this, along with alleged failure to consult staff on various issues before making decisions. Some of those holding management posts further down the hierarchy also perceived that they were not trusted by senior management:

> Well, I think they don't trust us, even Heads of Department, they don't trust us completely with money...I'm talking about elementary decisions....I think the system's gone too far in that direction.
>
> Focus Group, Science Learned Society

The extent of this lack of trust in universities, which is a significant issue in many public service organizations (Misztal 1996; Clark, Chandler, and Barry 1998; Nyhan 2000; Albrecht and Travaglione 2003), is born out by other evidence. Though devolution of finance to cost centres such as departments is now quite widespread in UK universities, the resource allocation models we encountered in the NM research rarely, if ever, included any autonomy on new staffing decisions and mainly what was devolved was the responsibility to raise money and to worry about deficits. Not only did middle managers feel that they were not trusted. This feeling extended, in our case study data, to perceptions of a range of other employees too, all of whom felt that they were not trusted and that transparency tended to run in one direction only, from the bottom of the organization to the top but not the other way round. This may reflect a more general unease with current systems of supposedly accountable university governance (Ackroyd and Ackroyd 1999).

The sense of remoteness of senior management teams seemed to apply equally, in our data, to relationships with the student body other than Student Union sabbatical officers (the latter tend to sit on official negotiating bodies with senior management). Thus we found it was not uncommon for senior manager-academics to see students as rather abstract entities, for instance as units of resource or potential sources of complaints and litigation (Johnson and Deem 2003), rather than as live members of a common academic community. This tendency was particularly strong in some pre-1992 universities.

So far as Vice-Chancellors are concerned, and as we saw in the last chapter, the role is undoubtedly changing (Smith et al. 1999), with the academic leadership dimension becoming less important and greater attention paid to crisis management, fund-raising and contacts with influential people outside the university, as well as strategic planning, although in practice firefighting may predominate over strategic activity (Bargh et al. 2000). More UK VCs, PVCS, and even Deans are now being appointed by headhunters (which may suggest either that institutions find it difficult to attract applicants under their own auspices or that universities are seen as more business like and therefore needing to adopt private sector methods of recruiting senior staff) and VC posts are now often fixed-term contracts, which are not always renewed. Though having an academic background is still very common amongst VCs, the subject range is changing away from an earlier predominance (in the 1960s–1980s) of scientists to a wider range of disciplinary backgrounds including social scientists (Farnham and Jones 1998; Smith 1999) and a very small number of those appointed to major universities recently have come from the private sector, not academe. The latter may well increase in future. The divide then, between senior manager-academics and their academic communities, and between knowledge workers and knowledge managers, does seem to be growing. So too, it would seem, are the divisions between one university and another.

Divisions Between Universities

Much of what has happened to UK higher education policy over the last couple of decades is underpinned by a growing lack of consensus between universities and the state (Kogan and Hanney 2000), a phenomenon not confined to the UK but increasingly evident in many countries with state-funded higher education systems (Kwiek 2005, 2006). Current UK higher education policies on research selectivity have also intensified competition between institutions at a national level, and also at international level (Jarrar and Mohamed 2001; Dill and Soo 2005; Liu and Cheng 2005; Merisotis and Sadlak 2005). This intense competition is replicated in the search for students, whereby UK institutions of higher education compete for international students with other European, North American and Australian higher education sectors. Within the UK context, the RAE, teaching quality and academic standard audits, and market conditions for students have encouraged universities to compete with each other rather than collaborate. The proliferation of media league tables of UK universities based on a variety of indicators from library spending to student dropout, has exacerbated this. The results of the newly intro-duced National (undergraduate) Student Satisfaction Survey in England, Wales, and Northern Ireland in 2005 (Higher Education Funding Council

2005) were rapidly turned into a league table. The government appears to embrace such competitiveness. For example, in September 2002, the then Higher Education Minister for England, Margaret Hodge, told university vice-chancellors that the government was not prepared to support universities in financial difficulties:

> Allowing a freer market may create more turmoil in the sector. But actually if students and research funders do not want what is on offer, why on earth should we carry on funding it? ... The current regime is one size fits-all but if you fund according to that, you inevitably fail to encourage excellence. But as far as the public purse is concerned, we will not carry on putting money into failure.
>
> Thompson and Baty 2002

Yet at the same time government has insisted that all universities comply with all government policies on higher education (Brehony and Deem 2003) even if they do not sit easily with their missions or are riven with contradictions. Examples of this include the 2001 New Labour manifesto commitment on widening participation in higher education to socially and economically disadvantaged groups of students, a policy which has included a wide array of sometimes contradictory initiatives (Brown 2002; Comptroller and Auditor General 2002), including the establishment in 2004 in England of the office of Fair Access (OFFA) run by a former university Vice-Chancellor, intended to regulate the undergraduate admissions policies of supposedly autonomous universities. Faced with contradictory policies and a plethora of special initiatives on widening participation, it is not difficult to see why division rules and collaboration is proving difficult, unless this takes the form of a merger (Beasley and Pembridge 2000), as for example with the fairly recent UK examples of London Metropolitan University which was formed from London Guildhall and North London Universities and the University of Manchester Institute of Science and Technology merger with Manchester Victoria University. The proponents of institutional mergers sometimes talk about the importance of building very large universities if they are to compete globally, although there are many other reasons for mergers such as financial problems of one of the merging institutions and a growing literature on their merits and demerits (Rowley 1997; Skodvin 1999; Harman and Harman 2003). It is not, however, entirely clear that size alone, rather than resources or reputation, enhances the knowledge work of universities (Beasley and Pembridge 2000; Patterson 2000). In the UK it seems more likely that there will remain big divisions between the remaining institutions, whilst league tables reign supreme and collaboration is largely left to rhetoric and exhortation. Thus both the divided university and divided universities seem likely to remain for the foreseeable future.

Conclusion: Managing Knowledge Work in Divided Universities

Until quite recently, paying attention to research on the organization and management of universities was not something which attracted either those who manage the UK higher education system or academics themselves. This may explain why, although there has been recent concern amongst UK and many other academics about how universities are organized and managed, some of those engaged in university management, particularly at more senior levels, have seemed willing to comply with the requirements that universities be managed more like private sector organizations, even if this means using practices which are not always appropriate to the work and values of the staff of publicly funded universities. Nevertheless, it has been suggested that to counter this, some academics have become knowledgeable players of the audit and assessment game in teaching and research. Indeed, this game-playing may be at the core of the identities that those new to academic life are forging for themselves. However, although all institutions are apparently engaged in similar knowledge activities and games, considerable divides still exist within UK universities, not only in the shape of traditional subject divides but also in respect of those based on pay, contracts, collegiality, gender, research and teaching tensions, and remoteness between senior manager-academics and other university staff. UK Universities are also still divided from each other, encouraged by government policies to compete with each other for national resources and 'global reach'.

What then are the prospects for changing how UK universities currently work and are managed? Will Reed's notion of neo-technocratic Managerialism remain the predominant orthodoxy for running higher education for the next decade or so? Does the future lie in even greater regulation and performance management or in seeking different ways to run universities and foster creative knowledge work? Universities in the UK and in a number of other Western countries currently stand at a crucial watershed. With less and less funding from the state, either now or in prospect, they are nevertheless subject to increased control and regulation by the state, a steering at a distance approach (Kickert

1995) which senior manager-academics in turn use on their staff. An important first step might be for universities and their managers to listen carefully to their staff about their concerns. They could also seek out new models of how a range of organizations operate, whether in the voluntary sector, the public services or in the private sector (particularly culture industries). This may, of course, fly in the face of what government and other agencies want for higher education, yet large teaching factories for undergraduates in underfunded classrooms, libraries and laboratories and world-class knowledge work and creation (whether in teaching or research) do not sit easily together. Universities in the UK have not been very effective at lobbying government in recent years, nor have they spoken with anything approaching a single voice. Perhaps they never can. But allowing for diversity between universities is not new and it may still be possible to share ideas on how to manage higher education institutions that go beyond the 'slash, burn, and divide' policies which sometimes pass for academic reorganization today.

Many academics are concerned about the loss of trust and autonomy from their daily work and the heavy workloads they are now expected to carry, whilst being poorly financially rewarded and increasingly intrusively managed and regulated. Whilst it can be argued that academics do still retain more autonomy than some other professionals employed in public service organizations, there is no doubt that loss of trust and discretion, low salaries, and high workloads are serious concerns. They are concerns that need addressing. Absence of trust, low pay and heavy workloads are features of contemporary academic knowledge work that may turn out to be far more central to the invoking of a crisis of the purposes of universities than many of the other concerns voiced by commentators writing about changes to the purposes of universities. 'Doing more with less' could easily lead to 'doing nothing with nothing' or 'doing nothing that matters'.

The divided university and its academic knowledge workers are in urgent need of fresh and radical thinking of the calibre of that shown by Newman and Humboldt in the nineteenth century. This does not mean putting back the clock. The universities that Newman and Humboldt talked about were elite institutions, whilst most twenty-first century universities are not. Visions for contemporary universities should instead take seriously Delanty's notion (2001) of the scope for universities becoming new forms of public communication, concerned with future cultural directions (rather than simply reflecting and developing national cultures) and using the potential of new modes of knowledge production to develop models of culture which can exploit the democratic potential of knowledge transformation. Such institutions would also embrace learning, teaching and research, and develop the synergies between these. They would trust, value, and reward all their staff (not just 'star' academics on permanent contracts) without regard to irrelevant social, economic, and cultural divisions. The twenty-first century vision of a university could usefully encompass the many potential cultural and social, as well as economic, benefits of higher education for a global society. Only then can we be confident that we have found a new vision and purpose for the university. How far such new visions and purposes are reflected in the identities of the manager-academics we researched is the subject of the next chapter.

4

Manager-Academic Identities, Practices, and Careers in the Contemporary University

Introduction

In the previous chapter, we explored what is happening to the knowledge worker in the contemporary UK university as an organization and noted how increasingly divided knowledge workers are from each other in their institutions and how in turn institutions are divided from each other despite exhortations to collaborate with each other. In this chapter, we explore how the sedimentation of varieties of New Mangerialism have suffused the accounts that manager-academics themselves give of their work, roles, and identities and examine the extent to which manager-academic lived experiences reflect at the micro-level, the systemic moves from regulated autonomy to institutionalized distrust described by Reed in Chapter 1. Neoliberal forms of Managerialism emphasize the universal imposition of free market forces and private sector market discipline upon public services. Neoliberalism suggests that only a managerial approach enables public services to break free from the power and control of professional 'producer/provider cartels' and sustain a dynamic of entrepreneurial-driven change and transformation. The imposition of market mechanisms and disciplines on the design, delivery, and management of public services is advocated by this approach, with the goal of greater strategic effectiveness and operational efficiency. In contrast, neo-technical Managerialism is a broad ideological movement that emphasizes 'managing' and 'management' as socio-technical practices and makes visible the organizations and agents enacting them. Neo-technical Managerialism regards managing and management as indispensable to the achievement of economic progress, technological development, and social order within the modern political economy. Management from this perspective is viewed as a generic activity that is argued to be necessarily, technically, and socially superior to any other previous form of social practice and organization of work such as craft or professional community.

The two models of management, neoliberal and neo-technical and their bearing upon manager-academics' working lives, form a basis for the analysis presented here. The chapter draws upon data from the ESRC New Managerialism project in order to examine responses to change in the UK higher education sectors and to examine to what extent NM has been accepted and internalized (or rejected) by contemporary manager-academics. It addresses four major themes: the identities of manager-academics, generic principles and values about the role of academics in the university, practical characteristics of everyday life in universities, and finally how academics are turned into manager-academics and their understandings of their careers. At the end of the section on the practical characteristics of everyday life in universities, there is also a brief discussion of technologies of management. These four themes allow the rhetoric, practice, and skills of different manager-academics to be explored in relation to different forms of Managerialism and the extent of its permeation of UK higher education.

Manager-Academic Identities

There is a long-standing debate in social science about identity theories and there is no space to examine this literature here. Some theorists argue that identity is now such an elastic concept that it is of very limited use (Anthias 2005: 39). Nevertheless, in our context, we feel that the concept of identity is worth using because it draws attention to the complex identities of academics who become managers and leaders in universities and the tensions between these that many manager-academics experience. We utilize a concept of identity adapted from Henkel (2000), who herself draws on several authors, including a leading New Labour sociologist (Giddens 1991) and develops the notion of identity as a reflexive and oft-revised project of the self-contained individual in autobiographical narratives and accounts. Henkel also utilizes philosophy (MacIntyre 1981) to introduce the idea of these accounts being embedded in histories and communities that together bear certain kinds of traditions. This is helpful in relation to our respondents because our interviews with manager-academics encouraged them to provide, as one element, an autobiographical account of their academic careers (and other employment careers where relevant). In addition, we worked with the assumption that academic identities are also worked on against a backdrop of personal and institutional experiences as well as disciplinary communities.

Investigation of academics' lives suggests that both research and teaching are central to their work identities (Henkel 2000; Musselin and Becquet 2005; Deem and Lucas 2007), although we also know that their discipline or subject (Moses 1990; Becher and Trowler 2001), gender (Acker and Feuerverger 1996; Brooks 1997; Morley 1999a; Brooks and Mackinnon 2001; Acker and Armenti 2004), and ethnicity (Carter, Fenton, and Modood 1999) are highly significant too. The notion of a profession, a sociologically much contested concept (Larson 1977, 1990, Freidson 1994, 2001), is also relevant, as observed in other studies of academic identity (Henkel 2000), although the academic profession in the UK, as noted in Chapter 3, is a very divided and fragmented occupational group. Finally, as Henkel (2000) notes, academics tend to have a strong loyalty to their basic unit (usually a department or school) that is also central to their identity.

The core activities of research and teaching, although a very significant element of what both academics and universities do (Deem 2006b), are often in tension with one another, relating to 'the deployment of resources in higher education systems, as well as a battle for supremacy and status of teaching versus activity research in the academy' (Deem and Lucas 2007: 7). Manager-academics have to take on these tensions, as well as undertaking the procurement and management of the necessary resources for their department, faculty, or university. They must also engage in dealing with the personal contradictions and tensions of trying to combine research and teaching (certainly in the early stages of their managerial journeys) with management, leadership, and administration in relation to their own time (Deem and Hillyard 2002), as well as that of their staff. Simultaneously, those who intend to continue a management career must begin to prioritize their leadership, management, and administration over and above their other academic work, thus acquiring new identities and perhaps slowly relinquishing old ones.

We take it for granted that all our respondents, in common with other academics, have multiple identities, which we were able to share in only momentarily through our research. The specific focus of our interest in identity here is about whether and if so, in what respects academics who become leaders and managers shift their identities to reflect that change of role and if so, how they do this and what that shift represents. In the context of the rise of NM, the significance of management and the changing relationship between trust and control referred in Chapter 1 are crucial. Furthermore, manager-academics themselves may or may not consciously adopt the regimes and values of NM. There is a possibility that some simply become bilingual (or even trilingual) as found in research with senior teachers and head teachers in English state secondary schools after radical policy reform (Gewirtz, Ball, and Bowe 1995).

It is also worth noting that our research identified a number of 'reluctant' managers at the HoD level (Deem et al. 2001), especially in the pre-1992 universities, who were taking their turn as head of their academic unit but who fully intended to return to being 'just' academics at the end of this time. Reluctant managers have been found in other kinds of organizations too (Scase and Goffee 1989). Both the reluctant managers and those we have termed 'good citizen' managers (Deem et al. 2001), who take on management positions out of loyalty to their institution, often towards the end of their career, may not want to fully embrace a new identity as a manager, in contrast with those who wish to embark upon or are already engaged in, a career as a manager-academic. We found that the majority of reluctant and 'good citizen' manager-academics in our sample were less likely than career managers to want to embrace NM. Those who are planning a managerial career may well wish to embrace NM, although some of this group may also resist it and search for alternatives. The latter are not easily found. The emphasis in books on how to manage contemporary universities often stresses the importance (to use Clark's term) of a central steering core (Sporn 1996; Clark 1998; Shattock 2003), though not all writers assume that this has to be accompanied by particular kinds of organizational regimes. Shattock (2003) makes an impassioned plea for the preservation of collegialism but this is somewhat contradictory to his otherwise quite centralist emphasis on how universities should be managed.

Given the range of motivations for becoming a manager-academic amongst those we interviewed, which varied from career ambition and love of institutional politics to feeling that other candidates would be worse in the role and the antithetical nature of some of the aspirations of NM to those of academics qua academics, one might expect that there would be a degree of resistance amongst some manager-academics to taking on the mantle of manager and though we found a substantial minority who eschewed this label at all, over half were prepared to concede that their job involved some management, even if this was not their preferred descriptor of themselves.

> Interviewer: And so why were you appointed?
>
> HoD...well the chap before me had done his sentence and had been reprieved and they needed another victim...I want to spend my time writing because I quite enjoy writing...and teaching whatever. But I also do like this power thing, and I like interacting with people and doing things, so I'd like to be plugged into the {institution} at some level doing something that is more than simply teaching undergraduates.

> HoD, Social Sciences, pre-1992

> I got a letter from the VC in December asking me if I would be head of department, which I did not want to do, I felt completely trapped, and...if you have a full-time post at the university and accept promotion, then I don't think it's fair to refuse to do that task, nobody wants to do it as far as I can see. And, so I said I would, with great misgivings, because it's had a terrible effect on my research output.

> HoD, Arts, pre-1992

Research on UK academics holding leadership positions in the late 1980s showed the 'manager' label to be strongly resisted (Middlehurst 1993). By the time of our study in 1998–2000, this had somewhat lessened and around two-thirds of our sample conceded that their job involved elements of managing, though few below PVC level saw management as an attractive or all-encompassing identity. Even at PVC level, manager-academics often wanted to hold on to their academic identity in relation to their original discipline or subject. Less than half of our HoD intervie-wees wholeheartedly accepted the role of manager, and most of those who did were in the post-1992 sector and had a permanent (not temporary) appointment as HoD:

> Yes, I do consider myself to be a manager, a manager of human resources and a manager of a small budget, the way in which universities' budgets are carved up.

> HoD, Health Sciences, post-1992

Other HoDs, particularly in the pre-1992 sector, including many of those who were in post only temporarily, saw themselves as providing acad-emic leadership of equals rather than management, in effect the collegial approach to running universities that the 1985 Jarratt Report tried to replace with corporate management (Jarratt 1985):

> I don't really understand what the concept of a manager is, I see myself as leading a group of people who are essentially equals, you know?...I like to see myself as providing some sort of leadership, but really I think mostly encouraging others to do things, and creating sort of areas where they can do things.
>
> HoD, Humanities, pre-1992

> you actually caught me spending about an hour and a half doing research which is not something that I find time to do anymore. My remit was when I was given the job that it was a 50% job and the other 50% should be spent on research and teaching. But as you have probably been aware, the university's going through a very significant restructuring exercise....
>
> HoS, Science, pre-1992

At Dean level there was less ambivalence about being described as a manager and only eight of thirty-five respondents eschewed the 'm' label as their primary identity because at this level incumbents are managing not simply their own subject but a group of subjects and also have generally taken a conscious decision to be in a managerial role, which is not always true at the HoD level. Most of our Dean interviewees, though, also wanted to hang onto their subject and academic identity in some way:

> if I had to put a label on myself, I'm still an academic, I still do some teaching, I still do as much research as I can. I manage because I think I'm reasonably good at it and think that somebody has to do it.
>
> Dean, Arts/Humanities, pre-1992

> you then join what is essentially the management camp but you do a little bit of academic or service staff to maintain your street cred and so that they can't throw at you the fact that you don't know what's going on and you've forgotten what it's like.
>
> Dean of Medicine, pre-1992

> the reality is I am a manager in this job but there are all sorts of connotations to management which I don't like...in academia...a manager is someone who has limited knowledge about what the people on the ground, if I can put it that way, are trying to achieve. You come in, you set targets that are unrealistic, the whole thing's completely out of context with what the workforce if you like, feel they are trying to achieve. I think all of that is the sort of negative side of management. I think the positive side is that the reality is that in any organization, unless there's some sense of direction, some form of goal setting

as well, there's a tendency for either the institution to lose sense of direction or for individuals within it to lose a sense of direction.

Dean, Applied Sciences, post-1992

The discipline, background, and identity of manager-academics, while crucial at the HoD level, where maintaining and nurturing the subject is one of the key aspects of the job, is still important for those managing several cognate subjects at faculty level but becomes much less significant for those at PVC level who may be managing activities across a broad range of subjects. Disciplines did seem, however, from the accounts of our respondents, to shape who (what kind of academic, a lone scholar, or a team worker) and what (from laboratories to archaeological digs) was managed at department and faculty level, something noted by other researchers too (Bourdieu 1988; Blackmore 2005). The intuitive understanding of what knowledge workers in your own discipline might require is a crucial part of the armoury of the HoD:

> if you listen to people as well as talking to them you hear it and you know which people, even within a discipline...you know whether they're solitary book people, whether they're people who need a line of postdoctoral research assistance or what is the nature of the grant that they might ideally apply for...because of course, the getting of research grants has become more important.
>
> HoD, Humanities, pre-1992

Being part of the subject context is important also to Dean's managing cognate disciplines:

> I think I would feel very uncomfortable if I didn't feel that I understood the day-to-day experience of people in my department and I'm lucky in the sense that I've taught English, I've taught Languages, I've taught Sociology...and I'm still very research-orientated myself.
>
> Dean, Arts/Social Sciences, post-1992

However, actually keeping up with a discipline when your main role is management may be more difficult in some disciplines than others, with laboratory-based and fast changing subjects the most difficult of all in which to sustain any real credibility:

> I gave up any expertise on the technology, personal expertise on the technology about 7 or 8 years ago, because the technology moves so quickly it's impossible to maintain anything like a credible level of expertise unless you are fully versed in that and nothing else.
>
> Dean of Business Studies, post-1992

For those who go further than Dean, the disciplinary context begins to recede and the project of the self shifts direction even though the subject may still be a significant element in personal identity:

> your research takes a battering...the time you've got to research and that's the great regret I have. I was able to keep it going during my Head of Department years by giving myself less teaching and to a lesser extent while I was Dean...I'm finding it rather difficult now, I must say, in my present role, to maintain a strong research profile.
>
> PVC, pre-1992

> I think people try and transcend their disciplines, I mean they have to if they are in senior jobs but you always carry I think the methodologies of that discipline with you, I mean the way in which you approach a problem. That's why incidentally I think it's very important in terms of the senior team you actually have a mix of people who bring...different backgrounds, different methodologies, different value systems into that agenda.
>
> VC, post-1992

As well as discipline, the other factor that we found to be important in our respondents' identity was gender. This is well established in research on women academics (Acker and Feuerverger 1996; Brooks 1997; Morley 1999*a*; Brooks and Mackinnon 2001; Acker and Armenti 2004), as well as in analyses which focus on manager-academics (Eggins 1997; David and Woodward 1998). Two-thirds (68%) of our female manager-academic respondents and just under half of our male respondents (44%) considered that gender (which was often interpreted by both male and female respondents as equivalent to 'being a woman' or 'being a mother' was relevant to their careers, with male interviewees tending to see not being female as a distinct benefit to both themselves and their male colleagues:

> it would be extremely difficult {to do this job if you were a woman} and I, you know, I, I think...I mean, I remember one of my colleagues at my last university saying 'Really, this is a profession which, it should be regarded like a mask of devotion, you just spend all your time doing it, teaching and research'.
>
> Male PVC, pre-1992

> let's look at one of the other people I've got promoted: he works enormously long hours. I know he's here till late at night, takes a lot of work home, but he can do that, whereas if you've got a family at home, you know, you've got your children and you have to spend time with them, but the result is that your output is actually less, and trying to put that into, balancing that up is, becomes very difficult, because people tend to look at the paper{s}, you know.

If this person has done, has got three grants, you know, published 20 papers in the last two years, and somebody else has got one grant and published three papers in the last year, you know, on paper it appears one is much better than the other.

Male Dean of Science, post-1992

Women manager-academics, by contrast, were aware of both the advantages and disadvantages of being female and how this affected both their identities and the way in which they were judged as managers, whether their personal circumstances involved them in activities like childcare, the care of other dependants, and housework. There was a view from over half of our female respondents that being a woman manager meant you were more visible than men and judged by different standards:

I think women are under pressure because they are very visible, there are too few of us, there's no emerging role model, there's a handful of women vice chancellors, all of whom I know and they are so variable in their style... and I think some are more helpful than others as role models. So it actually is very difficult and women are still an object of interest, 'how will she react?' And you know 'can we push her in this way? If we can make her angry that will be good because she'll get a bit shrill' {laugh}. And of course shrill's a word that's {only} used of women.

Female PVC, post-1992

the vice chancellor has senior team meetings on a Monday morning and I've been at this four years now, I thought it was because I was a new girl, but they are all anxious to get in and say the most innocuous, facetious stuff. And I'm sitting there thinking what the hell did he say that for?... And they bring all this stuff to the table and they all start rising up in their seats. And sometimes I think I could be getting on with some real work here. But there seems to be the importance in actually, in front of the Vice Chancellor, as being a good boy you know, and getting your oar in. Or doing somebody else down, as if that gives you more brownie points.... There is still a lot of testosterone about, you know, this macho management and 'tell them to do it'. You know, 'tell them to do it'. Fine, I'll tell them to do it, a complete waste of breath you know {laugh}. I really do think that the male view of the world is one that's been structured from childhood, 'get out of my way, I'm a tank'.

Female PVC, pre-1992

The identities of manager-academics are fairly complex, reflect some of the divisions of the academic community reflected in Chapter 3, and often consist of sedimented layers that are acquired at different points in a career biography, with managerial elements coming in often at a later

109

stage and (for our interviewees, at least) rarely dominating until quite late in their careers. We now turn to examine some of the ways in which our respondents defined the values of academic life, since this may help us to understand the extent to which (if at all) they have begun to take on the mantle of neoliberal and neo-technocratic NM.

Generic Principles and Values about Academic Life

This section addresses the principles underpinning academic life as a manager-academic as expressed by many of our respondents. These included comments on collegiality, trust, goodwill, and autonomy, values which as Reed noted in Chapter 1 are directly challenged by the institutional and system-level changes which have taken place and the accompanying shifts in material context and organizational culture. The principles mentioned also included, as one interviewee noted, 'decency and openness, and transparency, and leadership, and integrity. These are all principles' (Dean, Management, post-1992). Unravelling these in more detail, unusually, given the continuing strong emphasis in UK universities on meritocracy (Bagihole and Goode 2001; Knights and Richards 2003) as reflected in the importance of competitive selection and promotion on the basis of merit, a strong trend of egalitarianism was emphasized by a senior manager in one post-1992 institution:

> We want people to feel proud about working here, you know. We try to be a single-status employer as far as we possibly can, so a cleaner is on the same contract as the Vice-Chancellor, you know, as far as possible. We try and do things that way...we try to, you know, make it so that everybody shares and is comfortable with this notion of what we are. I don't say we succeed with everybody.
>
> PVC, post-1992

Though this particular post-1992 university was unusual, our research data showed that a number of post-1992 institutions we researched had invested heavily in internal management development (supplemented by external forms too) for both in-post and potential manager-academics, since they felt it helped to integrate all staff into a broadly similar way of being managed. Since then, in England in particular, the HE funding body has made money available for management development along with other aspects of human resource management and a new UK-wide

Leadership Foundation for Higher Education has been established (in 2004). The differences in approach to management development and training that we found at the end of the twentieth century existed because at least some of the post-1992 institutions place considerable store by management qua management as part of their view of themselves as still developing a reputation. By contrast, the pre-1992 universities appeared more confident in their depiction of themselves as research and teaching institutions (and hence did not feel in need of 'management development') but also seemed more likely to value collegial decision-making by peer academics. Indeed Shattock argues that it is essential to retain collegiality in universities in order to sustain and nurture the academic endeavour (Shattock 2003). However, as the first quotation above shows, some post-1992 university respondents also set store by collegiality. This may be a more all-encompassing version of it than the one that most academics tend to espouse (Bensimon 1995), which historically has excluded part-timers, support staff, and sometimes women. The kind of principles described in the quote from the PVC given above are supposedly the same ones that now underlie the current UK HE Framework Agreement (Joint Negotiating Committee for Higher Education Staff 2003) which seeks to put all staff in higher education institutions on a single pay spine and to align other working conditions of different grades of employee.

The discursive model of academic-led decision-making which appeals to notions of collegiality, discussion, tolerance, and goodwill was reflected in a number of other responses from both pre- and post-1992 university manager-academic respondents, particularly at HoD level, where incumbents must often face both ways, towards their colleagues but also towards the centre of their institution but are surrounded by their immediate colleagues (this becomes less and less the case as manager-academics ascend the career management ladder):

I think academic life is all about the encouragement, the free flow of ideas. I think talk-down managerial styles are an absolute anathema within a department and also upon a department. If you're reduced to ordering people about or pressuring people into doing things then I think you have done something damaging to the life of a university. You know, you can't always have a consensus, there will always be disgruntled people who feel they've been, they have lost out or whatever on things I think on their way. That will always happen, but I think if your people relationships are good enough, folk will put up with you disagreeing with them.

HoD, Humanities, post-1992

111

Johnson offers a definition of collegiality that appreciates the complexity of the term (Johnson 2002). The suggestion made here is that the value of collegiality, as the above quotation demonstrates, lies in the quality of relationships that it espouses which are deeply meaningful for many. However, the ambiguity of the term makes clearly articulating its meaning problematic. In the case of this Head of Department, trust in colleagues, which is a key element in a number of different kinds of organizations (Misztal 1996; Lane and Bachmann 1998) but one that as previous chapters have noted, is increasingly disappearing, rested upon good working relationships. Of course, the definition of trust is problematic and shifts, as trust operates at different levels:

> I was looking at the managerial part and I feel that they don't really trust even up to the Head of Department, they don't really trust you. Maybe people have different systems, but in terms of the academic staff, I would argue that we're more professional.

> Focus Group, Science Learned Society

Further insight into perceptions of the contemporary situation was provided by references to the immediate past (though as we saw in Chapter 2, the extent to which our respondents understood what had happened in any kind of historical rather than romantic context was limited). A changing environment, for some, was not so new:

> Changes are a normal state of play; this is experienced much more keenly in a School like this, whose curriculum is very, very, fast moving. But I don't find it helpful to regard change as a separate concept.

> HoS, Science, post-1992

For others, the appearance of frequent change and the prominence of managers was a more recent shift in university life:

> When I started in university work, managers were not part of the university set-up really, it's something that has developed, I think, in the past 12 to 15 years or so, a far more refined concept of Managerialism within the university.

> HoD, Humanities, post-1992

For some, the emergence of 'Managerialism' had been to the detriment of what were expressed as traditional emphases, such as upon the student:

> Do you know what I think has been horrifying? We have had a strategic review in this university and in the document the word 'student' was mentioned twice. And I think one of the key things about management in the university is

to actually build into management thinking this respect for students, to get across to anybody that if you don't have students, you don't have a job, do you understand?

HoD, Social Sciences, post-1992

Indeed an analysis of what our manager-academic respondents thought about students revealed that many of them saw students largely as an abstraction, a source of complaints, or as a unit of resource (Johnson and Deem 2003) rather than part of the academic community. So, in this instance, the emerging prominence of management inside the university has the potential to produce conflicts with traditional expressions of value. Nevertheless, particularly within the post-1992 sector, the value of the student and the need for widening access to HE were held up as central values. One associate Dean described his own experience of arranging an open day visit as 'the kind of thing we should be doing more, getting people in to say "well this is higher education but you can be part of it as well"' (HoD, Health, post-1992). Similarly, a dean of social sciences within the same university described widening access as the university's 'strap line' strategy.

In relation to the increasing prominence of management within HE, the uniqueness of the university setting and its product emerged as a theme in a number of responses across all the sixteen institutions. There was particular emphasis on issues to do with the autonomy and the management of professionals. One Head of Department reflected upon his role thus:

> There are great advantages to {managing} professionals on the whole and in particularly university academics are, on the whole, self-managing, they have broad guidelines and they don't like close supervision.

HoD, Science, post-1992

The importance attached to autonomy becomes all the more evident when threatened:

> The latest thing was they {the senior management} want to make a log of exactly what staff development activities people are undertaking, have a summary and check up on people. Well, there's a lot of staff development, all kinds. I mean people get offended at being checked up on. It's not conducive to a good working atmosphere.

HoD, Social Science, post-1992

In this sense, the notion of Managerialism expressed by manager-academics presented a danger to core academic values as it might obscure the values and objectives underpinning the university:

I think we have to be careful that in HE our core value, our core service, is still to develop and deliver knowledge and people and I think we need to keep an eye on the balance between that endeavour, those intentions, and the skills that are required, you know like the new types of managerial abilities that are required to actually operate successfully.

HoD, Management, post-1992

One of the most significant changes was associated with the introduction of assessments and evaluations of academic work—quality audit measures such as quality assurance and enhancement of teaching (Brennan and Shah 2000; Morley 2003) through the UK HE Quality Assurance Agency institutional audits of academic standards (and in the late 1990s, teaching quality audit by subject) and also the RAE (Lucas 2006) which first took place in 1986. The historical development of the RAE and external quality assurance mechanisms in the UK HE systems have been discussed in Chapter 2. In terms of its impact upon the present day, for the Head of Department, the obligations to ensure a good RAE return for the department as a whole can, on occasion, run contrary to the best interests of individual researchers. One Head of Department provided one such example:

I have a young guy coming in . . . a similar set of opinions would suggest that he is the Nobel prize winner potentially. I am going to have a very difficult job as a manager to protect that individual, to allow him to do the research which might bring a Nobel prize . . . to protect him and to allow him to do that and at the same time say to him 'The Research Assessment Exercise is coming up, can I have your four publications?'

HoD, Science, pre-1992

Changes such as those described, to values like trust, collegiality, autonomy, and the management of performance were seen to be taking place in a general context of change, which collectively held the potential to clash with generic values and principles underpinning academic life. Unravelling the tensions in more detail and their manifestation upon the everyday working lives of manager-academics is the focus of the next section.

The Practical Characteristics of Manager-Academics' Everyday Lives

The Everyday Activities of Head of Departments

Being a HoD is not an easy task, as both contemporary and older research accounts of it show (Startup 1976; Moses 1985; Wolverton et al. 1999; Knight and Trowler 2001; Morgan 2001). The everyday workload of a Head of Department in contemporary UK universities often covers a very broad remit:

> I am Head of Department, I am leader of the MA in X, I am head of undergraduate programmes, I am leader and responsible for all Faculty research.... I have a senior management team which meets fortnightly with a proper business agenda, but we might be covering everything from, I don't know, purchasing policy, buying computers to use of space.
>
> HoD, post-1992

The logistics of running complex departments can be a substantial task in itself:

> Unlike a heavy undergraduate department which might only have three or four major programmes in it, we have 25 or 30 discrete programmes. So the routine business of academic monitoring and management is onerous.
>
> HoD, post-1992

Although one-fifth of HoDs interviewed resisted the term 'manager', the position of HoD implicated them in decision-making processes above the level of their own department—and sometimes towards taking seemingly contradictory decisions:

> I know what finance comes into the Faculty and the sources it comes from and where it goes to and, in fact, this School partly subsidises some of the others... and I'm only just now beginning to get a clear picture of which bit's subsidising what... but the problem for me of that is that it means that I'm actually saying, 'We need to spend all the money that we earn' at a time when the institution is saying, 'Well, of course, we should be making efficiency gains'.
>
> HoD, post-1992

Budgetary responsibilities and logistical and administrative responsibilities of running a department were discussed by a number of Head of Departments. In the above example, the Head of Department looked internally towards the interests of their own department. In terms of other activities, in spite of potentially onerous administrative responsibilities, there were pressures to remain research active and to teach. In some post-1992 institutions, teaching overrode obligations towards the next Research Assessment Exercise submission:

> I do believe it's important. And when looking at priorities I place that higher up the pecking order.
>
> HoD, Science, post-1992

In terms of everyday techniques or technologies through which HoDs interacted with their staff, several Head of Departments described how they actualized their roles:

> I much prefer to go and see people if I can or pick the 'phone up and sort it out actually.... I don't really like... conversations on e-mail and it keeps coming backwards and forwards and I think it's pointless, you know. It's better to actually pick up the 'phone and sort it or have a short meeting.
>
> Female HoD, post-1992

However, sustaining an 'open door' policy for departmental colleagues to reach them at any time was not always possible for other Head of Departments:

> I try to have an open door, but it got to the stage where it was very difficult... things happen and maybe that's because I'm not good enough at just saying, 'Clear off!' It's very hard to say, 'Clear off!' if crises crop up and somebody's at the door.
>
> HoD, post-1992

The very physical location of the Head of Department within their own departments was therefore beneficial in some instances and problematic in others. Visibility and praise were technologies used by some HoDs to celebrate colleagues' achievements:

> If somebody's had a good publication I write round and tell everybody. If somebody's, if one of my staff won an award for the article of the year, if somebody's successful in getting a particular research contract, if somebody's invited to speak in a prestigious event or whatever, I publicise other people's success ruthlessly because I know how much it means to me to have my success publicised and they can't be that much different.
>
> HoD, post-1992

The use of praise to reward good performance or achievement was, however, only relatively rarely cited. Alternatively, expressing thanks or an interest in colleagues' activities was used by some Heads of Departments as a means to avoid any connotations of direct intervention:

> It's dead easy, morale boosting, saying, 'thanks, I appreciate that'. It hardly ever happens to the extent that I get into the habit of repeatedly saying, 'thanks, I appreciate that' or whatever or just saying to people, 'what are you doing at the moment?' or 'What are you working on for yourself?' (by the way that's the expression I would use) rather than the chores that you've got to do, 'what are you doing because you're interested'.

> HoD, Humanities, post-1992

So an element of artifice also comes into Head of Departments interactions with their staff, which can also extend to social activities:

> I'm a Professor and I've got a group of Professors and I enjoy meeting them and we do go out and meet together and deliberately with young staff.

> HoD, Management, pre-1992

So whilst HoDs identified with the best interests of their own departmental unit and sought to maintain a visible profile within a department—albeit with a degree of artifice—in terms of key decision-making, support beyond the level of the department was not always forthcoming:

> I did actually take someone through a disciplinary procedure, just shortly after the Faculties merged and in my view, it was a very clear case for disciplinary action... but my experience of the procedure taught me that it's not worth bothering again and most Heads of School think the same.

> HoD, Science, post-1992

To summarize, the role of the contemporary Head of Department exposes them to tensions outside of their immediate department (resources, quality assurance procedures, teaching/research links and tensions and the Research Assessment Exercise), whilst leaving some latitude for their everyday internal running of a department, albeit in the above case, autonomy without sufficient authority. Though academic middle management has some special features, in many ways middle management in a range of organizations faces similar problems and tensions (Clegg and McAuley 2005). In terms of the chapter's opening themes of neoliberalism and neo-technical management, there was some evidence that the impact of market forces was in line with a neoliberal model upon universities. However, in respect of the role of Heads of Department carrying forward a neo-technical agenda, it was argued by most of our interviewees that insufficient power was devolved for them to implement the control technologies that a neo-technical managerial model necessitates, even if they wanted to do so.

The Everyday Activities of Faculty Deans

The role of the Dean has been relatively little researched outside of North America (Fagin 1997; Newsome 1997; Wepner, Wilhite, and D Onofrio 2003) and whilst, some see them as middle management (Hancock and Hellawell 2003), it could be argued that this depends on how the role is defined, with some deans having financial accountability to the senior management team (so-called executive deans) and others having more academic powers and autonomy. What kind of academic departments they manage may also affect how they operate and whether their authority is challenged (Bourdieu 1988; Shattock 2003). Shattock for example argues that social scientists and arts/humanities academics are more likely to question and challenge their deans (Shattock 2003: 72), whilst Bourdieu suggests that different disciplines are more or less likely to produce academics who seek status through academic capital (such as administrative roles and office holding of various kinds inside and outside the academy) or scientific capital (status acquired through research), with scientific prestige being more commonly sought after in the sciences and academic power more commonly sought in medicine and law, whilst social sciences and arts tend to have people specializing in both. The question of where the role is positioned, that is between the Head of Department and more senior figures such as Pro-Vice-Chancellors, raises dilemmas for those in the role:

> I find actually deans are in a funny position um, because they are between the sort of top level, vice-chancellor, deputy vice-chancellor, chairman of the Council, those things. So deans are actually with the vice-chancellor and pro vice-chancellors, there's six of us in this university and so we're actually on the committee of deans which is a sort of major, strategic committee...I see myself as not in a narrow sense representing the Arts Faculties interest but certainly doing that as part of the job, but trying I would hope to see you know my Faculty's interests alongside those of the university as a whole...equally sometimes I have to take negative sort of decisions and views backwards which they don't like and so I find myself sometimes in a rather odd position, I'm neither as it were a sort of hound or hare.

> Male Dean, Arts, pre-1992

The exact remit of their role was the subject of some variation between institutions and also in terms of how the role was interpreted:

> We now have a formal definition of the role, but that doesn't particularly worry me. I mean I would have been upset I think if I'd been asked to do a job where everything was clearly defined, because I always work on the basis that the more open a job is the more opportunity you have to do it well and to do the best possible thing, whereas if you're highly constrained sometimes it's very difficult to do anything.
>
> Male Dean, Sciences, pre-1992

This in turn had the implication that their roles could be very broad:

> I find it extraordinarily demanding {there is a} very great deal of pressure, er there is often stress, there are also great periods of delight and satisfaction. Er, so it is a sort of roller coaster of emotions inevitably, because you see all shades of life really.
>
> Male Dean, Sciences, post-1992

It also permitted some freedom for individuals to define and interpret their everyday activities:

> my ideal is that the actual running of the institution should function so smoothly that the vast bulk of my colleagues aren't constantly harassed and in the end somebody has to do that. And its better that its done by people who are actually themselves still practising academics because then you get a sense of, you don't get a dichotomy between the concerns of management and the concerns of um, the academics . . . 95% I expect is salary expenditure and I can't, I don't have powers to hire and fire.
>
> Female Dean, Social Sciences, pre-1992

The practicalities of their working day revolved around meetings, both group and individual. However, for those in post-1992 positions in particular, becoming a Dean did not exclude teaching responsibilities:

> The dominant thing of my week are the meetings I have to go to. There's an extremely heavy, I would say that about fifty per cent of my week that I have either meetings in the School or university-type meetings or meetings outside which are, you know, something to do with the university and I still manage, I still try, because I think it's important that managers should do this, I still try to get into the classroom and teach as well.
>
> Male Dean, Social Sciences, post-1992

One addition, in more recent times, was the level of communication via email:

> I'm driven by e-mail which I hate. I now get it all printed out and go through it all on paper, I don't look at it at all {on screen}. We get absurd amounts of e-mail.
>
> Male Dean, Sciences, post-1992

Whilst not all Deans were in a position to 'hire or fire', they were almost all directly involved with addressing staff who were perceived to be under-performing:

> I don't like that. I don't mind it, but I don't like it....I remember one of Moss Canter's lines, 'You shouldn't delegate nasty jobs', so I sometimes feel responsible for doing those. I equally recognise that part of my role is to develop other managers in the place....If they don't like it they have to go to {the VC} and it's a real big one that one and {the VC} will support me, I know he'll support me.
>
> Male Dean, Business, pre-1992

In this sense, the role of the Dean involved the implementation of change through more junior members of staff:

> I think the biggest struggle I have is with the members of staff of my own gen-eration and the business of change. They're reluctant to change, they don't see the point of change, they see that, they have this halcyon view of a university as it was when they were students etc and the external pressures of QAA or HEFCE or various other, internal senior management quality audit etc, etc...they see these as burdens and unnecessary burdens and I do find that that's the hardest job; trying to keep these guys on board, forward looking...because they do have an influence on younger members.
>
> Male Dean, Social Sciences, post-1992

This aspect of their everyday working lives often presented a challenge:

> you can't drive academics and tell them what to do, like herding sheep to work really. I mean they run around all over the place, don't they? And the more you try pushing them in one direction, the more obstinate they become. So I don't think the academic world works that way...you've got to influence people and convince them that your plan is reasonable and give them the opportunity to bring forward their plans. The area which I think is difficult and which I haven't solved and I've got in one department at the moment, is when you actually have everybody on board, senior staff bar one, and it doesn't matter how much work you put in, how many people, how many hours of explanation that one is never going to fit in....I don't think even the vice chancellor could persuade

them, with professors, to do things that they don't want to do. We can't sack them after all.

Female Dean, Sciences, pre-1992

As such, their role is as much as the carrier of change, as the presentation of academics' views to senior management:

I don't, I haven't actually sought the views of the lecturing staff generally. I believe, but I believe that I promote their interests vigorously.

Male Dean, Sciences, post-1992

Deans then, with their responsibility for a group of cognate disciplines, are located between HoDs who manage only one subject or discipline but have wide ranging responsibilities and Pro-Vice-Chancellors who tend to have a more specialized brief but across a wide range of subjects.

The Everyday Activities of Pro-Vice-Chancellors

The role of Pro-Vice-Chancellor is distinct from that of Heads of Department or even Deans. PVCs do not formally line-manage academics though they may manage a few non-academic staff. In addition, when the Managerialism research was done in 1998–2000, pre-1992 institutions tended to advertise externally for the role of PVC, whereas generally post-1992 institutions did not. However, this is now changing and more pre-1992 universities are advertising externally for PVCs. The mode of appointment can affect both the dynamics of senior management teams and how PVCs are regarded by academic knowledge workers. In terms of their working hours, long hours were a common phenomenon amongst all respondents (Deem and Hillyard 2002) and increased still further at this level:

I come into work at 8 and I go home at 6. And I would normally work between 1 and 2 hours each evening . . . the amount of time that's been demanded of me in my thirteenth, this is the end of my thirteenth year in the management of {this institution}, has increased, has gone up from perhaps forty per cent as a Head to perhaps sixty, seventy per cent as a Dean to perhaps eighty, ninety per cent as a PVC and this goes up in steps. Meanwhile your career options change and shift and in some sense narrow. I mean, I've gone on producing research, but the numbers of that have sort of dwindled and you could do it as a graph like that, whereas the other time would be going in the other direction.

PVC, Humanities, pre-1992

The everyday activities of Pro-Vice-Chancellors involved greater responsibility within the university as a whole rather than a department or faculty:

> I underestimated how much time would be spent on the University Management Group itself and on the group of the Vice-Principals which meets weekly as a kind of auxiliary to it and various functions that kind of flow from that, substituting for the VC and opening conferences.
>
> PVC, Humanities, pre-1992

University management groups or teams are often involved in resource planning (e.g. overseeing new projects) as well as crisis management and all of these raised issues of values and leadership:

> You've first of all got to declare values and standards and everybody has to know what those standards are. Not just paying lip service to them, but the extent to which they are really visible if you like in practice.
>
> PVC, Humanities, pre-1992

Such visibility sometimes included maintaining an active research profile (though this is dependent on discipline, as it is not really possible for laboratory-based scientists to do as much research, as say, a Humanities scholar):

> I don't need to do any teaching if I don't want to. I do happen to like it so I do a bit, but I can be very selective about it. In terms of research then yeah, I do still feel that as one of the senior members of, I guess, well if we talk RAE then for sure I have the responsibility to make sure that when we submit to the RAE that my name's there.
>
> PVC, Science, pre-1992

Additional responsibilities included staff recruitment, meetings with Head of Departments, Deans, or Heads of Schools, external relations, and chairing working groups as well as more strategic tasks within the remit of PVCs:

> Half of the time is to do with the more strategic aspects of moving ahead on those two initiatives the enhancement development of the Continuing Studies and business meetings, conferences, consultancy side and the postgraduate activities.
>
> PVC, Science, pre-1992

The roles of PVCs we interviewed clearly involved more strategic level technologies than those of HoDs or even Deans. We now move on to consider the chief executive of contemporary UK universities—the Vice-Chancellor.

The Everyday Activities of Vice-Chancellors

The role of the VC is usually supported by a Senior Management Team in the university, although the exact title of such a group varied. As we saw in Chapter 3, SMTs are not usually formal parts of the university structure and as such are often not formally accountable to anyone (Marginson and Considine 2000), but they provide an important forum for VCs. In terms of reflecting what has changed in respect of the role of VC, Bargh et al. argue that the UK VC was once perceived as a leading academic (Bargh et al. 2000) but from the mid-1980s onwards this role became more corporate and managerial. However, Bargh et al. argue that whilst VCs often argue they are being strategic, work shadowing of them often reveals a good deal of firefighting instead. In terms of role, the multifaceted nature of the Pro-Vice-Chancellors' roles also featured in the everyday activities of Vice-Chancellors. However, for VCS this also included fulfilling more traditional, diplomatic roles:

> There is an ambassadorial role of the Vice-Chancellor which I do not do well, although I do it better than I used to and this is called 'Eating the Dinners'. You could eat yourself stupid for the university...that is an old model of the Vice-Chancellor, where the Vice-Chancellor is the senior academic of the institution and goes round doing good works.
>
> VC, Science, post-1992

On a more, contemporary level, one Vice-Chancellor defined three constitutive elements demanded of the modern VC:

> I think in terms of the Vice-Chancellors' jobs I think there are probably conceptually three sort of elements, one is clearly the strategic, the long-term vision, perhaps the shaping of the opportunities, the ideas, the values, the beliefs about the university. There's a second element, which is, if you like, about the operational systems, which deliver that strategy, and there's a third element, which is essentially about the people.
>
> VC, Social Science, post-1992

The first and second of these elements, the 'vision' and its delivery, are closely entwined in the university context:

> You can make a decision, whether it actually is really shared is a different value, is a different matter. So I actually think it's worth, it's well worthwhile

universities, indeed any organization, just spending time in what apparently appears, this very abstract debate about value systems within which you want to operate.

VC, Social Science, post-1992

The implementation or delivery of decisions therefore involves a discursive element:

What I feel is that the process of managing change which I've been going through is as important as the outcome, that that process and that process of inclusion and that process of openness, transparency, taking people along with you, trying to get people to share those corporate values. I think that's what I want to see reflected in the way that Strategic Review then happens elsewhere in the university. But it's that process of trust, respect, academic respect, one for the other. Respecting and that means you have to be able to listen to disparate views, have to be prepared to be castigated in public meetings, all of those things, but you just say yes, you have the right to say that.

VC, Social Science, post-1992

In this case, the Vice-Chancellor is less the head of a democratic organization, than one in which debate and discussion are important features. In this process of discussion, the visibility of the Vice-Chancellor's commitment to their vision and the consistency of their own actions become vital:

You can talk until you are blue in the face and you don't always get it across. I mean people do, I'm sure the university's not unique in this, have a stubborn persistence despite being told otherwise, so I'm conscious that just sort of telling people what I'm trying to do is not enough you have to actually demonstrate it by action.

VC, Social Science, pre-1992

Echoing the importance for some PVCs to visibly attend to their own expression of values, the Vice-Chancellor's visibility around the institution bridges decision-making with its operationalization and, for some, is a preferred technology. As we noted from our case studies of employee views of university management, some VCs communicate with most of their staff only by email, which is not always as popular as more personalized and synchronous communications or 'management by walking about' as this VC expressed it:

I would like to think I know a lot of people around the campuses and they would certainly know me, spend a lot of time in that old-fashioned term, you know, management by walking about. I would much rather go and meet people in their laboratories, workshops, offices than I would necessarily have them here.

VC, Social Science, post-1992

This VC is here echoing some of the preferences expressed by HoDs who sought to operate 'open door' policies or resolve issues face-to-face rather than through correspondence or protracted emails, although clearly HoDs have far fewer people with whom they need to engage. Another important distinction between the role of a VC and that of a HoD is the number of different disciplines encompassed within their remit. The pervasiveness of the Vice-Chancellor's scope for decision-making into academics' everyday discipline-based activities is therefore restricted in this sense:

> A university depends on individual creativity as its absolute lifeblood, that is particularly true in research, but I think it's also true in education but perhaps to a lesser extent. I mean, I literally can't tell people what they should be doing because I don't know what they should be doing. You know, if my professor of, you know, organic chemistry whatever it might be, is meant to be working at the leading edge of his/her role, I don't know what they should be doing first, only they know that.

VC, Social Science, pre-1992

The chapter now turns to consider a less visible group of workers inside the university, namely senior administrators.

The Everyday Activities of Administrators

Senior administrators' roles have also shifted over recent decades. For example, some of them now often occupy a place on Senior Management teams, which while not a formal management structure, are an important site for institutional strategic decision-making. Boundaries between manager-academics and what Shattock (2003: 179) calls professional managers have shifted and blurred as management has become more central to universities, although at the same time some of their functions have become more specialized (Dobson 2000). The career biographies of administrators have also changed—in the past, some academics *became* career administrators (we had several of these in our sample) but a good number of the more recently appointed administrators we interviewed (including almost all those concerned with finance) had started their careers outside higher education. Those from the latter group whom we interviewed, as the following discussion will reveal, tended to find the shift into HE

125

quite a culture shock. Nevertheless, almost all the senior administrators interviewed by us tended to define their own roles with reference to their academic colleagues:

> My priority is to make sure . . . that what the support services are doing, is what the academic colleagues want us to do, to support teaching and research. Now that doesn't mean being supine, it does mean making suggestions, so say for the use of, it might be an internet or it might be more effective ways of enrolling students or processing research grants, applications, whatever it may be.
>
> Senior Administrator, pre-1992

The impact of 'Managerialism' in recent years was perceived to have influenced senior administrators' autonomy and also how their work was defined:

> It's partly a question of using a different term to describe what's always been essentially the same kind of role. Manager is a more, it's the more usual term now to describe what we do. I mean certainly when I started off administration was the normal way of describing things. . . . There has also been some change in the nature of the job and what's expected, towards a more, if you like, proactive Managerialism, if I can draw the distinction, as opposed to administration, which probably most people would regard contains a more reactive element.
>
> Senior Administrator, pre-1992

In this sense, Managerialism was felt to be a relevant and appropriate term to apply to their roles as senior administrators (very unlike most of the manager-academics we interviewed):

> Senior Administrator: I think of myself nowadays as a manager. There's been a change in thinking, which has clearly happened over the last decade. I wouldn't always describe myself as that for public consumption because it isn't necessarily productive to do so.
>
> SH: Is that because of what people associate with the term?
>
> Senior Administrator: Yes.
>
> SH: And what do you think they associate with the term?
>
> Senior Administrator: Managerialism.
>
> SH: What is Managerialism?
>
> Senior Administrator: In its bad sense it is somebody who is not as familiar with the academic subject matter as people who are actively engaged in teaching and research. And imposed Managerialism can push them into directions, which their academic careers and credentials and wishes don't want them to follow.
>
> Senior Administrator, pre-1992

This demonstrates a degree of internalization of Managerialism by senior administrators and suggests that, with the advent of NM, their roles may have become more empowered. Nevertheless, the direct employment of managerialist rhetoric was used by quite a few with considerable caution in the university context:

Interviewer: Would you be happy to describe yourself as a manager, is that something you'd apply or?

Senior Administrator: Well I don't have any difficulty with it and I don't have any difficulty with the term 'administrator' which does seem to be a slightly less acceptable world, word in this particular world...and of course the term 'manager' is not necessarily very PC in the university sector...you are trying to make people realise that it's pointless putting on a course that no student will want to do. We have a very successful hospitality department here that works for me, but it's not particularly popular within the university because it's {a} cold, hard glint of commercialism.

Senior Administrator, pre-1992

In some cases, Managerialism had extended the authority and remit of administrators over academics, for example, in relation to research and teaching quality (Morley 2003; Lucas 2006) or finance and personnel management. Yet whether this new empowerment was front stage or behind the scenes remains a question. For those who had been long employed in universities, their expressions of administrator status within the university structure remained very traditional:

I think 'support staff', 'support services' is absolutely fine, I've got no problem and I don't find it demeaning one iota for the personnel service to be a support service because the core business of the university is teaching and research and it always will be and it doesn't mean to say that I'm less significant because I'm a support service.

Senior Adminstrator, post-1992

Administrators or career managers are a vital part of universities and increasingly their work overlaps with as well as supporting that of academics and manager-academics. But as more administrators are recruited from outside of academe, so they may become both conduits for the entry of further managerialist principles and vehicles of value change in universities. The chapter now moves on to unravel the question of how manager-academics manage and the kinds of technologies they use.

Technologies of Management

The opening chapter outlined the theoretical basis of NM. In understanding the extent to which contemporary HE institutions accommodate or resist models of Managerialism, the role of technologies or techniques of management is central. Chapter 1 argued that controlling technologies as employed by managers were central to the achievement of neo-technical Managerialism. The following is an example of a particular form of managerial control technology used by Heads of Department:

> this is where I think the university really could help a bit. They pay lip service to the idea that you can be promoted and have a good academic career if you are good at teaching and ... so forth and I really applaud that. It's just that it's not really true.
>
> HoD, Social Science, pre-1992

The possibility of directly expressing what manager-academics sought from their staff was discussed in many interviews, although the secret of how to achieve this was hard to discern:

> You can't say 'Do better research' you can't even say 'Do more research' you can um, plead and you can encourage and you can support by providing {and} encouraging a good research profile, you lead by establishing {in} people's minds, how critical it is that this kind of research be done in the School.
>
> HoD, Arts, post-1992

Being clear, if not direct, was an important part of this process:

> What characterises good management in these professional contexts is that very clear sense of taking the organization forward, not in some airy fairy um, let's all be better, better world tomorrow kind of way, but in very practical ways 'Next year if we do this we'll be in this position, if we get this programme off the ground it will do these things'.
>
> HoD, Science, post-1992

In terms of 'carrots and sticks' in motivating staff, both were discussed, though it seemed sticks were sometimes more readily available than carrots.

> Well the fundamental tool of compliance is the contract, which then mediates as I've said to you this notion that everybody has a diet of activity.
>
> HoD, Engineering, post-1992

What I need to be able to give people is the time and that's what I can't give them. . . . That would be the real carrot and that's the one that's difficult.

HoD, Humanities, post-1992

The descriptions manager-academics gave of their control technologies suggested that only certain kinds of strategies work:

The people I see who have been bad at this {leading} are people who have tried to make everybody happy. Very often through consensus. . . . The bad example is where people try to come to a compromise for the sake of a quiet life.

PVC, pre-1992

One-to-one use of technologies employed to implement or encourage desired outcomes took place at all levels—from Head of Department to Vice-Chancellor but approaches to it differed:

I also don't carry grudges and I usually say to staff, 'If I've got to tell you off, don't go out there and sulk, because tomorrow morning when I see you it is "Hello, would you like a cup of coffee?" ' and we have moved on from whatever it is. If it is something that I feel the individual needs to learn from I usually say to them, 'this arose because you didn't do this, this and this. Now, I think we ought to monitor this for a week, for a month, for six weeks and then when I'm happy that you're happy with the way in which you're moving that issue forward, that problem forward, that module forward, then we can move on'.

HoS, Health Sciences, post-1992

This contrasts with the different management roles academics perform, for example HoDs are closely associated with their disciplinary base in their departments, whereas those occupying more senior posts have to work across a range of disciplines:

I've worked {in the USA} and at a {National Research Institute}. Actually I was student {here and} I came back to head a research group . . . and then as things went on I eventually became professor and head of the department. . . . My primary role was to run my research laboratory and to operate on the international stage. . . . As time progressed it fell to me to be elected Dean . . . and I discovered that I did get some job satisfaction from the more managerial side of universities and had to decide what a career move might be. . . . I was beginning to think well maybe I'd like to be a vice-chancellor of another university. And, by that time I'd ceased being Dean and I was then appointed Pro vice-Chancellor. . . . In the meantime the creation of the Deputy vice-chancellorship . . . offered an opportunity. . . . That's how I ended up where I am.

DVC, pre-1992

Only a few of those operating at high levels of seniority are still involved with directly managing staff although Vice-Chancellors themselves can actually remove managers from their posts if they wish:

> We do not have tenure and our management staff, I can assign them to duties appropriate to their experience. So... it happened a little while ago, if I want somebody to cease to be a Dean, I walk into their office and sit down and say, 'Look, I'm sorry, but I don't want you to continue to be Dean. I want you to do something else'.

> VC, post-1992

The technologies employed by manager-academics sometimes appeared to us to be more direct and more managerial than might be considered consistent with the kinds of values and notions of trust mentioned elsewhere in the manager-academic interviews and explored in an earlier section of this chapter. The chapter now moves into the final section to consider how such technologies of management might have been acquired and the formation of routes into management careers.

Preparing for Managerial Careers and the Formation of Careers

Only about a third of our 137 manager-academics in the second phase of the research had received any significant formal training for their role, although most others had engaged in some kind of informal learning or attended very short training units or sessions. The nuances between such different forms of learning and academics' reflections upon their management learning experiences—indeed the very need for management learning—are discussed in greater detail in Chapter 5.

Preparing for Management

For some manager-academics taking up their first management role, the experience was daunting and represented a real sea change in their academic identity, since suddenly the 'day job' was no longer the main focus for their attention:

> It was a like a real baptism of fire....I feel almost that I've never learned to do the ordinary job, because I haven't had time to come to terms with what the ordinary job is and would be if all this wasn't going on.

> HoD, Social Sciences, post-1992

But the very process of being in post itself created for some, a learning environment and opportunities for reflection on best practice:

> There have often been times when I've thought, 'Although I've done this like this I don't like the outcome and, in retrospect, it would have been much better if I'd have done this, this and this.'

> HoD, Science, post-1992

However, not all Head of Departments felt unprepared. A number had actively sought some form of training in advance of their career development into management:

> I think part of it is sort of common sense, a way of going about things, but I did actually do an Open University certificate in Management before I came into post, because.... I decided that I was interested in moving in that direction and I thought if I was, that I ought.... I needed some theoretical underpinning.

> HoD, Health Studies, post-1992

> It certainly helped to have the {a certificate in management} background, because people make assumptions... that you know all sorts of bits and pieces of theory that support management, when if you're a Microbiologist there's no reason why you should ever have heard of any of it and when you come to do, if you come into larger groups or management learning courses in wider groups people assume things and certainly some of the things that were assumed, I'd picked up on the course and it was helpful from that point of view.

> HoD, Science, post-1992

For others, moving into management was perceived to involve 'life skills' that they had already acquired, with an emphasis on practice, not theory, a focus that other researchers looking at the management of higher education have also noted (Townley 2003). This did not necessarily mean, however, that those who emphasized their previous 'life skills' were not open to informally acquiring new skills, by listening to and observing others or asking them questions:

> I also feel that I have drawn upon a lot of my experience in bringing up two children, running a home, having to juggle the time to study, to plan and to organise my own life. And also I think one of the things that I pride myself on is I'm a very good listener. I watch people. I learn from my experience and I'm not frightened of saying to someone, regardless of however senior I am, 'I don't know. I will go and find out.'... The way to learn, the way to develop, is to find somebody who I respect, I see as a role model, I think have got good practices, things that I can aspire and either asking them openly, 'can I shadow

you for a while? Can I ask you some questions about how did you manage that situation?'

Female HoD, Arts/Humanities, post-1992

We noted whilst carrying out the research fieldwork that some of the institutions we were studying deliberately set up situations where informal contacts between manager-academics might develop, for example a regular 'heads' coffee or lunchtime, awaydays or even action learning sets. Other universities in our research did not appear to recognize how important it was to foster such networking were nor did they offer possibilities for regular informal contact other than a brief induction for those new to the manager-academic role.

Routes into Management and Changing Identities

The above section considered preparation for the initial move into management; this section looks at the impact of such moves (whether the move is temporary or permanent) upon academics' own identities. Routes into management reveal that there are particular channels that most academics we researched had followed before they became manager-academics, often with progressively more demanding administrative loads and recognition by others of particular skills connected with management and leadership:

> I have certainly acquired over the years a fair amount of the administrative experience at various levels and in various parts of the university. So in fact perhaps for the past 7 or 8 years my colleagues have said that when the post has come up 'would you be interested in doing it?'...So it wasn't something I especially wanted to do to be honest, it was something I thought I ought to do. And I think I was reasonably well qualified in terms of experience around the university.

Male HoD, Humanities, pre-1992

On the other hand, there were a few interviewees now occupying senior positions to whom management had not appealed earlier on in their careers:

> Interviewer: Was it always your ambition to run an institution?
>
> VC: No, I don't think I even thought about it until I become Pro Vice-Chancellor at {X institution}...even when I was Dean at {Y institution}] I didn't assume that I would end up as a full-time manager, I was invited to go back into research. And indeed when I came here I had a two year sabbatical,

to spend on doing whatever research I wanted to do for two years {laugh}, I mean, completely uncluttered money, so it was very much a case of making a conscious decision.

VC, from Social Science background, post-1992

Though there are different pathways or routes we could identify amongst our respondents, as discussed in Chapter 2, that is, the reluctant manager, the 'good citizen' manager, and the career manager (Deem et al. 2001), these were not necessarily watertight and some people moved from one to the other over time. In some instances, the transition into management provided a refreshing change and an opportunity to protect and preserve what was seen as important during times of turbulence or reform:

I've always had to find new ways of doing things because there were no obvious routes through for the kind of things I wanted to do, but it doesn't seem to me outlandish. I'm not having to take on whole new ways of looking on the world that I'm not happy with, I'm not happy to adjust, I'm not, questioning, I'm not having a lot of conscience problems, let's say, all the time. And finding ways that I can bring what everyone always thought was good through into new conditions, but that's what life's about isn't it? Things change and you find ways of still doing what's important.

Female HoD, Humanities, pre-1992

Some related their decisions to take up Head of Department roles to their stage in the life cycle and to family commitments and obligations:

Why I wanted to be head of School as opposed to a head of a specialist unit? Career, money, change, lots of little factors, my wife and I both have aged mothers {with us} living and working here {in the south}, we have young children, quality of life.

Male HoD, Science, post-1992

However, such explicit statements framed purely in terms of career objectives were seen by some female respondents as being particularly male in their outlook, with reference to serendipitous or 'by chance' careers, as noted also in research on female head teachers of schools (Evetts 1994):

I've never been a person that's said, 'In two years I'm going to do this and then I'm going to do that', I've never thought like that. I think that's quite a male thing actually ... the people that I've known that have done that have all been men and most of the women I know don't operate like that. They tend to, they get to a point where they think, 'It would be good to do this' and then do it.

Female HoD, Social Sciences, post-1992

133

However, the 'by chance' syndrome also seemed to be characteristic of some men we interviewed, so perhaps in this instance it is related to the extent to which senior manager-academics tend to emerge from the academic ranks, with almost no one we encountered saying that they had dreamed of being a Vice-Chancellor when young. The project of the self as a manager-academic amongst our sample tended only to arise at mid- or even late career stage. Once made at a later stage in a career it can be hard to reverse the process, so routes back to conventional academic life after a period as a manager-academic above the level of Head of Department are less evident and more difficult to pursue.

There were, perhaps predictably, some expressions of reluctance amongst respondents to allow new responsibilities to permeate personal or home lives, although we found that considerations of home-life balance were hard for many manager-academics we interviewed (Deem and Hillyard 2002):

> I've got to the stage where I've been working virtually every evening when I get home until I go to bed and part of the weekend and I don't think that's a sustainable pattern nor a desirable one . . . we've got plenty of interests outside, but the main thing is that they get squeezed.
>
> Female HoD, Humanities, post-1992

As well as the loss of time for home life, the move into more senior levels of management offers a very different working day compared with teaching and researching, suggesting that the community of practice into which senior manager-academics move is one distinct from that of academics in general because of the detachment from the core activities and academic subject or discipline that Henkel (2000) and others see as so central to academic identity:

> Having gradually come into a leadership position from being a junior academic in one university and a middle manager in another and now a {more} senior manager, I recognise that the further you go, to go much further than this I would lose day-to-day leadership roles over a recognisable unit. The thing about Pro Vice-Chancellors and Deputy Vice-Chancellors and Deans even, they don't actually interact with many people other than their immediate circle of administrators and the other managers that they manage.
>
> Male Head of School, Science, post-1992

However, for others the attraction of a route into management was this very taking on of more responsibility and influence at a broader organizational level:

I suppose I became more interested in the management of the institution and I wanted to change things I suppose. Basically I didn't really like the way it had become and I was interested in changing it and that's what, what got me doing these things.

Male Dean, Applied Science, post-1992

Alternatively, such a move could also hold negative consequences:

I'm part of an academic community, I'm an academic, I love it and I used to be an academic, I wish I was a good academic. I wish I was as good as I'd like to have been!

Male HoD, Management, pre-1992

Other motives expressed by academics include obligations towards colleagues and taking into account the time available before retirement:

it's simply related, I think to two factors. One towards the end of my career, I'm now sixty. It sounds very old fashioned, but I perhaps wanted to give something back to the university in terms of management. And I did bring an unusual blend of expertise, having been out at {on secondment to a research council} you know for sometime, so I know that sounds awfully old fashioned but I do genuinely feel that. And secondly I knew that if I turned it down that a younger colleague whose career should not be burdened at this stage by being a Dean would have been asked, and would perhaps have been lent on quite heavily. And this is an individual whose research career is blossoming at the moment and I simply didn't want that to be invaded in any way.

Male Dean, Science, pre-1992

The move into management was therefore motivated by a variety of factors: personal, family, and career elements. The interview data drawn upon in this chapter suggests that few academics accept that there is a generic management role in HE, rather there is a degree of reflexivity for most regarding their perceptions of NM. Explicit mechanisms of line management run contrary to the culture of UK universities despite the raft of recent reforms encouraging a more managerial approach:

I think the actual line management would be quite difficult because the style, the type of control is so different than the industry I'm familiar with which is a sort of clocking on, clocking off sort of industry where everything has got to be done by last Friday.

Female HoD, Arts/Humanities, post-1992

135

In some instances, the language used by academics can be used as an indicator of acceptance, internalization, or resistance:

> I think, notwithstanding any of the operational difficulties that you may have or any of the environmental or contextual difficulties that you may have, your first duty is to maintain professionalism and integrity in terms of what you're doing... you could not afford to be in a situation of which you felt nervous or you failed to sleep well at night because you thought really the quality of our degrees is going down or that our ability to sustain our research activity is really um, too difficult to deliver. I mean, if you couldn't have the confidence that there is integrity about what you are offering, what you are saying about yourself to the wider world, then I think you have a serious problem.
>
> Male PVC, post-1992

Here, the legitimacy of management is caught up with the expression of values, such as professionalism and integrity. The language used here demonstrates more than a degree of acceptance, in that the pressures to succeed in relation to indicators of success (teaching quality and research activity) are expressed in terms of legitimacy. In this sense, there is a risk that resistance is difficult and compliance becomes an accepted way of doing things.

Finally, 'bad' examples of management were used by some interviewees to determine their own, very different, practice:

> I think a lot, one of the early, biggest mistakes that people make in management is not saying thank you and not saying well done and not saying that's interesting.... Nobody, nobody, ever, at senior level has said, 'I see you're going to be in the next RAE, what things are you putting in?' No interest, no interest.
>
> Male HoD, Humanities, post-1992

For a few, feelings of management omnipotence were seen as very problematic as they suggested that no mistakes could be made or vulnerabilities recognized; aspects of management identified by other research on public service management as distinctive from private sector management (Alimo-Metcalfe and Alban-Metcalfe 2000; Alban-Metcalfe and Alimo-Metcalfe 2003a, 2003b)

> I sort of have maxims in my mind, like one of them is from Cromwell, Oliver Cromwell, which I had pinned up on my desk for a long time: 'Think ye in the bowels of Christ ye may be wrong' {laughs}. And as I have said to, you know, other women who have asked me various things about management, 'Just because you are put into the position of X it does not confer infallibility on you, if you think it does, forget it'. Or if you find yourself saying 'Oh that's

going to happen without even discussing it with people' rationale, you get to the danger point.

Female Dean, Social Science, post-1992

Even when management is seen as legitimate, an acceptable form of management is for some people, difficult to achieve in an academic setting:

I think there's a middle way, I hate to say that because I don't believe in it as a phrase. But I don't mean that in any sort of Blairist [reference to UK Prime Minister Tony Blair 1997–2007], sort of way. But I think its possible to be better run than the old universities ever were without heavy-handed, being heavy-handed in a managerial way, it's just bloody difficult to do it.

Male Dean, Science, post-1992

Conclusion

The chapter has discussed the working lives and identities of a purposive sample of manager-academics as expressed through their own accounts. We have moved from system and organizational levels of NM to the micro- and individual level, looking at how some of the broad trends in Managerialism in public services discussed in Chapter 1 and the changes to the UK higher education system and universities as organizations that were considered in Chapters 2 and 3 play out in the perceptions, practices, and values of individual manager-academics. Whilst the focus and context here has been that of the UK, the themes of Managerialism and academic work cultures are much more generally applicable and the processes to which our respondents referred are probably generic to many academic systems. However, in the case of the UK, some of the mechanisms of reform and audit, such as the RAE, are still somewhat distinctive, even though similar such systems are now developing in other countries (von Tunzelmann and Mbula 2003; Lucas 2006).

We also saw that the kinds of identities adopted by our respondents were indeed fluid and (mostly) related to reflexive projects of the self (Giddens 1991; Henkel 2000) but were also critically shaped by biographies and the institutions in which interviewees worked, by institutional histories and membership of various communities (MacIntyre 1981). Discipline background, gender and type of institution (pre- or post-1992) appeared to emerge as particularly important but so too did the kind of management role held, and whether it was regarded as a career move, a temporary role or even in some cases, an activity undertaken reluctantly.

There was still some indication of unease amongst many middle level manager-academic respondents about describing themselves as a manager rather than academic leader, although a majority accepted that their role had a management element to it. There were signs too, at the middle management level, of resistance to Managerialism and the holding of more traditional academic values such as collegiality, tolerance and integrity, with relatively little evidence except at very senior levels, of trilingualism, that is of appearing to hold, simultaneously, several different sets of values and beliefs set in contradictory discourses. Nevertheless, the very activities of contemporary manager-academics involve and invoke Managerialism and so de facto most of our respondents were at least bilingual (Gewirtz, Ball, and Bowe 1995), working with the values of their discipline and those of the contemporary neo-technocratic managerial academy.

Thus our data suggest some lack of congruence between the values manager-academics claim to espouse and those they actually appear to practice, something we also found in comparing manager-academic accounts with those of other employees in the case study element of the study, where manager-academic claims to be consultative and collaborative were not what employees perceived to be happening (Deem and Johnson 2000; Deem 2003). It is at this intersection of manager and employee that some of the most salient features of the divided university discussed in Chapter 3 make themselves evident. The unevenness and unpredictability of the implementation of NM in the sixteen UK universities we investigated is apparent in the differing extent to which our manager-academic respondents can be seen to have accepted and internalized new forms of management at various institutional levels. Important distinctions between very senior (Pro-Vice-Chancellor/Vice-Chancellor) manager-academics on the one hand and Heads of Departments and administrators on the other have emerged with middle level manager-academics less likely to have overtly embraced NM except for a minority of permanent HoD appointees in post-1992 universities. More senior respondents were much more likely to have embraced aspects of NM, by virtue of holding more senior demanding roles and because of the greater likelihood that they were embarked on a managerial rather than academic career. This lends support to the notion that identities of manager-academics are a constantly reworked project of the self (Giddens 1992; Henkel 2000) but also constitute a highly contingent and contextual activity. Academic identities and values are likely to shift as manager-academics working in the context we have been describing to perform the everyday activities of their roles (effectively, performing neo-technocratic

Managerialism), which increasingly involve the audit culture, monitoring of individual and unit performances, meeting targets, being visibly accountable, taking account of development plans and strategies and 'doing more with less'. For those that have taken on manager-academic roles in a permanent or career capacity, their legitimacy, authority, and self-identity progressively come to rest more on their role as a manager than on their scholarly activities. In terms of echoing a neo-technical model of management, this is a significant shift. At the same time at more senior levels of management, the issue of a profession (Larson 1977; Freidson 1988, 2001) emerges again, only this time a profession related to management of academics, not to academic work per se. Senior management teams may be beginning to resemble a community of practice (Lave and Wenger 1991; Wenger 1998; Wenger, McDermott, and Snyder 2002) quite divorced from the everyday activities and routines of academic knowledge work.

Chapter 5 develops the theme of learning to be a manager-academic and the training needs and requirements of those taking on manager-academic responsibilities. Whilst this theme was touched upon in this chapter, it warrants much further development if the longer-term implications of the uneasy and uneven influence of Managerialism on UK HE are to be fully understood. The issue of training and development also raises the possibility of making possible opportunities to position manager-academics in a more reflexive mode and discourse that sidesteps some of the negative consequences of neoliberal and neo-technical management.

5

Learning How to Do the Management of Academic Knowledge Work

Introduction

This chapter engages with two themes: what are manager-academics' perceived learning needs and what is the process by which manager-academics learn? The chapter employs data collected as part of our 'New Managerialism' research project as a means to explore these themes in depth, focusing particularly on interviewees already in management roles reflecting on their personal journeys whilst occupying those roles. It is argued here that whilst there is a definite place for formal training of manager-academics, informal learning with and from peers is also significant in professional learning (Eraut 2000). Hence, attention needs to be paid to what is sometimes called situated learning (Lave and Wenger 1991) as well as to formal courses. The perceived learning needs of manager-academics are considered first, followed by a discussion about how these needs might be accommodated. The chapter concludes by offering a speculative argument about what needs to be done to supply the university with knowledgeable managers. This final argument is two-handed. Firstly, it is argued that effective management learning is dependent on the *context and/purpose* of manager-academics' work (this partially relates to degrees of acceptance of or resistance to NM but also to the disciplinary background and level of management involved). Secondly, management learning ought not just to produce knowledge and skills but also to develop *reflexive practitioners* who can continually reassess what is 'appropriate' practice in a volatile environment and who are able to 'listen to others' as well as 'manage' them. However, there is also a third element, which concerns the extent to which learning and development are about helping manager-academics to work within the parameters of NM, whilst alleviating or ameliorating some of its worst effects of or whether learning and development could or should be about helping manager-academics to find alternative ways of leading higher education organizations to the prevailing orthodoxies.

When we began our ESRC research in 1998, although training was available both at institutional and national level for UK manager-academics (the latter largely but not exclusively through bodies like the Higher Education Staff Development Agency), we found that many of our respondents had started their managerial careers when there was much less training available than there is now. The situation with regard to training has continued to change. In 2004, a new institutionally funded leadership body for UK higher education was established, the Leadership Foundation for Higher Education (http://www.lfhe.ac.uk/), which, in theory at least, will make management training widely available to a range of staff (and governors) in all UK universities and colleges of higher education. But at the same time (and this is by no means unique to the UK systems), whilst there is no clear career route for manager-academics in general, which is still largely true of the pre-1992 universities where the majority of manager-academics are internally appointed, often on a rotating basis, then investment in training may not be regarded as worthwhile by everyone who takes on a managerial role. Furthermore, as Bourdieu has noted for the French higher education system (albeit in the 1960s), if there are only two routes for academics to follow, the scientific capital (or research) route and the academic capital (administration and teaching) route (Bourdieu 1988), then the kind of investments made by those following the latter route will tend to relate to networks of contacts rather than paying attention to the building up of cultural capital in the form of qualifications and knowledge (Deem 2006). Furthermore, if as we noted amongst some of our interviewees, a number is what we termed, following Scase and Goffee (1989) 'reluctant managers' (Deem et al. 2001), serving their fixed term of office as Head of Department rather unwillingly, then they may also be unenthusiastic about investing significantly in a route they do not plan to pursue in the future.

If we fail to create knowledgeable manager-academics and leaders who are capable of seeing beyond the present orthodoxies of NM, the alternatives are either to perpetuate a culture of amateurism (a criticism voiced by other staff in our four case studies) or to effectively hand power over to non-academic professional managers. The latter may have very different value systems, especially if they are recruited from outside higher education, and may also have difficulty in understanding the centrality of research and teaching to academic life. The question of academic values and the management of academic knowledge work are discussed further in the final chapter.

What Do Manager-Academics Think Their Learning Needs Are?

This section examines manager-academics' views on their learning needs, the context being one in which these views are associated with both recent changes to the HE context and senior academics' own changed or changing roles. We found a somewhat mixed picture with regard to training experiences. Most of our manager-academic respondents had undergone or been offered some training, often at the beginning of their first appointment to a managerial role, though this was rarely substantial, often amounting to a few days or half days. This training was also often front-loaded, that is, it was provided in the early days of a new post or even before it had begun, when real problems may not yet have arisen and when much else that is new is also being assimilated. Furthermore, the concept of learning implicit in a tutor-led, pre-prepared, generic short course can be problematic. Often only a short time is given for information to be presented and engaged with on a level supposedly sufficient to equip the manager-academic with some practical skills and knowledge and address any problems they may have. This cognitive approach to learning is typical of traditional approaches to undergraduate teaching which have been much critiqued (Brandes and Ginnis 1986; Boud 1988; Gibbs 1992; Rowland 2000; Walker and Warhurst 2000) because the learning achieved is often inflexible, not easily transferable to other contexts and rarely based on self-generated inquiry. From the perspective of manager-academics, the effectiveness of the short course approach is limited, because the issues of concern to them are primarily associated with specific contexts, and the material complexity of the institutional or departmental environment in which management is conducted, not with a generic set of more abstract concerns. This also applies to other forms of generic learning such as booklets, as this respondent recalled:

> Int: Have you had any training to be a Head of Department?
>
> HoD: I got a letter from the then Deputy Director, . . . after I was in post, with some booklets. There was some training centre at one stage, 'something House' {it was called}

Int: Did you go?

HoD: No.

Int: So, you haven't...

HoD: I had these booklets.

Int: Did you look at them?

HoD: Yeah.

Int: Did you read them? HoD: Yeah, a long time ago; they had green covers and I can't remember much else beyond that.

HoD, Applied Science, post-1992

The mixed, ambiguous, and half-forgotten nature of this manager-academic's experiences of formal management learning was shared by many other respondents:

> I went on a one-week course with all heads of departments, probably....I can't remember just where it was. It was a long time ago...you can only learn a certain amount in a week.

HoD, Engineering, post-1992

Others, albeit a minority, more explicitly expressed the positive aspects of management training courses, whilst also pointing out that there were elements that were just too detached from the real world context to be of use:

> Some bits were useful because {they} told you some of {the} things about university systems that you didn't know...and introduced you to people...in some of the central servicing faculties of the university. {It was} not so useful in that I would have preferred to have engaged in scenario training, 'what do you do if this happens?', 'what do you do in this situation?' There is very, very little about that on the course, {on}...how to deal with certain regular situations...that were difficult in terms of managing people and managing programmes.

HoD, Social Science, pre-1992

In this sense, many elements of such management training courses were found to be of limited usefulness:

> I haven't been to many courses that I've found especially useful. The university has had a number of courses run by outside people about management and different ways of planning, different ways of organising things, and I can find those quite interesting for a day. The trouble is that probably 90 per cent of what you do in that day doesn't relate to what you're doing in your

every-day life at the moment. So, you pick up the bits and you use the bits and the rest sort of recedes into memory. Courses that I have been to that have been good... involved a lot of role-play so it made you actually think about it.

HoD, Arts/Humanities, pre-1992

By contrast, the informal opportunities to network and to meet other manager-academics at such courses were seen to be one of the more positive outcomes of attending such courses:

The support initially was to go on a Head of Departments' course, which was three days long and.... {I} learned a lot. I probably learned more from meeting other young Heads of Department and finding out what they did.

HoD, Science, pre-1992

The senior management training programme... has been valuable, not necessarily to learn how to manage... but it has been extremely useful in interchanging ideas and views with other Heads of Department.

HoD, Arts/Humanities, post-1992

Quite honestly the greatest value I got from {the courses} then was on the one hand being able to spend some time away from this place with other Heads of School, and more particularly with Heads of School from a couple of other universities. So there were, if I can remember the days, there were maybe 20 new Heads of Department, Heads of Schools thrown together in a hotel somewhere... for about three days at a time with professional consultants in there.

PVC, pre-1992

In this sense, the more informal aspects of management training courses were useful for meeting the learning needs of new manager-academics but often as much for meeting others as for the content and knowledge or skills offered. This is indeed 'situated learning' (Lave and Wenger 1991) in which the new manager-academic gradually learns from her or his peers in a process of what Lave and Wenger call 'legitimate peripheral participation'. The informal nature of the process of learning was also echoed in the experiences of other manager-academics who had not attended formal management learning programmes, but picked up their skills and knowledge 'along the way' in an informal apprenticeship mode:

On the managerial side, I haven't felt any great weakness, although I have had very little form of management training. I've never felt it as a major deficiency. I think it is something that I have acquired over a long period of time.

PVC, pre-1992

This experience of learning-through-doing was not without difficulties, however:

Int: Have there been times when you've felt ill-equipped?

HoD: Oh, people, dealing with people....There was very little, if any, preparation for that. The assumption was that you would be able to manage these people. OK, there are procedures....for staff development and career review and so on, but it's not that, it's just being able to manage people and to relate to the kind of personal difficulties or problems that they have. They're not performing well, why are they not performing well? Being able to help without seeming to be patronising or wishy-washy about it all. Or, if they're actually difficult problems, being able to face up to these and challenge people and say, 'This is not on'.

HoD, Social Science, post-1992

This situation was also further complicated because the skills associated with management positions have themselves changed from requiring someone who could provide gentle and collegial leadership for their academic colleagues (Startup 1976) into the need for a more overt 'manager' who can deal with complex budgets and personnel issues (Knight and Trowler 2001; Deem 2004). The financial aspects of university management came as a shock to some at the start of their management 'career':

In the period prior to becoming Head of Department, I'd had management responsibilities, often they were course management type responsibilities, or research management responsibilities. The crucial difference was the shift into financial management responsibilities, definitely that had never crossed my mind previously.

HoD, Health/Social Science, post-1992

However, this was not such a break from the past for those in laboratory-based science and technological disciplines who had needed such skills when managing large research projects:

I did my PhD....I went {abroad} as a post-doc for about ten years....Then I was offered a post {here,} so I've been here since the inception of this department....So I've come up through the ranks: started off as a trooper, lecturer. Got a personal chair....and I guess I didn't really consider myself as managerial potential, I considered myself as a researcher. I was very happy getting on running big programmes, supervising graduate students and post-docs.

HoD, Science, pre-1992

145

The positive aspects of learning by moving up the career ladder were also reflected upon by a number of respondents, by some as a gradual progression of taking on more responsibilities, with the benefits of an increase in salary:

> I did postgraduate work,...started working as Assistant Lecturer,...{then} started here as a Lecturer...and I moved up to be a Senior Lecturer and...Principal Lecturer with responsibility for a combined honours programme....I became, eventually, Director of Undergraduate Studies...in charge of all the undergraduate programmes. {When the department was formed}, I was the only candidate to {want to} be Head of Department....I think the opportunity then came to do something I'd never done, which was to actually manage a group of staff and I thought this was a good career move: the opportunity to do something different and {gain} a considerable increase in my salary.
>
> HoD, Social Science, post-1992

Personal career trajectories and the context of change also contributed to the attraction of seeking more senior positions for some:

> I guess once you get your personal chair, you think, 'well, you can't go much higher as far as salary or promotion {are} concerned'. It allows you to sit back and take a more holistic look at the department. I guess with it being a very, very, competitive university for survival of departments—research funds, Fellow of the Royal Society {awards}—if the department's not run properly, then you're all in serious trouble.
>
> HoD, Science, pre-1992

The process of management learning implicitly promoted here is therefore of a natural progression, taking forward knowledge and skills acquired through taking on more significant administrative roles over a period of years. The knowledge and skills are then carried through to more senior posts. There were, however, caveats made between different departments and the relevant type of management:

> The fact that I've done a few different things in my career has made it easier to think of what other people are doing. I did Maths {in my first degree},...the Professor of Mathematics talks to me as though I'm a human being rather than some alien creature....At the level of making policy decisions on academic development, I work with the people that I've appointed to head the different disciplines within the School....Philosophy is run on a slightly more democratic {basis}—they prefer to have a sort of rotating Head of Section....They don't hold huge resources, so in a way that's perfectly all right, you know.

I think it might be difficult if you had large budgets involved. You know, I think the Humanities are slightly easier because you tend not to have a lot of money that is used at the academic interface and much of it is in the infrastructure.... Our quality systems are {such} that we hold central principles of quality, but the Languages people, who work in one way, don't implement them in the same way as the critical theorists who work in another.

Head of a mixed-discipline School, pre-1992

In summary then, there was some ambivalence amongst our respondents as to the exact value of formal management learning processes. The strengths and weaknesses of short courses are evident in some of the literature on professional development (Eraut 1994, 2000). The effects of short courses are unlikely to last long and seldom lead to significant change in organizations. The training courses offered to manager-academics in our sample often seemed to have taken place before much of the work of a manager-academic had happened, so that applying the knowledge and skills offered was seldom possible immediately. More informal methods of acquiring management skills characterized the favoured learning of many manager-academics interviewed. However, in terms of the legitimacy of management per se, the importance of—or need for—management was acknowledged:

> Int: What would you think {have} been the main experiences that have been of benefit to your movement up the ladder to this position?
>
> DVC: My experiences? I suppose it's because I do what I do well.... I combine an ability to lead, to manage, to run major projects, to plan major change, to remain empathetic to the main purposes of the university, remember what we are here for, not because it's just interesting to play management games.

DVC, post-1992

In this respect, the environment of the university in which our manager-academics found themselves were acknowledged (by a minority) to require management skills and such views provide some evidence of the permeation of NM within the universities studied. However, as discussed in earlier chapters, *what one needs to know* reflects what has changed, for example, the increased emphasis upon financial skills. This articulates a potential breakdown of traditional public service academic values in which competition for resources becomes more significant, so that values expressed in terms of teaching or research are no longer congruent with such a shift. The dilemmas that manager-academics have to grapple with are often also associated with achieving cultural change (Pollitt 1993), in a setting that may be resistant to such change or invoke diverse reactions (Trowler 1998). The focus on cultural change can sometimes be combined with manager-academics becoming seen by others as agents of change, a role which some of our respondents welcomed but others found highly challenging:

> DVC: I think you learn all the time. In terms of the traditional university academic, . . . I was managing my PhD students, myself, {and} was also a Warden of a Hall of Residence. . . . But in terms of managing an institution—I sometimes think about when I went to be HoD and I shudder at times, because I'd had no management experience whatsoever; I knew my subject and I was good at my research work . . . but I'd no professional training to be a manager other than that I'd picked up in different parts of experience, really. Going from HoD to Dean wasn't a major problem, it was a good exercise because I was given a blank sheet of paper and told there are seven departments there, form them into one School and they won't like it, so off you go. . . . It wasn't quite made clear to me what it was like. No, it was very enjoyable actually. I mean it was hard to start with. . . .

> DVC, post-1992

The changes to the HE context articulated by the manager-academics we interviewed can be summarized under four headings. First, there was a perceived shift from emphasis on the provider to emphasis on the consumer (typically the student) and the associated measurements of accountability related to this change. For example, there are now measures of such internal and external quality assurance of teaching and institutional audit of academic standards which seek to assess the 'quality' of learning and teaching provision but which position academics in a new hierarchy vis-à-vis those who are charged with assessing quality (Morley 2003). Second, in this new environment, there was seen to be a need to act entrepreneurially, in order to gain resources, even within one's own institution, a trend clearly recognizable in other contexts too (Slaughter and Leslie 1997; Clark 1998; Marginson and Considine 2000). A third point was the introduction of incentives and penalties (the latter sometimes applied with great force) for the performance and financial health of academic units, but within which middle manager-academics' scope for manoeuvre is strictly limited. Finally, the new role of dealing with devolved budgets creates a need for manager-academics to develop strategies in order to cope with potential risks and possible financial crises.

Returning to the question of resistance to and evidence of the permeation of NM, the first, second, and third of the changes noted above are indicative of a general shift towards centralized power and corporatization of decision-making with regulated accountability at the centre and incursive performance measurement at the periphery. The processes by which these shifts have occurred were discussed in Chapters 1 and 2. The fourth point reflects changes taking place in HE more generally, as a result of the impact of government policy on funding higher education, coping with financial insecurity, and becoming accustomed to greater competition between institutions and the pressure for institutional mission differentiation. There are also many contradictions inherent to the conditions of organizations operating under NM such as instability, unpredictability, and volatility. These contradictions highlight the tensions between organizational belonging, cohesiveness and fragmentation, or expressed another way, raise questions about what quality standards *should* be aspired to within the modern HE environment. In addition, on a theoretical level, the decentralization process of devolved budgets but without any real empowerment at the periphery experienced by manager-academics at department level did not seem helpful for nurturing either knowledge workers' creativity or care for students.

The next section moves onto engage in more detail with what is and what *should* be the process of management learning.

What and What Should Be the Process of Management Learning?

What views did our sample of manager-academics have on the availability of support for their learning; the perceived need for such support and the quality of support experienced? These views are examined in this chapter and are also discussed relative to the role held by respondents (such as HoD, Dean/PVC, and VC) and according to subject or discipline. We have seen that a good many of our respondents expressed some scepticism about the usefulness of formal courses, although the capacity to meet and talk to peers at such events was generally appreciated. This is consistent with the view that academics in management roles might be more interested in networking with others doing similar roles than in acquiring new cultural capital such as management qualifications (Bourdieu 1988; Deem 2006). On the other hand, most of our interviewees felt that they had learned a great deal through a kind of informal apprenticeship model or situated learning (Lave and Wenger 1991). Yet their institutions did not always support this latter approach very well and only a couple of universities of the ones we studied deliberately provided opportunities for manager-academics to meet informally on a sustained basis or encouraged the formation of action-learning sets of peers in similar roles.

Learning needs at the HoD level were often expressed in the most acute terms. At this level, the role is complex, may be the individual's first experience of the management of a unit rather than a course or research project and is likely to include a workload full of new and ever-changing dilemmas. Also as noted earlier, not all HoDs are willing recruits to the world of management:

> I suppose the change comes from being just an ordinary academic to being someone with real management responsibilities. I was surprised by how much that just changed overnight. Literally overnight. One suddenly is expected to be taking decisions that I didn't really feel competent to take, but there was no point in simply saying I couldn't take them because if I didn't nobody would. So I was surprised by how quickly that came, about what a steep change it was. The types of things that I found hard were suddenly having to make sensible choices about people's careers.... One is responsible for the careers of a dozen technical staff and ten secretaries who've all got their own aspirations and way of working.... I was surprised that people suddenly started coming to me for advice.... people who I would have regarded as being academically senior to me suddenly were in my office asking me about what they should do to advance themselves.
>
> HoD, Social Science, pre-1992

The new responsibilities and also workload level associated with the HoD role were a common experience across different disciplines and made some manager-academics feel ill-equipped or turn to those with more experience to help them out:

> I think it's not so much that I haven't got the skills, it's more that there are too many things hitting me at once. I mean, that links to the skills, because it's about prioritising and time management, but I sometimes think that, however good you are at those things, there's actually too much coming at you to handle and without better support it's actually quite hard. And then you don't know how much it's to do with you and your capacity and how much of it's to do with circumstances and support.
>
> HoD, Applied Science, post-1992

> I have to say that on the informal side I've always found my colleagues, both at Head of Department level and above, very, very supportive in being prepared to share experience and being able to say to colleagues, 'Look, I've got this

problem. How would you have handled this?'.... There's a great deal of training that can go on on an informal basis where it's very difficult to train on a formal basis.

HoD, Humanities, post-1992

You can do the mechanics of it, but it teaches you nothing about the judgements that you're going to need to make and what to bear in mind when making any particular judgement, and I think ultimately that's something that only comes with experience.... You can say, 'This is what the procedure says', but that's a world away from how you actually handle an individual at a time of crisis.

HoD, Humanities, post-1992

However, as already noted in respect of different orientations to research and to teaching, distinctions did arise between disciplines. This is not at all surprising since academics' identities are closely bound up with their discipline or subject background (Henkel 2000; Becher and Trowler 2001; Deem and Lucas 2007), as noted in the previous chapter:

The difference in things like problems in student recruitment are very... substantial}. Some of the schools have quite a long tradition of research and others very little. So there are quite significant differences.... I think we've learnt to work with each other and as a result we can co-operate very well.

Head of applied science in teaching-oriented post-1992 university

What is being managed does tend to vary significantly by discipline. Thus many HoDs in science need to manage laboratories and large research teams, whilst in humanities archives, music rooms, theatre spaces, classrooms, and lone researchers may be more significant elements. So learning attuned to context is important. The subject background also affects which skills may be needed and which ones have already been acquired (Kekaele 1999). Those from a scientific background are likely to be at home with large budgets, numbers, and statistics, whilst those from a non-science background may want help with such skills but be better at writing long reports or memoranda and dealing with routine administration.

I think that the training that I've had in marshalling large amounts of information and writing clear summaries and accounts of it is of great value to this work. I can write better memorandum than most people here, that's one of the reasons why I hold this job, I am unfazed by large volumes of paper but that's partly the historian's strengths and it's partly just a personal strength, and it would be wrong to suppose that that is a necessary strength for the

151

post. Others could do this job perfectly, as well or better, with other kinds of disciplinary strengths. I am, for instance, un-intimidated by figures but not especially sophisticated in my grasp of techniques and confrontational processes.... So I don't think that being an historian is a necessary condition of doing the job well but it does give you, I think, some strengths.

> DVC, Historian, pre-1992

it is the transferable skills of the chemistry that I've been using and not the specific skills ... it's probably only once or twice a year that I can use any specific chemistry skills, there are occasional times when one uses an understanding of chemistry but it's not frequent. So, um, it is, I'm a particular type of chemist, I'm an analytical chemist and analytical chemists are always problem solvers. And therefore I spend quite a lot of my time problem-solving and to have developed problem-solving skills was a big asset.

> PVC, Chemist, post-1992

well we always regard psychology as being a very useful discipline when you are transferring the skills and quite a high level transferable skills, not simply the basic ones but you know the critical thinking and this, that, and the other one.

> HoD, Psychology, post-1992

my management experience as a Nurse Manager and the way in which you used to be prepared for management roles within the NHS was that you do a first-line management course, then a middle management course. Both my first degree and my Masters have large components of management within it and I felt those are very useful.

> HoS, Nursing, post-1992

I certainly had this experience myself of overnight being told I was responsible for a few million pounds budget without any background at all. And I wasn't too bad cause I had maths, I mean, I was numerate, I could add up and I could deal with a spread-sheet.

> DVC, Statistician, post-1992

In terms of those who progressed further beyond the role of HoD to more senior roles, the discipline or subject gradually becomes less crucial but the stage of being a discipline-specific HoD was still seen as a key learning experience:

> Well, I thought I was always very fortunate that I had an apprenticeship as {temporary} Head of science, while the incumbent Head was off being Dean.... You had as much responsibility as you wanted to and if you felt a bit nervous about something you could always hide behind the fact {that}, 'Well I'm not really the

Head, he's just down the corridor' {laugh}. It was a comfort, and so from that point of view I think it was a good apprenticeship.

DVC, post-1992

At the more senior level of PVC and Dean, the expressions of the learning process often put a lot of emphasis on 'learning-through-doing' and some felt that this offered sufficient training in the sense that they were able to relate academics through their (shared) academic background, even though the latter tends to be from a particular disciplinary perspective. In terms of creating an effective collective and institutional strategy, this is a skill sometimes explicitly developed in a senior management team. Such teams have grown in importance outside the UK (Marginson and Considine 2000) as well as inside it (Deem and Johnson 2000; Deem 2003). How the members of such teams develop depends a good deal on how people are appointed to or selected for their senior roles. In pre-1992 universities the senior team is often 'home-grown' (with the exception of the Vice-Chancellor who is only rarely an internal appointment) and hence the sense of belonging may be as or more important than expertise, a particular set of skills and knowledge, the classic Bourdieuian academic capital route?

It's invariably the case that Pro-vice-chancellors are chosen amongst the four Deans in the university and the Deans, in turn, are chosen from amongst Heads of Department.... The vice-chancellor will say that his view of Pro-vice-chancellors is that they are elder statespersons—or, as he would say, elder statesmen—of the university who have seen a wide variety of different facets of the university and how it operates.... Simply because we have been there, got the T-shirt, we've done our role as Head of Department and we are continuing to operate as a tutor and as a lecturer and working within a department.

PVC, pre-1992

The move to this level of management within an organization does not necessarily imply a sense for the incumbents that they have become detached from the realities of university life, although this is not always how others see it (Deem and Johnson 2000; Deem 2003). For many of our respondents there was an emphasis on remaining a part of the whole academic community:

I think that I now see my position as being: endeavouring to represent an academic rather than a detached managerial view in a university that is aiming to re-establish itself as a mainstream institution, probably in the upper twenty-five per cent of universities in terms of research and teaching.

PVC, pre-1992

Many of the senior professors who I worked with ... had great managerial skills and, you know, plain common sense: how you make things happen, don't get too bogged down in bureaucracy, where there's a will there's a way, you know, those kind of approaches.

PVC, pre-1992

Their perceptions of the *process* of management learning and *what* is appropriate or necessary learning is positioned in terms of two conflicting cultures or at least, two contrasting imperatives: those of the professional-academic and those of the the managerialist. For PVCs and Deans, the managerial skills that they possess are acquired from this blend of their own past experience of managing smaller units within their current or a previous university and also their own personal characteristics and capacity to manage:

I suppose ... 80 per cent or more of what you do as a manager, you are depending upon two facets really: one is, what you've learnt by your own skills and experience in terms of your own historical development to that particular position, but secondly it's an ability to deal with those sorts of problems. You know, there is something innate, inherent about your character.

DVC, post-1992

Even the VCs we interviewed mostly shared this view of management: that the ability to 'manage' is about people skills and being an effective leader but acquired through experience, not via formal training:

Int: In terms of ... the kind of skills that you employ in doing this, do you think your background in {discipline} been particularly useful? I mean, have you had any formal skills, training along these lines, or is it something throughout your career you've just developed personally?

VC: More the latter than the former. I mean I have undertaken one or two management development courses but they have had to involve formal skills training. I see it that I've learnt from experience and different situations. I've also learned a lot from observing other people's management at universities. ... I found that invaluable and actually giving me material on which to reflect, if you like. So I think I've learnt a lot from observing what other people do as well as finding my own learning situations.

For many manager-academics then, the emphasis appeared to lie more with existing personal abilities, and 'learning by doing' rather than anything acquired through a formal learning process or training. In respect of new managerialist discourses, when VCs identify themselves as 'chief executives' (Bargh et al. 2000), they may appeal to an attribute that is often based on previous experience, and also assume that their strength of character is what is really required to persuade others or to take hard decisions:

> I suspect that part of the personal support I had was being {a scientist}...and virtually all of the research I carried out had a very strong link into industry and so I was accustomed to dealing with people who operated in managerial circumstances.
>
> VC, pre-1992

The chapter now moves to look more closely at manager-academics' views on what makes for *productive* management learning. The discussion up to this point has suggested that management learning cannot consist just of pre-prepared training courses, but also that it should not purely be about experiential training or occur by default through an absence of support structures or processes.

Ideally those who become manager-academics need to become reflexive practitioners who are able to create sensible and critical management practices that are appropriate to the management of knowledge workers, whilst preserving the generic idea of the public and academic purposes of the university. In this sense, they can then provide a legitimacy for a reflexive leadership and management, rather than offer an unreflective compliance with the tenets of NM Exworthy and Halford 1999.

> I've come to realise—maybe it's just the change in times, or maybe it's the change in my role, the whole thing revolves around the lack of finance that Government is providing.... And... we've definitely had to react to that by developing our commercial accounts, developing a research income in order that we can just simply sustain the activities at what we would deem to be the right level. So that's been the main challenge, and.... I wasn't prepared for that in any shape, form, or description. I've no training in terms of financial management. I guess the other key aspect would be linked to that, the sort of strategic management side: crystal ball-gazing and trying to get things right in terms of what is happening in the sector and how you need to move in order to stay fit and active... {and} beneath me in the School there is another tier of senior staff who we call 'the management team'; but the idea of

management and the...important words like...strategy, development, defining priorities, assessing effectiveness, they don't relate to {these} at all, or very little.

HoD, Social Science, post-1992

Manager-academics need regular access to challenging and supportive focused learning environments where their assumptions can be challenged, as well as talking through current dilemmas. They also need situations where vulnerability, more often found in public service contexts than in the private sector (Alimo-Metcalfe and Alban-Metcalfe 2000; Alban-Metcalfe and Alimo-Metcalfe 2003), can be shown:

> Approaches that have worked in the past do not work now and I think people are struggling around what to do about it. I would like to see that being made explicit, that it's recognized that that is an issue, that it's legitimate for people to say to each other, 'I don't know what I'm going to do about this'. So, in that sense, I think that there is a need to not just drop people into these situations and expect them to get on and see whether it works, but I think there is a need to manage that process of change....I think what happens at the moment is it's a case of sink or swim and...it's recognized that the responsibilities have changed, but nobody is managing that change into place, supporting the staff to be clear about what the new responsibilities are, and giving them appropriate staff development opportunities that support them in those responsibilities.

HoD, Applied Science, post-1992

The discussion has demonstrated that active and applied learning is also highly compatible with the notion of the 'self-educating' academic. For this reason, it seems an appropriate concept of management learning to take forward. The problem in this however, is one of identity politics. Here the chapter echoes arguments developed elsewhere in the book. In Chapter 1 there was a discussion of visible, invisible, and 'middle' managers, and in Chapter 2 an analysis of the significance of shifting tangible aspects of working lives such as job titles. There is a need to reflect upon whom we create as manager-academics through the provision of management training. For example, what sort of manager is credible in the eyes of other academics? It is clearly not the same as one who complies with NM. Is NM really the only alternative for universities?

A further option is needed in order to resist NM. The relative absence of formal courses, structured identifiable learning programmes, and/or requirements for formal qualifications amongst manager-academics until very recently calls into question the legitimacy of manager-academics in others' views (e.g. support staff) since they can be dismissed as amateurs.

Yet, as the discussion has shown here, there may also be ambivalence amongst manager-academics (particularly HoDs) towards formal training, qualifications, and structured programmes, which could be seen to be a salient point about the significance of their 'identity' as academics and the protection of this identity, for sustainable and achievable management practice in an academic context.

The final section of this chapter ends with discussion of how manager academics need to learn about management *early on in their academic careers*. This approach to management learning is framed in terms of inclusive practices that enable others to participate in decision-making and is also consistent with ideas about distributed management (Gronn 2000, 2002; Gronn and Hamilton 2004). For instance, early-career academics unwittingly do management work by leading teaching units and programmes or by running research projects. This serves to achieve effective management learning (at an early stage), but in doing so leans towards the acquisition of a management identity that is acceptable to the academic community. That is, their credibility as academics is not compromised and loyalty to and empathy for, academics and knowledge work, is retained. They are not yet identified as 'managers', which comes if at all, only at a later stage.

There are, of course, dilemmas associated with such an approach. Such an unaccredited form of learning may not be recognized by professional administrators either as at all credible, or, as productive of credible management identities. The relationship between administration and academics was reflected on by a number of senior administrators:

> I see myself as trying to bring them down to earth and steer them in a logical direction but that very often is over-taken by politics and academic freedom which I always argue is freedom of thought, not freedom of action, but others wouldn't agree with that {laugh}.... I've got mixed feelings about academics as managers. I think most of them are appalling, but then perhaps my professional bias would come through in this {laugh}, they are gifted amateurs, not all of them, but a lot are therefore um, I think very often they will welcome the public support that you give them, but they are also hyper-critical because they don't really understand and don't want to understand the big picture either. They don't think realistically at all.
>
> Senior Administrator, pre-1992

> There are people I have met in academe who see it as their job to make life of the Administration, as they call it, 'Hell', because they see themselves as being better. I mean, I've had an academic, you know, sort of shouting at

me and saying, 'It's none of your business to be giving us this, you're just an administrator, an officer, that's an academic decision'.... It was Jarratt who talked about the integration of academic, financial and physical planning and clearly, in any business, it doesn't matter what the business, but if you don't integrate the business planning with the financial planning and with physical resources i.e. whether it's a university, a factory, an office block or whatever, the end result is chaos and that's no different for a university.

Senior administrator, pre-1992

In this sense, credibility in skill or identity is in question by senior administrators to a great extent anyway. Such tensions would need to be resolved in the promotion of any form of management learning. The chapter now moves towards a conclusion with speculative argument about what needs to be done to supply the university with the knowledgeable managers that are required.

Conclusion

The chapter's concluding argument is progressed along two lines. Firstly, that effective management learning is contingent on what view of the context/purpose for manager-academic's work is taken and the values underpinning it. For example, are the core motivations academic or managerial or even neither? Expressed in another way, are we creating people who are only effective in a newly managerialized academic world? How do we encourage those who want to know how to create an academic organization that sustains itself as an academic enterprise productive of knowledge work and, nevertheless, is robust enough to deal with the realities of the New Managerialist policy context whilst resisting its incursion?

This first point is closely associated with the second emphasis. The suggestion pursued here is that what is needed is management learning that is productive of reflexive practitioners and thus both helps manager-academics continually reassess what is *appropriate* management practice in a volatile environment for action whilst not necessarily opting for the current technical orthodoxy about how public organizations should be run. The question of the values underpinning the management of academic knowledge work will be discussed in greater depth in Chapter 6. The emphasis here is upon aiding manager-academics to 'listen to others' whilst at the same time occupying a role that is often seen by others as one of control or regulation. It is an emphasis that is reflexive in learning about models of management other than reactive compliant or 'imple-menting/carrying' strategies in response to volatility and/or institutional or policy imperatives.

If this form of management does not emerge, then there is a risk of the implosion of HE in the sense that only professional managers or industrialists rather than academics may end up being appointed to senior management posts. This is far from so at present in the UK but it is a possible future scenario. Such appointments would then reflect the value systems of some of the professional administrators we interviewed, whose only performance measure would be likely to be performance-related or financial. In this sense, NM would have been successfully implemented and academic autonomy, as it is currently understood, curtailed if not lost. The question of whom should be appointed to head academic institutions has been the subject of recent controversy in the UK, with some arguing that administrators may have as much claim as academics (although few non-academics have ever been appointed to such posts) and others arguing that academics alone can provide academic leadership (Opinion 2006). The process of management learning advocated here is resistant to any simplistic notion of 'management training' whilst advocating a more formal process of learning that is balanced alongside the 'learning-through-doing' experiences of many of the manager-academics described in this chapter.

We now turn in the final chapter to the question of how the manage-ment of academic knowledge work in publicly funded universities relates to the values held by manager-academics and we will also explore some of the wider implications of our analyses not just for the UK but also for European universities in general.

6

Values, Public Service, the University, and the Manager-Academic

Introduction

In the previous two chapters we have focused closely on the backgrounds, views, perceptions, practices, satisfactions, anxieties, and learning needs of a sample of UK manager-academics as portrayed in accounts provided by them, having previously discussed theories explaining some recent trends in public service organization management and examined some of the recent history and current situation of UK universities, both at a systemic level and at an organizational level. This final chapter follows up our in-depth exploration of manager-academics by analysing issues about values related to the governance and management of universities as public service institutions and considering the consequences for those who manage universities, both now and in the future. As Chapter 1 noted, the different variants of NM are cultural as well as structural in their effects, and their proponents seek to change the cultural climate of publicly funded institutions. This chapter therefore examines a further dimension of the culture of publicly funded universities. The chapter also places the debate about the management of academic knowledge work in a wider, European, perspective. Indeed, some of the matters raised are undoubtedly capable of being applied to other higher education systems outside Europe, providing that due attention is also paid to the local context of such systems (Deem 2001; Deem, Lucas, and Mok 2006). Europe is used as a reference point here since the UK is a member of the European

The chapter is based on a paper first presented to the Higher Education Research Network of the European Conference of Educational Researchers in Hamburg, Germany, September 17–20 2003.

Union and has been a signatory to a range of European initiatives on higher education.

Public and Private Higher Education

It is now the case in the UK, as in many other western countries, that competing pressures on the public purse and the process of massification of higher education have erased much of what used to identify universities as a unique form of public service organization (Kwiek 2005). Public expenditure pressures have also affected other public services, bringing in forms of quasi-private provision such as the UK public–private finance schemes for new buildings (McKendrick 2002; Pollock, Shaoul, and Vickers 2002; Pollock 2004*a*) or even replacing some elements of public service with completely private provision. This has had the consequence that the use of the concept 'public' has come to be seen as problematic (Newman 2006) and the terms public and private are now much more blurred and overlapping than they once were. Newman notes that 'the publicness of . . . services is viewed as somehow outdated, part of the old world of the universal welfare state rather than the new world of modernity, flexibility and consumerism' (Newman 2006: 1). So some might conclude that discussing the connection between academic management, values, and universities as public institutions is no longer a useful debate in which to engage. However, it might equally well be argued that a blurring of public and private may have been a deliberate intention of those who have been at the helm of recent public service reforms (Giddens 1998, 2000) and that it is therefore something important that we should not ignore.

There is certainly, as Marginson has noted, a set of conceptual confusions around what exactly public and private mean in relation to higher education (Marginson 2004). The concept of public has often been associated with the state and private with the market, though another equally plausible definition might link private to business or activity for profit, and public to civil society. Nevertheless, neither of these definitions is exclusive. Thus, governments set up quasi-private agencies and may encourage the establishment of markets whilst some philanthropic or voluntary organizations also fund and support services, for public good such as housing, social services, or education. Not everything that happens in civil society is for the benefit of all (e.g. family practices include some citizens and exclude others) and some businesses donate money to public or charitable concerns (though the extent of the latter is affected by different countries' taxation policies, some of which reduce tax liabilities in return for corporate donations). Economic definitions of public and private goods, Marginson observes, often focus on rivalrous and non-rivalrous goods (the latter are those that can be consumed by any number of people without depletion of the resource and without anyone being excluded) so from this perspective, a public service view of a university would be one that sees it as offering its services freely to all. No UK university would now pass that test and even those higher education systems in countries which are still fully state-funded and charge no fees have a tendency to select their students. Marginson contends that public service can usefully be defined as something having a significant element of non-rivalry and non-exclusivity. Thus knowledge, for example, could be seen as a global public and collective good. Since knowledge is a component of both research and teaching, this could provide a useful frame for a debate about higher education as a public service and the values held by those who work in higher education.

Some discussions about public higher education begin with funding issues such as who should pay for higher education or the costs of particular kinds of public policies (Callender 2002) or alternatively, concentrate on consumers of education and how they benefit from higher education (Naidoo 2003), which are equally valid approaches to the topic. However, since this book is principally concerned with the management of academic work, it seems sensible to view the public service dimension from the perspective of those who work in publicly funded higher education, whilst bearing in mind Marginson's comments.

The accounts given by the manager-academics we interviewed in our research, of the perceptions and values underpinning the governance and management of academic work in higher education, are examined here for indications about how publicly funded higher education is regarded in contemporary times. This is a key aspect of the discussion about public service and higher education, given that there are considerable ideological differences surrounding views about such phenomena as performance management, targets, audits of research and teaching quality, league tables, and privatization of higher education, in an era when public expenditure on higher education is increasingly held up to scrutiny. The desire of governments and universities worldwide to achieve global recognition means that similar processes of reform involving such features are also taking place in many other countries too, with a number of unintended consequences for the higher education systems involved (Deem, Lucas, and Mok 2006). The meanings attached to public service higher education in the UK are clearly in considerable flux, especially in the context of competition from corporate and other private universities, in relation to changing definitions and conceptions of knowledge, and since public funding for higher education is no longer necessarily regarded as a good thing.

In England, since 2003, there are some indications that there may have been something of a recent sea change in whether manager-academics regard universities as public service organizations, following the recent controversy over so-called top-up or variable fees for undergraduates, which have been introduced in England and Northern Ireland with effect from autumn 2006 (they are also being introduced in Wales from 2007). There appears to be enhanced sensitivity over whether UK universities, even though they remain in receipt of significant public funding, are still regarded as public institutions. This is particularly so as students (and often also their parents) become a growing source of funding for teaching and as knowledge becomes differentially available to students dependent on their ability to pay (Deem 2006b). The UK variable fees can be deferred until after graduation (when repayment becomes income contingent) by taking out a loan. For students from low-income households (and for the academically very able), there are also supposed to be university-awarded bursaries. In addition, there is a possibility that a handful of English institutions will not charge the full variable fee or will not charge it for some courses. However, the introduction of substantial fees for undergraduates potentially puts undergraduate student recruitment on a more commercial basis. It reinforces the view of some commentators that students are being repositioned as consumers (Naidoo 2003; Naidoo and Jamieson 2005), who see education simply as a instrumental activity involving the purchase of a positional good (and involving packages of ready-parcelled learning) rather than as a developmental process of advanced learning and study which is provided as a public service.

Managing Knowledge Work in Publicly Funded Universities: The UK and Europe

The UK's position as a member of the European Union is highly relevant to the question of higher education as a public service. A number of developments in Europe are germane to this matter. For example, the Bologna Agreement signed in 1999 set out a framework for bringing undergraduate and postgraduate education qualifications, credit transfer and quality assurance closer together across different European countries. Ostensibly this set of issues is not about management and governance or about whether education is a public service but the Bologna process is aimed at publicly funded higher education systems and is also likely to have some impact on how European universities are managed and how their role and purposes are interpreted in the future. The Lisbon European Council in March 2000 produced a Heads of Government commitment to work towards a new strategic goal by 2010 of making Europe 'the most competitive and dynamic knowledge-based economy in the world, capable of sustainable economic growth with more and better jobs and greater social cohesion' (Corbett 2005). This involves developing knowledge-based economies, modernizing the European approach to social development and welfare, developing citizens, tackling social exclusion, and sustaining healthy economies with good growth prospects. The Lisbon process is based on what is termed an 'open method of coordination' in respect of relevant policy areas and services, together with agreed common objectives and evaluation strategies. This is, as Corbett notes, an unusual approach for an area of policy like education, which has always been regarded as a national responsibility (Corbett 2005). The Lisbon process acknowledges this but it has also noted that as part of this process 'the Community shall contribute to the development of quality education by encouraging cooperation between Member States and if necessary by supporting and supplementing their action' (Corbett 2005). Subsequent discussion, such as the Graz declaration by European university leaders in 2003 (European University Association 2003) and the Bergen communiqué in 2005 (European Higher Education Ministers 2005) as part of the Lisbon process, has focused on developing and refining the Bologna process, the creation of a European Research Area and the development of a European Higher Education Area. Discussion has involved setting out the role of national governments in this process and working out how to differentiate European higher education from other systems of higher education in a global context (European University Association 2003). The focus on quality assurance, student mobility, and the three levels of degree qualifications (or first, second, and third cycles) in respect of the Bologna declaration focuses principally on what can be achieved in public universities. This is something which Kwiek argues could be seen as ignoring both the issues posed by public underfunding of many European universities *and* the burgeoning private sector in some European countries, including the recent accession nations in central and Eastern Europe (Kwiek 2004). Nevertheless, recently, the inevitability of introducing fees for all university students in publicly funded higher education institutions in Europe, even in countries that currently do not charge them (e.g. Germany), has begun to be acknowledged at European level (European Commission Representation in UK 2006). This is further evidence of the blurring of public and private in European higher education. The vision of research being developed in Europe is a more overtly privatized one, in which much of the research is expected to be funded by private sources (Wilson 2004), with the possible implication that some of the knowledge generated will not necessarily even be available for public use (even though this seems in opposition to the collaboration involved in the open method of coordination) Indeed, any research funded by industry will almost certainly have rivalrous and exclusive elements. The focus on a European research area is also closely bound up with globalizing forces affecting higher education systems, whose effects include developments in international league tables ranking universities (The Times Higher Education Supplement 2005; Shanghai Jiao Tong Institute of Higher Education 2006) and the quest for 'world-class' universities (Altbach 2004; Marginson and Sawir 2005; Mok 2005). In tackling this objective, the issue of the relation between public values and university research is highly unlikely to be centre stage.

Quite apart from global and European moves, and financial pressures of governments, and changing trends in management and governance, the shift away from elite to mass enrolment of students in higher education systems also brings other pressures to bear on traditional notions of what constitutes a university. A recent government White Paper in England (Department for Education and Skills 2003b) suggested that it would soon be possible to apply for university status in England without first having acquired research-degree awarding powers (as has previously been necessary). In 2004, this new approach to university status formed part of the Higher Education Act in England. So far, most institutions acquiring titles under the legislation have declared their intention to undertake research and offer research degrees (Deem 2006b) but the attempt to manipulate what constitutes a university by removing the research element challenges many historical notions of what a university is about. It also raises some important questions about for which students non-research universities are intended and about the kinds of knowledge that are likely to be created and transmitted as a result of this process of distinguishing between different kinds of universities.

Debates about the management and governance of publicly funded universities also raise issues about the accountability of universities to their stakeholders. Traditionally, in much of Western Europe, internal regulatory and control structures and processes have facilitated knowledge creation and transmission and ensured institutional integrity, both internally and externally. Furthermore, recent reforms have often bolstered the formal autonomy of institutions from the state, albeit it is the case that most governments have also retained the right to interfere in higher education (de Boer, Enders, and Schimank 2005; Huisman, de Boer, and Goedegebuure 2005). But there are increasing threats to traditional governance forms and patterns in the UK and elsewhere. In the UK in the 1980s and 1990s, two distinct models of higher education governance developed, one in the established chartered universities and the other in the incorporated higher education institutions which, as former polytechnics, acquired university status only in 1992. The latter placed more reliance on the involvement of business people in their governing bodies and less on staff involvement, and tended to have smaller governing bodies. Recently, the pre- and post-1992 university structures have begun to blur, partly as a consequence of common audit and funding mechanisms and partly because of a recommendation in the 1997 Dearing report on higher education that governing bodies should not generally have more than twenty five members (National Committee of Inquiry into Higher Education 1997). However, the 2003 government White Paper on the Future of Higher Education in England and the subsequent 2004 Higher Education Act seems likely to introduce new distinctions to the cultures of the management and governance of higher education, as universities are encouraged to concentrate on either research (albeit still with significant teaching) or teaching. The concern about new forms of higher education management and governance, as we have seen in the previous chapters, is whether they can actually still enable academics to work creatively and effectively in the current conditions, whilst also providing accountability and continuing to support knowledge creation and transmission. This is a crucial question not only for UK higher education but for all publicly funded universities, whether in Europe or elsewhere.

What Does It Mean to Say that Higher Education Is a Public Service?

One of the current threats to publicly funded higher education in general is from world trade negotiations over services. Much of the debate about the possible extension of the World Trade Organization's proposals for a

General Agreement on Trade in Services (GATS) to universities was about concern that this could mean the end of publicly funded universities, with the possibility of corporate, and international, as well as national, private institutions requesting a share of public monies or public funding being disallowed. GATS came into existence in 1995. GATS comprises a set of multilateral rules (which can be legally enforced, i.e. they are not just advisory) governing the liberalization of international trade in services, which include education as well as a host of other things from transport to leisure, in countries throughout the world. There has been quite a strong reaction from some commentators to including schools and higher education in GATS (Barblan 2002; Nunn 2002; Robertson, Bonal, and Dale 2002; Sauve 2002), as it can be argued that it turns education into just another commodity and may ultimately result in the end of publicly funded education systems at all levels. GATS includes definitions of four supply modes for services:

1. *Cross-border supply* (in HE this translates as programme mobility, such as distance education)
2. *Consumption abroad* (in HE this translates as student mobility, e.g. students from one country studying in another)
3. *Commercial presence* (in HE this translates as institutional mobility, e.g. a university based in one country having a campus in another country)
4. *Presence of natural persons* (in HE this translates as academic mobility, e.g. where academics travel temporarily to another country in order to teach or do research)

GATS could thus in theory be applied to both research and teaching in higher education. Verger Planelles (2006) suggests that Northern, high-income countries are more likely than Southern low-income countries to want to include education in their trade negotiations, as for the latter there is less competitive advantage in so doing. Modes one and two are those most commonly forming the basis for negotiation over education. Verger Planelles also argues that for higher education only, there seems to be a correlation between countries with a high proportion of private education and those having few GATS commitments. This may, as Verger Planelles notes, be because such countries see their existing supply of education as adequate or because well-established private higher education institutions may be able to exert greater pressure on governments than public institutions not to further liberalize the existing system. The current GATS methodology in use at the time of writing (2006) has been changed from its earlier formulation, so that any country making a request of another country cannot simply be refused and sector-specific negotiations for different sectors have also been introduced. Verger Planelles argues that this appears to be a deliberate attempt on behalf of the higher income countries to persuade less affluent and southern countries to participate in negotiations.

Returning to the UK itself, is the aspiration to recruit more undergraduate students from disadvantaged backgrounds, as is current policy in the UK, sufficient to guarantee that higher education remains seen as a public service? As noted earlier, the public and private dimensions of higher education are increasingly blurred (Marginson 2004), as they already have been for some time in other areas of public service provision such as housing and leisure services. Universities are increasingly privatizing both their teaching (particularly in respect of overseas students, who pay not just top-up fees but for the whole of their tuition) and research (applied research for industry and spin-off companies are just two examples) as the strength and reach of what has been termed 'academic capitalism' grows in parallel with a decline in the public unit of resource (Slaughter and Leslie 1997). Can values about higher education as a public service survive these various onslaughts from within and outside national systems? Would the values still be appropriate if they did survive?

This raises a broader question—do academics see their own role and that of universities as one that has a strong public service element? A survey conducted in 1997 amongst members of the European University Association about what European universities would like to see by in higher education by 2010 (Meijers and Nutgteren 1997) found that four core values emerged from the survey responses. About half the institutions contacted responded. The core values broadly supported by respondents were that freedom of research and teaching must be the fundamental principles of university life, that university contributions to sustainable societal development should become more prominent aspects of university missions, that research and teaching must remain inseparable at all levels of university education, and that national governments should bear as much responsibility for HE in 2010 as they did in 1997. Two of these, on sustainable development, and funding responsibility, significantly address the public service function of universities. However, the descriptions and content of these values did not arise spontaneously from respondents but were set out in the questionnaire itself. Indeed they are taken directly from the precursor document to the more recent Bologna agreement, the Magna Charta of the European University in 1988, signed by nearly 300 rectors of European Universities (UNESCO European Centre for Higher Education 1989). Furthermore, the responses represent only the views of the heads of institutions, not their academic staff as a whole.

We actually know relatively little about what academics in general think about the public service function of universities. It is a quite different question from asking them how they would like their institutions to be managed and governed. Much of the research on academic identities and academic work emphasizes the attachment to discipline or subject (Becher and Trowler 2001), and to teaching and research as the core of academic activity (Henkel 2000). However, these attachments are not necessarily accompanied by particular kinds of values about higher education as a public service. Additionally, as we have seen in earlier chapters, there are also debates about the deskilling, declining status and proletarianization of academic work (Halsey 1992; Smyth 1995; Cuthbert 1996) and the changing conditions of such work (Enders 2001). But these bodies of literature rarely, if ever, talk about public service *per se*. Furthermore, there is little or no research that tells us whether academics in higher educa-tion institutions funded by the state actually have noticeably different identities from those who work in privately funded higher education institutions (Tierney 2005). Tierney argues that for-profit organizations may have more flexibility to make key decisions without always involv-ing academics in key decisions but perhaps some academics in publicly funded institutions feel that this happens in their universities too. We certainly found this in our four case studies of employees in the ESRC research (Deem 2003). Tierney also argues that publicly and privately funded institutions differ in their missions, environment, and strategy. The missions might well be different: outside North America, it is not uncommon for private universities to focus only on teaching (even in the USA the huge distance teaching university, Phoenix, does no research) but then we have also seen in the UK that the English government is keen to designate universities which have no research role.

Of course, those in private and public universities may have different political values in relation to their work, which might in turn support a different view of the role and function of universities. An important ele-ment in notions of public service may be the capacity for critical thinking, long argued to be a principal form and foundation of academic freedom. Some commentators have suggested that increasing commercialization of higher education threatens critical thinking: 'Since the 1980s universities have been urged to adopt commercial models of knowledge, skills, curriculum, finance, accounting, and management organization...in order to deserve state funding and to protect themselves from competitive threats....These measures threaten what many people value in universities, e.g. the scope for critical analysis'(Levidow 2002). It has also been argued by Sennett that those working in public services often have a strong element of long-term commitment, both to the service itself and to the people who use that service, rather than being principally concerned with service innovations or the interests of stockholders, as would be the case in the for-profit sector (Sennett 1998, 2002a, 2002b). Not taking risks, trust, probity, a sense of accountability and a concern with predictability and stability are also likely components pf public service values. But Sennett, though an academic himself, is not writing primarily about higher education, where a relatively high level of autonomy amongst its key workers has often been evident, as compared with some other public services.

In the UK, during 2002, the House of Commons Select Committee on Public Administration voiced concerns that some of what it sees as core public–service values may already have been swept away by public–private partnerships and other reforms to public–services involving degrees of privatization of services or the service infrastructure (Butler 2002). The committee called for the creation of a public service code of conduct for staff and organizations in order to re-establish public service values comprising: observation of high ethical standards, accountability to elected representatives, a high quality of service, fair and equitable treatment of staff, respect of the citizen's right to good administration, and the belief that public service means serving the public, not serving the interests of those who provide the service (House of Commons Select Committee on Public Administration 2002). However, as Pollitt notes, the kinds of values and ethics attached to a public service are not totally generic and depend a great deal on the nature of the service itself, as well as whether the public can and does access the service directly (Pollitt 2003). Nevertheless, a number of elements of this group of values, particularly high ethical standards; a sense of accountability; a high quality of service; fair and equitable treatment of staff and the belief that public service means serving the public not serving the interests of those who provide the service fit well with notions of public goods as non-rivalrous and non-exclusive. These elements are also appropriately applicable to higher education.

Teaching in higher education has an obvious client group in a way that research does not, despite the urging of research funding bodies to take account of research users. However, the potential client or student comes in highly diverse forms, from the rich and privileged middle and upper class young to those who are relatively poor, mature, disabled and/or working class or from an ethnic minority. Attachment to teaching and research *per se* do not by themselves constitute either a public service ethic or a set of values about education as a public service, especially if the focus of the attachment is based on individual careers, reputation, and status, all key features of the academic game (Bourdieu 1988). Furthermore, as the notion of the academic as a politically detached actor (Hammersley 2000, 2002) gains strength from recent trends in social theory and the belief that neoliberalism is inevitable (Bourdieu 1998), as well as from attempts to privatize and change the culture of public service professional work (Exworthy and Halford 1999; Farrell and Morris 2003), the likelihood of more academics holding values which are supportive of public service is not strong. In addition, even though in the UK and some other European countries, higher education institutions are being urged to take on more students from disadvantaged backgrounds, the extent to which this has been achieved (and is seen as desirable by academics themselves) is very variable. It differs, at least in the UK, by institutional type and mission and is underpinned by contradictory policies, a surfeit of initiatives and unforeseen policy consequences, such as the fact that the largest category of students in UK HE with disabilities by 2002 (and this remains the case in 2006) were those with dyslexia (Brown 2002; Comptroller and Auditor General 2002). In any case, widening the social basis of access to higher education does not of itself solve the problems experienced by non-traditional students once admitted to higher education (Quinn 2004; Thomas and Quinn 2007), as has been particularly noted in studies of what happens to students with disabilities once they become students (Riddell and Tinklin 2003; Riddell, Tinklin, and Wilson 2005). In this regard, the quality of the service offered and serving the interests of students (representing the public in this instance), as well as facilitating access to knowledge in a non-rivalrous manner might be expected to be paramount, whereas Riddell's and Quinn and Thomas's work, for instance, suggests that this is not always the case.

Yet a commitment to higher education as a public service should surely embrace an accessible process of higher education for disadvantaged groups, as well as support for their initial entry. A public service commitment in higher education in research might be expected to embrace high ethical standards (not just those required by research sponsors or by the Data Protection Act), high quality research, and a commitment

171

to free access to research, knowledge. The latter is a stance that would cause many so-called 'enterprise managers' in universities, never mind academics, to become very anxious about loss of money from intellectual copyrights and patents. As Fuller has noted, much academic research has not yet even embraced the cyber-revolution to the extent that it is freely published on the web rather than in commercially published books and journals (Fuller 2002), although a substantial number of open access academic journals do now exist (Lund University Libraries 2006; Peters 2006). Frequently, academics do not even benefit from the commercialization of publishing, often providing their services free or for a token amount, and it considerably limits unrestricted and non-exclusive access to knowledge. Some publishers in the UK have now agreed that academics' own published journal articles (either in a pre-refereed or post-refereed form) can appear on their personal websites or in institution-specific repositories but even this has taken a long time to negotiate. What is more, as Fuller points out, competition for money, status, and reputation, rather than concern with non-exclusive access to knowledge by the public, remains dominant values amongst so-called star-researchers, a point noted by other commentators on the contemporary university (Barnett 2003). That is not to say that there are no academics with a commitment to public service but rather to suggest that the commitment, where it exists, may sometimes be limited only to teaching, and not extend to research. This is because most academics in research mode tend to focus much more on individual career strategies, playing research games (Lucas 2006) and participating in extensive contestation of academic fields (Bourdieu 1988) rather than engaging with the notion that research might be considered a public service.

There are, however, at least two important ways in which considerations of public service in respect of research may arise. Firstly, some researchers may wish their research to serve some kind of social or public purpose, and secondly, academics are often concerned about the overall state of their discipline or cognate disciplines in their particular country. Thus, Henkel found UK scientists concerned about the state of British science (Henkel 2000: 202). However, these wider social and discipline-related concerns are some way from beliefs constituting a public service commitment for all or most academics working in higher education. Furthermore, whether academics hold public service values in respect of higher education, what is the position with manager-academics themselves? We turn now to examine this possibility, in the context of recent policy changes to UK universities, looking at the extent to which the views and values of academics in management roles that we interviewed reflected concerns about and interests in the public service functions of higher education.

Recent Policy Changes in UK Higher Education

The UK higher education system consists almost entirely of publicly funded institutions (universities and colleges of higher education, plus some higher education activity in further education colleges), with only one institution entirely privately funded. But the system is not as unitary as it might sound, since each of the four countries of the UK has its own higher education funding arrangements and individual universities in each country also have quite diverse histories. Devolution has affected higher education in a different way from schools (Deem 2004) since only some aspects of higher education policy are devolved in Scotland and Wales. Science policy itself (including exercises to assess quality of research) is UK-wide whereas most (all in Scotland's case) other higher education system decisions are devolved. As devolution has proceeded, so policy differences between each country's higher education system have begun to widen (Scotland has historically had a very differently organized system but Wales and Northern Ireland did not), though the full extent of this is not something researchers agree upon (Keating 2001; Mooney and Poole 2004).

All publicly funded higher education institutions in the UK supplement public funds with private money, including research funding, entrepreneurial activity of various kinds (e.g. conference lettings and, spin-off companies), and recruitment of overseas students. The pre-1992 institutions, which includes universities as diverse as ancient universities like Oxbridge, the big civics like Birmingham, the 1960s universities such as Sussex, former university colleges like Keele, federated universities such as London and Wales, and ex-colleges of advanced technology like Salford, all have charters to award degrees and have been in receipt of public funding from central government for both teaching and research for several decades. The post-1992 institutions were mostly formerly polytechnics run under local government control until 1988, when they became independent corporations (Pratt 1997). The process of change and the former institutional types of the post-1992 universities were slightly different in Scotland and Wales. The polytechnics were officially publicly funded only for teaching, not research, until after they gained university status in 1992. Before becoming universities, many polytechnics specialized in vocational or semi-vocational degrees, though most had a broader curriculum than this would imply. The differences between these two types of university are not now as marked as in the early 1990s, when the ex-polytechnics were much more oriented to undergraduate teaching rather than a mix of first and higher degrees and research. Since 1999 UK undergraduate students have paid standard tuition fees, initially these were set at £1,000 but rose to £1,150 in 2004–5. Tuition fees are remitted or reduced on a means-tested basis. But in England, and Northern Ireland, as noted earlier, from autumn 2006 onwards, variable tuition fees (often referred to as top-up fees) will be payable by all undergraduates. The Welsh Assembly has said it will not introduce variable tuition fees until at least 2007. Scotland has a completely different system of (lower cost) graduate endowments payable after graduation.

Since the beginning of the 1980s, following the election in 1979 of a Conservative government under Prime Minister Thatcher, committed to deregulating, privatizing or exposing all public services to markets, the UK higher education system has undergone some dramatic changes, as we saw in Chapter 2. These have included greater government control coupled with resource reduction (e.g. a 36% fall in public funding per student between 1989 and 1997), considerable expansion of the percentage of the relevant age cohort attending higher education (in 1972 only 13.8% of 18–30-year olds went into higher education, now it is 43% in England and slightly higher in Scotland and Wales), the rise of decentralized cost centres in higher education institutions and the development of an elaborate set of quality control processes for teaching and research. There has been, as consistent with theories about NM as an ideological approach (Deem and Brehony 2005) to managing publicly funded institution (Enteman 1993; Clarke and Newman 1997; Deem 1998; Exworthy and Halford 1999; Clarke, Gewirtz, and McLaughlin 2000), and as noted in previous chapters, a strong emphasis on attempted cultural change in universities and particularly amongst academics, as well as organizational and funding changes. As a configuration of ideas NM stresses performance management, target setting, the erosion of discretion on behalf of professionals, public–private partnerships, the importance of management per se to public services and devolution of financial responsibility to lower and lower levels of organizations. It has been widely adopted (Pollitt and Bouckaert 2000; Pollitt 2003) in western countries. Its permeation of UK higher education has, as noted earlier, been only partial (Deem 2001, 2003; Reed and Deem 2002). However, its effects are evident in the adoption of an audit culture which stresses extensive documentation and inspection of procedures and outcomes in teaching and research (Shore and Roberts 1995; Shore and Wright 1999; Strathern 2000) and puts pressure on individual academics to engage in self-governmentality as well as overt performance management and inspection regimes, as for example in quality audits of teaching and academic standards (Morley 2003).

The changes in HE begun in the 1980s have continued since the election of a Labour Government in 1997 (Brehony and Deem 2003), although recently more money has begun to go back into the sector (particularly for teaching) and the emphasis has shifted towards seeing higher education as a tool of the economy (though this is neither non-rivalrous nor non-exclusive), with consequent greater stress on further widening of participation to under-represented social groups and raising the quality of teaching. Some other aspects of public service provision such as quality of service and accountability have been imposed on academics from external agencies such as the Quality Assurance Agency for Higher Education.

It has become apparent that in England at least, there is a desire on behalf of government to continue radically changing the face of higher education and to exert control over the activities of universities, even though public funding is not the only means of financing activities in HE. This pattern of attempted intervention is certainly not specific to the UK (de Boer 2005; Kehm, Lanzendorf, and Gerlof 2005; Lanzendorf, and Dellwing 2005), though it has had a smoother ride in the UK than elsewhere. In a White Paper published by the Department for Education and Skills in England in January 2003, a number of aspects of radical proposals for change were developed further. One of these proposals is particularly relevant here. This is the attempt to separate research and teaching from each other as activities that have no necessary or desirable connections with each other in higher education, even though what evidence the White Paper draws on is either old and based on American sources (Hattie and Marsh 1996) not readily applicable elsewhere or comes from a curious brief reference to the current situation in the Chinese higher education system, not an obvious comparator for the UK. The recommendation on separating research and teaching has subsequently been reinforced by funding policies that are increasingly selective for research and by increasingly initiative/competitive bid based activities for teaching (such as the 2004 competition in England and in Northern Ireland for Centres for Excellence in Teaching and Learning, with promised annual funding of up to £500,000 per year per centre).

So far as change in research is concerned, the process has been uneven. A set of recommendations in a 2003 report on how research quality might be assessed in the UK in 2007 (Roberts 2003) suggested that instead of subject departments in almost all higher education institutions entering a single RAE, there would be three different routes: one for institutions that have little intensity of research, a second for those departments that are still developing their research, with an emphasis on building research capacity, and the third route focused on research quality amongst departments that already have a good track record in research. But this set of recommendations was not adopted. Although some changes have been made to the 2008 RAE (e.g. by grouping subject panels in cognate groups and by introducing a graded profile based on assessment of all the publications from a particular unit in each subject rather than a single grade for departments), these are not as radical a departure from previous RAEs as was once anticipated. However, in 2006 it was announced that the 2008 RAE would be the last and that it would be replaced by an analysis based on metrics alone. The metrics proposed in the consultation paper in summer 2006 were largely based on funding income (Department for Education and Skills 2006), a strange move to make when previous RAEs have been based much more on outcomes such as publications. The move to metrics has its proponents, especially amongst vice-chancellors of elite universities and those in science, technology, engineering, and medicine but also has its critics (Sastry and Bekhradnia 2006) who point out the distorting aspects of a metrics-based system. There is also concern about how well metrics will work in the social sciences and in the arts/humanities. At the same time, universities have been under pressure to engage in more research collaboration with industry (a rivalrous and highly exclusive approach to knowledge) for some years but especially after the publication of the Lambert Report on higher education and industry links (Lambert Committee on Business-University Collaboration 2003). Universities in England have also been encouraged to collaborate with each other in Regional Development agencies, a somewhat more public service-oriented initiative, but it is unclear how much progress has been made in this. There is some support for the view that regional collaboration in several areas has been slow and somewhat ritualistic (Brown 2004).

Of course, the function and purposes of universities is not something that can or does remain unchanged. There have been many changes to how universities are conceptualized in recent times, not least as a consequence of changes in social theories which have altered conceptions about the universalism and particularism of knowledge and its progressive detachment from national cultures (Delanty 2001). There have also been changes to national economies, with greater interdependence on other countries being a feature and a widening of the social groups that can reasonably expect to attend university. This plus pressure on public expenditure is bound to have an effect on universities (Kwiek 2005). Yet those who have predicted the demise of universities (Readings 1996) have not yet seen their predictions fulfilled. However, if a publicly funded university can be constituted as an institution solely concerned with teaching, then the view that the public service function of universities lies solely in teaching, not research (which thus becomes an exclusive and rivalrous good), is considerably strengthened.

The Values of Manager-Academic in UK Universities

It was in a context of higher education policy flux after the 1997 report on UK universities (National Committee of Inquiry into Higher Education 1997) which was supposed to find solutions to the higher education funding crisis but did not do so, that our ESRC research was undertaken (Deem et al. 2001). We found in our interviews and focus groups that many academics in management roles did not project a strong view of higher education as a public service. When such respondents were in retrospective mood, they tended to look back at the apparently glowing past in higher education and reminisce about the times when only an elite was educated, academics were relatively well-paid and highly autonomous, universities were generously funded, and institutions were free of an audit culture which emphasized short-term outcomes of teaching and research (Strathern 2000). Though the loss of autonomy, trust, and the relatively easy passage of public money through institutions were mourned by a number of our later-career respondents, it did not seem to be the case that most also regretted having lost a sense of universities as public service. When values of or about higher education were mentioned, both in the manager-academic interviews and in the learned society focus groups, the kinds of things discussed tended to be about declining levels of trust in universities or the fate of collegiality (the latter is a kind of academic self-governance largely reliant on unspoken verbal agreements or on committees composed solely of academics) and how these two phenomena are now in tension with more managerial approaches:

> As far as accountability goes, we aren't trusted at all, we have to be accountable for everything. We're judged against criteria all of the time and a certain

amount of that was extremely good, but I think we're perhaps verging on carrying it slightly too far.

Science Learned Society

My Pro-Vice-Chancellor...prefaces many meetings by, 'We are a managed institution, that's the bottom line, that's what we are', but within that if you cannot have that creative trust and collegiality and so on...you *can't* do things that you want to.

Social Science Learned Society

There is a contradiction at the heart of HE management processes, and we as Deans are at the 'tilt point'. Either universities are run through a line management system, or they continue to use committee processes, but one or the other is simply redundant.

Arts/Humanities learned body

However, not all respondents thought that collegiality as a democratic process had ever existed, though some interviewees nevertheless still believed that there *were* considerable tensions in running contemporary universities, including concerns about fair and equitable treatment of staff in the running of institutions:

If by collegiality you mean shared vision and values, that's one thing and that's one thing, which we all strive enormously hard to try to maintain. If you mean by collegiality the sorts of...democratic processes, I mean I think (this is historically), but I mean, I mean it was largely an illusion in many universities anyway....Um, so in a sense, I think the tension is between how you, how you try to maintain and move along with largely disparate and dispersed communities with a shared vision and values and wrestle with the problem of how you actually enable people both to make some influence and genuinely listen to what they have to say and to make decisions.

Generic academic body

Only a handful of respondents in the focus groups explicitly mentioned the public service role of higher education; the view expressed below was thus atypical:

Because we're a public service, because we're a people business, you actually can't. I mean I, I'm struggling currently with directions I'd like the university to go in terms of the subjects we offer, aren't we all? I just went through the exercise of applying a business model to that, because my governors asked me to; here's the product, here's the outcome. What stops me from going from A to B is that I don't want industrial action.

VC, post-1992 University, generic academic body

What some of the manager-academics we talked to did regret was the increasing tendency they observed of governments and funding bodies seeing universities in competitive and market terms, with (in their view) the issue of finance driving almost all decision-making. There was a further concern about the dominance of administrative and managerial matters over academic ones, which might be interpreted as a concern to retain some public service values, though it was rarely expressed like this

> very often when I go to work I have to pinch myself and say, 'Look I'm sure I originally was an academic, but gosh I now feel like an accountant, I spend all my time, it seems to me, talking about issues about money'...we become managers by default and very often I've got in a position of being in an antagonistic relationship within an institution with the part of the managers...the academics are quasi-managers at loggerheads with the real, full-time managers who have a different career structure and a different career path.
>
> Social Science Learned Society

> I think there's been a much clearer focus on what you might see as sort of business priorities. In terms of that we now are all engaged in forming strategic plans, which are very much driven with financial objectives...balancing the books is one of the major priorities for anybody.
>
> Science Learned Society

Those working in business schools and science/technology subjects where a high surplus was being generated, often from applied research and consultancy, tended to demur from this view that universities are too finance-dominated. They usually had no problem seeing higher education as exclusive and rivalrous whereas others did have a problem with this:

> Well, it's an entrepreneurial business- (if you like) led ideology, which has led to a great deal of devolvement of accounting, for example, so that individual Heads of Department are at least in theory extremely autonomous and encouraged to be entrepreneurial and go out and create new educational wealth if you like...it's not just the Vice-Chancellor either, it comes from a group of people associated with the University; both employees of the university and people on the Council and perhaps it derives from the history of the institution or perhaps it's just accidental, I don't know....in fact the ideology or the ethos of the institution is in fact very imperfectly realised and the actual practice of being a Head of Department is a constant clash between what you perceive you're supposed to be doing and actually the many ways in which your freedom to

act is limited by circumstances and so, completely devolved accounting would work very well if all of the accounting units were more or less performing at the same level. But when you have some that are doing very well and some that are not doing so well, then the dreaded collegiality comes in and basically the rich are robbed to pay off the poor.

Applied Science Learned Society

In our manager-academic interviews we found much the same pattern of response as in the focus groups. Where interviewees did touch on public service, it was often in relation to students and issues of their access to higher education. This issue was most frequently raised by those working in the former polytechnic sector, though the final quote below is not from that source, and is hence somewhat unusual in that respect:

In an institution like this for instance {there is} a responsibility to try and make sure that higher education reaches students whose aspirations have not for family, domestic, social reasons, you know we need to ensure that more people from the kind of class background I came from, feel that higher education is for them as well.

Dean, Social Sciences/Humanities, post-1992

I think it's fundamentally right that we have got to include those into the HE system and get benefit from the HE system for the benefit of the community, the benefit of the region, right? I don't think many people yet have sat back and thought what that means.

PVC, post-1992

Well, they {universities} want to try and keep links with other sectors of society and certainly outreach programmes and links with schools, I think, are very important and it's important that the schoolchildren realise that, get that from earlier on, get a view of continuing education.... I have for many years gone out to schools and there's one school that's only about seven minutes from here on the motorway and I had never been there in my life, but it's a third world, it's just another place altogether and it meant so much to the staff and the pupils in that school to be able to come and talk to you...then we did have a few children from that school coming to university and I mean, what it costs them to come, you know, and all their peers were at best working in a Safeway. So bridging these kind of social gulfs I think are terribly important.

HoD, Arts/Humanities, pre-1992

There were also references in some interviews to care of students and commitment to teaching, which are redolent of concerns about the quality of the service offered and the concern to put the needs of the public (in the form of students) first but these concerns were mainly mentioned by those working in the post-1992 sector:

> if there's then a tussle between doing the paperwork and seeing to the well-being of the student, my immediate inclination is to go towards the well-being of the student and I do see a conflict there as we become more and more proceduralised.
>
> PVC, post-1992

> I think there's a strong set of shared values which are very substantially concerned with teaching and learning. I think there's a strong commitment to teaching and people care about it and by and large do it very well.
>
> VC, post-1992.

> yeah, I do believe it's important {teaching}. And when looking at priorities I place that higher up the pecking order for me personally than research publications....I do believe that I absolutely have to maintain that teaching role.
>
> HoD, Sport Science, post-1992

> I see students who maybe are not achieving all that I think they could do and then I realise that they are probably working three days a week and then I come into sort of conflict with the system because I think it is nearly impossible for some of them.
>
> HoD, Arts, post-1992

Contrasting views were sometimes provided by those working in environments that were heavily influenced by commercial and business considerations, such as this statement from a head of a business school

> My aim is to keep the overheads down and be lean.
>
> HoD, Business, pre-1992

Alternative perceptions also came from a few of those who saw academe in more traditional terms, as being about ideas and with knowledge available to all:

> I think academic life is all about the encouragement, the free flow of ideas.
>
> HoD, Arts/Social Sciences, post-1992

There were also a few veiled criticisms of elite institutions and exclusive approaches to higher education:

> In a sense I think the university, a large part of the university saw itself, still sees itself as sort of the Imperial {College London} of {this part of the country}

as it were. This elite institution that really didn't need to bother with things like access and widening participation and so on and so forth. So yeah, time to change.

PVC, pre-1992

my feeling is that in UK universities in general the majority of people who you deal with internally and externally are you know let's put it bluntly, in general middle-class, contented people.

HoD, Medicine, pre-1992

Our data and the differences between respondents from pre- and post-1992 universities, particularly with regard to students and teaching, suggests both that institutional cultures and historical trajectories are important in shaping the views of manager-academics. More speculatively, a process of self-selection may operate, whereby those with more elitist views end up working in institutions which reflect these values.

In the four institutional case studies we carried out in the research, where we talked to a range of university staff from those working in technical, secretarial and manual occupations through to junior and mid-career academics, the kinds of words used to describe what motivated manager-academics in their own institution, were those related to ambition, money, and external research success (Deem 2003, 2004). These characteristics clearly reflect rivalrous and exclusive values. Other attributed characteristics of manager-academics that surfaced in these discussions included: being defensive, remoteness, amateurism, being untrained, appearing insensitive to others, and even, on occasions, acting in a bullying manner. Whilst such descriptions were not applied to all the managers in an institution, the fact that they were used at all, whilst not in any way precluding managerial views on universities as public service institutions, does seem a long way from the kinds of descriptions used by the House of Commons Select Committee on Public Administration referred to earlier. Some of these characteristics included 'high ethical standards' and 'fair and equitable treatment of staff' (House of Commons Select Committee on Public Administration 2002).

Overall, our research data (which may not be representative of the whole UK sector though there is no particular reason to suppose they are not) suggested that a good many of the manager-academics interviewed (and especially those from pre-1992 universities) did not express any values that appeared consistent with a notion of higher education as a public service or public good. For those that did express such values, mainly from the post-1992 universities, their focus was almost exclusively on teaching students and access by under-represented groups to a university education. Research was almost never included in statements about public service. This clearly has implications for not only GATS discussions about research but also wider issues about what constitutes a university, what the public service function of a university is or should be, how research and teaching relate to each other and the extent of public funding spent on research. If teaching can be seen as non-rivalrous and non-exclusive but research is not, then the prospects for future linkages between the two are poor.

Managing the Contemporary Publicly Funded University: Issues for Higher Education

The kinds of views reported here as expressed by our respondents need to be seen in the context of developments in the management of UK universities discussed earlier in the book. The climate of recent UK higher education policy has considerably affected the extent to which higher education is still seen as a public service and additionally, political devolution has had some impact, so that we now have four largely separate systems linked only by science policy which is UK-wide. These organizational and policy contexts, as consistent with some of the tenets of NM documented elsewhere in the book, include an enhanced emphasis on management (of resources and people) rather than academic leadership of teaching and research. There has also been a quite rapid spread of an audit culture (Power 1997; Shore and Wright 1999; Strathern 2000) in which individual academic performance in research and teaching is frequently monitored, with quality measured by short-term outcomes (academic publications over four or five years, student responses to programmes of study immediately after completion). This performance management does address issues of the quality of the service offered to the public and value for money, but in the main, this drive has not been led by academics. There has also been a focus on the privatization of services and facilities (e.g. catering and student residences) that has raised food prices and rents. Over the last three decades a policy emphasis on doing more with less (e.g. taking on more students but with less resource and no more staff) has developed, accompanied by passing on of more of the costs of a university education to the students themselves via tuition fees or an after-graduation contribution, which in itself emphasizes higher education as a private rather than public good. Additionally, there is a somewhat contradictory concern within UK universities, which, on the one hand, hands financial responsibility to academic units through devolved budgets, whilst on the other hand retaining all hiring, firing, and big purchase decisions at the centre. This emphasizes loss of trust in academics, which echoes similar views held by policymakers and politicians.

It should be emphasized, however, that many of these developments are not specific to the UK. Indeed, if we examine what is happening in other university systems across the world, we can see some of the same developments occurring, though in the UK there appears to have been less resistance to them and more collusion or co-option of academics than in other countries such as the Netherlands, Germany, or Austria (de Boer, 2005; Huisman, de Boer and Goedegebuure 2005; de Boer, Enders, and Schimank 2006). Parallel developments in other countries inside and outside Europe include the restructuring of higher education along market lines, with corporate autonomy given to institutions in return for seeking more private funding. The latter is particularly striking in East Asia (Mok 2000a, 2000b, 2005; Mok and James 2005; Mok 2005a). In Europe higher education reform has often been accompanied by 'steering at a distance' measures by governments (Kickert 1995) which ensures that the new autonomy of universities is not accompanied by freedom to research and teach what they like. Such measures include research quality exercises to measure quality of research publications and research activity in countries as diverse as New Zealand and Hong Kong (French, Massy, and Young 2001), the development of performance management tools for academic work, as in the Netherlands and Belgium (van den Bosch and Teelken 2000; Teelken and Braam 2002; de Boer 2005), and the development of quality assurance systems for teaching in many countries, including France, Italy, Finland and the Netherlands (Brennan and Shah 2000; Shah and Brennan 2000) as well as in East Asia and elsewhere. The prevalence of such measures may suggest that there are now relatively few alternative possibilities for how contemporary universities should be run. Nevertheless, in practice, there may actually be more variations in what appear similar practices, as demonstrated in studies of middle management (Clegg and McAuley 2005; Santiago et al. 2006) and as shown in international comparisons of how research funding is determined (von Tunzelmann and Mbula 2003), whereby several European countries do not yet use research performance data for funding purposes.

Despite all this evidence of considerable institutional and system diversity in Europe, some writers suggest that there are no organizational alternatives for the management of publicly funded organization to NM. Indeed, NM has received wide support from political parties and governments of different political persuasions across the western world (Pollitt and Bouckaert 2000; Pollitt 2003). It is particularly the most recent version of NM, which earlier in the book we termed technocratic Managerialism, that has become particularly widespread and persuasive. Yet if we are to preserve a public service ethos in the UK and in other university systems elsewhere, then alternatives to the dominance of Managerialism and overt performance management need to be found which can support and promote teaching and research as collective services worthy of public funding because they play a genuine role in public life.

Whether it is possible to use the Bologna process as a starting point for this in relation to teaching is unclear. As we saw earlier in the chapter, the original 1988 agreement was fairly broad, whereas the agreement signed in June 1999 at a Confederation of the European Union Rectors Conference and the Association of European Universities and its later versions (European Higher Education Ministers 2005) has as its main objectives, to reform higher education systems, to facilitate overall convergence at the European level with respect to student mobility and credit transfer, to respect autonomy and diversity of systems (which might imply that huge variations might remain), and to find common answers to common European higher education challenges. These issues are not obviously about how universities should be governed and managed. Also, as mentioned earlier there is an assumption that all future European undergraduates will need to pay fees for their higher education (European Commission Representation in UK 2006). There are other developments, such as discussion of common issues in the European Research Area[4] created in March 2000 in Lisbon by heads of state from the then fifteen EU member states

[4] The aims of the European Research Area are:

- Networking of national and joint research programs and organizations,
- Integration and development of existing initiatives,
- Mapping of leading research centres in Europe (Mapping of Excellence),
- Improved environment for private research investments and partnerships,
- Coordinated quality and impact assessment of national research and development policies in the areas of research and development,
- Creation of a trans-European high performance data network (DataGrid) for scientific communication,
- Removal of barriers blocking mobility of researchers in Europe; measures against the brain drain of highly qualified researchers, and
- A European 'Community Patent' system for protecting intellectual property rights.

and developed further by heads of universities in the Graz agreement in 2003, and the wider Lisbon process discussed earlier in the chapter, which might also be used as vehicles for change. But most European Commission moves on research across Europe seem aimed more at marketing research and gaining world status for it than protecting it as a public service (Deem, Lucas, and Mok 2006; European Commission Representation in UK 2006). Indeed, one of the aims of the Research Area refers directly to private research funding.

Furthermore, as was hinted earlier in the chapter, it cannot be assumed apriori that most academics regard research as having a strong public service element. It may be that many see it in terms of their own careers, status and disciplines or as a game to be played (Lucas 2006) and do not want non-rivalrous and non-exclusive access to the research knowledge that they create. In addition, as Reed has argued, NM and forms of NPM contribute to and reinforce this individualistic view of research by introducing forms of performance surveillance and control over research activity as well as teaching, leading to a self-governmentality mentality amongst many academics. Morley has noted that quality assurance of teaching has also had these kinds of effects amongst UK academics (Morley 2003). Smith and Webster have suggested that one of the effects of Managerialism is to make academics see their institutions as simply a place of work rather than as an academic community of scholars (Smith and Webster 1997: 100).

What then are the major issues for European universities in relation to the public service function of higher education? They appear to include:

- How to sustain public funding of higher education without at the same time using management and governance approaches which erode academic autonomy, trust, probity, and discretion, such that higher education becomes just another workplace indistinguishable from those of for-profit organizations;
- How to ensure that universities and the academics who work in them continue to do both research and teaching and benefit from and emphasize the synergies and connections between them;
- How to ensure that a majority of academics working in publicly funded higher education institutions are aware of and committed to the public service role of academic work in respect of both research and teaching. Including non-rivalrious and non-exclusive access to knowledge;

- How to develop forms of managing and governing publicly funded higher education institutions which do not privilege managerial, market, and competitive concerns over academic ones but which do facilitate academic work as a set of collective, political, social and cultural processes and activities;

- How to ensure that manager-academics remain academic leaders not bureaucrats and have adequate support and preparation for their roles

- How to ensure that increasing resort to private sector funding by publicly funded higher education does not erode any remaining public service values held by academics and others working in higher education; and

- How to ensure that governing bodies of publicly funded higher education institutions do not see for-profit employers as both a principal source of governors and as their only major stakeholders or regard for-profit organizations as the main role model for universities.

At the moment, the only significant arenas for discussion of public service values and the issues for European universities mentioned above, other than at academic conferences, are national organizations of manager-academics and international organizations such as the Confederation of the European Union Rectors Conference and European Universities Association. Members of such bodies and representatives from publicly funded universities at events associated with such organizations are however, highly likely, by virtue of their senior management roles, to hold views that are consistent with prevalent trends and fashions about how universities should be run and to be particularly concerned with reducing resource dependency on national government. They may not always be the best source of radical ideas about how universities dedicated to public service could be managed and governed in future. But such radical ideas are sorely needed. Though collegiality has had its problems, a more collective approach to managing and leading higher education may still have much to offer. We ideally need philosophies and forms of HE governance and management practice that facilitate long-term 'institution building' but are also realistic about the need for effective, shorter-term, 'negotiating and renegotiating order' political-cum-cultural capacities and skills and the constant need to strike a pragmatic balance between the two.

Conclusion

The chapter began by examining possible threats to the idea of higher education as a public service, considering developments in Europe as well as in the UK alone. Next notions of what might constitute a public service university were considered. It was suggested that high ethical standards, high quality service, a sense of public accountability, a responsibility to service users and non-rivalrous and non-exclusive access to knowledge, were all important elements of this. The analysis considered the extent to which academics and manager-academics in publicly funded higher education institutions might regard public service as an important part of their identity and activities (in respect of both teaching and research). It was suggested that in so far as such views did exist in our sample of manager-academics, they might tend to cluster around teaching and students rather than research, was the latter is often seen in terms of individual careers and reputations. Where our respondents expressed views perceiving higher education as a public service, teaching and students tended to figure far more prominently than did research and most of those holding views consistent with public service notions came from post-1992 universities. Finally, some of the issues that are facing publicly funded higher education institutions in Europe were outlined. It was suggested that whilst the Lisbon and Bologna processes and the creation of a European higher education area might be seen to be moving in the direction of forms of convergence between European universities, public service and forms of management and governance were not necessarily prominent in these, especially in relation to developments concerning research. It therefore remains a priority amongst those committed to higher education as a public service to find ways of taking forward an agenda around the public value of higher education in the future that will engage the managers of academic knowledge work to the same extent as academics themselves. Otherwise Readings' view (1996) of the 'university in ruins' may finally come to fruition.

Our preceding chapters have noted the ways in which different varieties of NM have permeated UK higher education at system, organizational and more micro-levels, a process which is now being repeated in many other countries both inside and outside Europe (Mok and James 2005; Mok 2005*a*; de Boer, Enders, and Schimank 2006). The opening chapter examined some of the theoretical attempts made to explain the movement to NM in public services. The discussion focused particularly on some of the organizational changes associated with NM.

Chapter 2 examined the recent history of the shift to NM in the UK higher education systems and Chapter 3 concentrated on universities as organizations, drawing on empirical research to explore the extent to which universities are now divided both internally and from each other. In chapters four and five we took a closer look at the accounts and experiences of the manager-academics interviewed in the ESRC project on which the book is based and also explored their careers and learning needs. In this chapter, the focus has been on questions of values and how this relates to current developments about higher education in Europe.

In the book, we have documented how the accounts of our sample of manager-academics and administrators in sixteen universities, our national learned society focus groups of academics, administrators and manager-academics and our case studies of employees in four universities bear out the theoretical arguments introduced in Chapter 1. We have also extensively illustrated the hold of neo-technocratic Managerialism over UK universities and government policy on higher education. Though we have also observed that there is resistance to this from academics, support staff and some manager-academics themselves, there is little sign that this resistance has produced any significant new ideas about how to manage universities, that would set aside the tenacious grip of NM. As 'institutionalized distrust' has replaced 'regulated autonomy' as the dominant set of conditions of public service professionals under the auspices of NM, so professionals like academics, local government officers, teachers, social workers, and health service workers have experienced considerable ideological, political, and cultural challenges to their identities and status and a loss of public trust in them (Exworthy and Halford 1999; Dent and Whitehead 2002). Not everyone who has experienced NM has necessarily rejected it, however, and some have benefited from career and promotion opportunities opened up by it. There is also a new enthusiasm for training manager-academics in the UK, despite the scepticism expressed by some of our interviewees but whilst this is in some ways to be welcomed as a way of extending the 'learning from doing' approach noted in the last chapter, if the new training merely serves to reinforce NM and if the increasing use of headhunters for senior posts in academe also means merely searching for those who are clones of those already implementing technocratic Managerialism, then change is unlikely. There is surely scope for examining how other kinds of organizations such as voluntary organizations and those in the creative industries field are run. There also needs to be an attempt to break free from the grip of

NM in higher education, before academic knowledge workers become completely overburdened and disillusioned. For governments, NM may have become seen as the only possibility for running public services but as more and more countries' higher education systems are forced into similar moulds, the possibility that this is the wrong road becomes ever stronger.

If we really do want to preserve higher education as a public service, then NM, privatization, increased use of performance indicators and further loss of trust in academic knowledge workers are clearly not the route to achieving this. Who our future manager-academics are, how they are appointed or selected, how they manage academic knowledge work, and how they are supported whilst they do this, are critically important. The future of public higher education does not lie in the over-managed institutionalized mistrust that currently bedevils it but in rethinking what the academic enterprise is about, how it relates to the public realm and how it can best be organized to release research and teaching-focused creativity and energy. Only then can the real potential of the contemporary university and academic knowledge work be released.

FOCUS GROUP AND INTERVIEW QUESTIONS USED IN THE ESRC PROJECT

1. Phase 1: focus groups with learned societies

Themes for discussion

The meaning of the term 'management' (and whether it is viewed as neutral, positive, negative, or all three).

How management practices are characterized and whether they are currently changing (or whether they have already changed).

Identifying what pressures in institutions lead to more emphasis on management.

Whether academics from different disciplines have different views about management.

What characteristics successful academic managers now need and how their careers are likely to have developed.

Whether there is a glass ceiling preventing women academics from entering the ranks of senior manager-academics in significant numbers.

Whether it matters from what discipline background manager-academics come.

What constitutes collegiality and whether it is seen as something still present in universities, something that is fast disappearing or a myth about a non-existent golden past.

Whether academics are still (or were ever) characterized by professionalism (and what does the term mean) and how much autonomy academics still have.

Whether there are enhanced pressures on academics and manager-academics to be accountable and if so how and to whom.

2. Phase 2 questions (for Deans/Heads of Department), adapted as appropriate for Pro-Vice-Chancellors, Deputy Vice-Chancellors and Vice-Chancellors/Principals/Chief Executives

A. Biography

Development of career as manager

Was it always your ambition to work at a management level?

Have you been appointed or elected to this position? Is it permanent? Could you explain how you came to be a Dean/Head of School—what happened to you, or what were the decisions that you took which led to your progression?

What experiences have you had that have been of benefit to your progression to seniority within higher education?

What, in your experience, may have mitigated against your progression—and how did you set about overcoming those obstacles?

Do you think your career would have been different if you had been a woman/man (as applicable)? If so, how and why?

Could you identify a point at which you felt least equipped or skilled to deal with the demands that were placed on you? How have you learnt how to manage?

How might you have been better prepared? What forms of support, if any, have been useful to you during your progression?

B. Role/context/change

Defining role

What do you think is the purpose of management at the level of Dean/Head of School?

In relation to your faculty/school, do you consider yourself to be a leader, resource handler, representative academic or hands on head of a unit, or are you all those things?

How has that function evolved—have you been able to define your role and function for yourself? Have you been able to develop and influence how others in the institution interpret your function?

To what extent, and how, do you feel that the job of being a manager at this level is different in respect of your previous experiences at other levels? To what extent has your experience of doing the job of Dean/Head of School differed from any expectations you might have had about what work at this level involves?

How much does your role bring you into contact with administrators? At what level? Do you like working with administrators?

Managing in this institution

What sort of institution do you think this is? How would you conceptualize it?

Do you identify yourself with this institution?—Is this how you would like the institution to be? How does your work within the school contribute to or relate to change and development within the institution?

Does your role extend to and contribute to work 'at the centre'? What are the main limitations to your influence in the centre?

Could you describe a situation in which your loyalty—to the school/faculty and to the centre—was divided?

Change

What does change mean to you? What is the function of the Dean/Head of School in relation to internal or external change? Is this mostly organizational change, cultural change, or something else?

C. Assessing the tasks of a Dean/Head of School

Faculty/school contexts—present experience of management

What would you say are the main reasons that you were selected to be Dean/Head of School here? To what extent do you feel that the job of being a manager is different here, in comparison to your experience of managing within other HE institutions?

Managing and relations with other people

What is your relation to Heads of Department? Do you have power and influence in a hierarchical sense? How would Deans or Heads of Department interpret your role? Does their interpretation present you with difficulties in respect of managing this school/faculty?

What power and influence do you have over people for whom you have responsibility, and how have you obtained this? Are you in a position yourself to manage and direct their work?

Over which staff do you have most direct influence? What would help you to improve or increase the level of authority you have in relation to other academics?

Do you mostly work with men, women, or both? Is there such a thing as a glass ceiling for women in this institution?

To whom are you accountable? Are you managed by anyone or by sets of people?

Whom do you trust—is trust a significant issue?

Tasks

Is there a regular pattern to your work over a period of time, say a typical week?

What do you do on a day to day basis—what tasks constitute weekly business and schedule of a Dean/Head of School? What are the most vital tasks?

What degree of influence and choice do you have in determining and choosing the tasks that you have before you?

What are the tasks you enjoy most? And which least?

What tasks draw on your strengths?

What factors are involved in deciding how to handle particular tasks and situations? Do you rely on personal experience about what works, is there a rationality or overall rationale to the way you work?

How do you like to be managed?

How do you set yourself goals and objectives for the tasks that face you?

What are the key means by which you know how successful you are in your role?

D. Enabling and constraining management and managers

Resources

What are the main resources you have that enable you to manage?—what are the tools with which you can have control or influence? What would improve your ability to manage?

Are there rational means and channels available to you and on which you can depend in order to exert control?—or is it necessary to continually assess, develop and evolve different means and strategies for dealing with each task or situation that faces you?

What stops you getting your own way?

Tensions and contradictions

What are the main struggles that you experience in your work?—could you typify the sources of struggle or characterize the nature of your struggle?

Are these problems that that you feel are essentially contradictory? What can you do to mediate or alleviate the consequences of these contradictory situations?

Could you describe an event in which you felt that your approach—the resources you drew on or the strategies you developed were inappropriate?

Could you describe an event that demanded action with which you felt personally uncomfortable?

E. Support, home/work, and the future

What forms of support would bolster and sustain you in your job—What forms of support does a Dean/Head of School need?

How easy is it for a Dean/Head of School to find support? Is support something that you feel able to actively seek?

Do you have a partner? Children?

Do you find any tensions between your job and your out of work life? If so what are these?

What are your own career ambitions for the future?

3. Administrators: phase 2 questions

A. Biography and career

Was it always your ambition to work at a senior level in a university?

How long have you held this position? Is it permanent? Could you explain how you came to be in this role? Where did you work before coming to X university? (if from outside academe originally) What were your expectations of working in higher education? Has the reality been different?

Do you think your career would have been different if you had been a woman/man (as applicable)? If so, how and why?

B. Role, managing, and change

Defining role

What do you think is the purpose of management at this level of administration?

Do you think of yourself as a manager? If not, what would be a better descriptor?

How have your current role and function evolved—have you been able to define these for yourself? Have you been able to develop and influence how others in the institution interpret your function?

To what extent, and how, do you feel that the job of being a manager at this level is different in respect of your previous experiences at other levels? To what extent has your experience of doing the job differed from any expectations you might have had about what work at this level involves?

How much does your role bring you into contact with academics? At what level? Do you like working with academics?

Managing in this institution

What sort of institution do you think this is? How would you conceptualize it? Is this how you would like the institution to be?

Do you identify yourself with this institution?

How does your work contribute to or relate to change and development within the institution?

Does your role extend to and contribute to what academics do?

Change

What does change mean to you? What is your function in relation to internal or external change? Is this mostly organizational change, cultural change, or something else?

Do you think that universities are easy to change? How do they compare with other organizations (in the public or private sectors)

C. Assessing the tasks of a senior administrator

What would you say are the main reasons that you were appointed to your current role? To what extent do you feel that the job of being a manager is different here, in comparison to your experience of elsewhere?

Managing and relations with other people

What is your relation to senior academics here? Do you have power and influence in a hierarchical sense?

What power and influence do you have over people for whom you have responsibility, and how have you obtained this? Are you in a position yourself to manage and direct their work?

Over which staff do you have most direct influence? What would help you to improve or increase the level of authority you have in relation to other staff?

Do you mostly work with men, women, or both? Is there such a thing as a glass ceiling for women in this institution?

To whom or what are you or do you feel accountable? Are you managed by anyone or by sets of people?

Whom do you trust—is trust a significant issue for you in this organization?

Tasks

Is there a regular pattern to your work over a period of time, say a typical week?

What do you do on a day-to-day basis or weekly basis?

What degree of influence and choice do you have in determining and choosing the tasks that you have before you?

What are the tasks you enjoy most?

What tasks draw on your strengths?

What factors are involved in deciding how to handle particular tasks and situations? Do you rely on personal experience about what works, is there a rationality or overall rationale to the way you work?

How do you like to be managed?

How do you set yourself goals and objectives for the tasks that face you?

What are the key means by which you know how successful you are in your role?

D. Enabling and constraining management and managers

Resources

What are the main resources you have that enable you to manage? What are the tools with which you can have control or influence? What would improve your ability to manage?

Are there rational means and channels available to you and on which you can depend in order to exert control?

What if anything ever stops you getting your own way?

Tensions and contradictions

What are the main struggles that you experience in your work? Could you typify the sources of struggle or characterize the nature of your struggle?

Are these problems that that you feel are essentially contradictory? What can you do to mediate or alleviate the consequences of these contradictory situations?

Could you describe an event in which you felt that your approach—the resources you drew on or the strategies you developed—were inappropriate?

Could you describe an event that demanded action with which you felt personally uncomfortable?

E. Support, home/work, and the future

Is there anything about your job that keeps you awake at night?

What forms of support would bolster and sustain you in your job? What forms of support does someone in your job need?

How easy is it to find support? Is support something that you feel actively seek?

Do you have a partner? Children?

Do you find any tensions between your job and your out of work life? If so what are these?

What are your own career ambitions for the future?

4. Phase 3: case study questions for focus groups and interviews with university employees

You

Why do you work in higher education?

Why did you choose to work at this institution?

What makes it worthwhile to work here: what are the rewards, the satisfactions?

And what are the downsides?

To what or whom are you most committed?: work area, people, institution?

Your work

What are the pressures, demands, and constraints of your work?

What conditions/behaviours are supportive, constraining, frustrating?

What would have to change to improve your working conditions/levels of success?

In your area, is there a team culture?

Do people have to 'fit in'? What are they joining in with?

Do women and men both get on here equally well?

What objectives do you have? Who sets them?

What strategies are necessary in order to achieve these?

What drives / directs your work?

What levels of autonomy and discretion do you enjoy?

Your university as an institution

What is the culture of the institution? Strong, weak, confused, conflicting, changing?

Are there dominant cultures and subcultures?

Are there institution specific idiosyncracies, rituals, traditions, languages, jokes?

Are there institution-specific myths, stories, beliefs?

What is the public face of the institution?

What is the internal character of the institution?

What is the work culture: stable, traditional, ad hoc?

Are there traditions and conventions of work? Are these positive or negative?

Are there traditions and conventions of management? Are these positive, negative or neutral?

Who are seen as 'the managers'?

Who does 'the management'?

Has there been a notable crisis here? If so, how did the institution respond?

Was this response defensive, speculative, successful, unknown?

Other people

Who are the main characters in your daily work life? Who has greatest influence on your work?

What levels of trust, goodwill, politicking are in evidence?

Are people focused on structures?

Do structures and processes of work lead to competition or collaboration?

How are academics, students, and non-academics characterized?

What is the relationship between academics and non-academics?

Bibliography

Acker, S. (1997). 'Becoming a Teacher Educator: Voices of Women Academics in Canadian Faculties of Education', *Teaching and Teacher Education*, 13(1): 65–74.

—— and Armenti, C. (2004). 'Sleepless in Academia', *Gender & Education*, 16(1): 3–24.

—— and Feuerverger, G. (1996). 'Doing Good and Feeling Bad: The Work of Women University Teachers', *Cambridge Journal of Education*, 26(3): 401–22.

Ackroyd, S. and Ackroyd, P. (1999). 'Problems of University Governance in Britain: Is More Accountability the Solution?', *International Journal Public Sector Management*, 12(3): 171–85.

—— Kirkpatrick, I., and Walker, R. (2007). 'Public Management Reform and its Consequences for Professional Organization: A Comparative Analysis', *Public Administration*, forthcoming.

Aitken, R. (1966). *Administration of a University*. London: University of London Press.

Alban-Metcalfe, J. and Alimo-Metcalfe, B. (2003a). 'Leadership Culture and Change Inventory', *Selection and Development Review*, 19(5): 7–10.

—— —— (2003b). 'NHS Leadership Qualities and the Public Sector Version of the Transformational Leadership Questionnaire (TLQ)', *Selection and Development Review*, 19(3): 23–6.

Albrecht, S. and Travaglione, A. (2003). 'Trust in Public Sector Senior Managmenent', *Journal of Human Resource Management*, 32(1): 1–42.

Alimo-Metcalfe, B. and Alban-Metcalfe, R. (2000). 'Heaven Can Wait the Requirement for a Leader to be a Charismatic Superman Was One of the Mythologies Debunked in a Major Survey on Qualities Needed at the Top', *Health Service Journal*, 26–9.

—— and Alban-Metcalfe, R. J. (2000). 'A New Approach to Assessing Transformational Leadership', *Selection and Development Review*, 16(5): 15–17.

Allen, D. and Newcomb, E. (1999). 'University Management and Administration: A Profession for the 21st Century', *Perspectives*, 3(2): 38–43.

Altbach, P. (ed.) (1996). *The International Academic Profession: Portraits from Fourteen Countries*. Princeton, NJ: Carnegie Foundation for the Advancement of Teaching.

____ (2004). 'The Costs and Benefits of World Class Universities', *Academe* (January–February) http://www.aaup.org/publications/Academe/2004/04jf/04jfaltb.htm

Alvesson, M. (2004). *Knowledge Work and Knowledge-Intensive Firms*. Oxford: Oxford University Press.

____ and Wilmott, H. (2002). 'Theorizing the Micro Politics of Resistance: New Public Management and Managerialism', *Organization Studies*, 26: 683–706.

Amaral, A., Jones, G. A., and Karseth, B. (eds.) (2002). *Governing Higher Education: National Perspectives on Institutional Governance*. Dordrecht, The Netherlands: Kluwer.

Anderson, R. (2006). 'Universities, the State and Markets', Unpublished paper given to the 'Universities and Ideas' Institute of Advanced Studies Seminar series, University of Bristol, 2 February.

Anthias, F. (2005). 'Social Stratification and Social Inequality; Models of Intersectionality and Identity', in F. Devine, M. Savage, J. Scott, and R. Crompton (eds.), *Rethinking Class: Cultures, Identities and Lifestyle*. Basingstoke, UK: Palgrave.

Association of University Teachers (2002). 'UK Academic Staff: Ethnicity, Nationality and Average Pay 2000–01', Retrieved October 2002 from http://www.aut.org.uk/pandp/briefings/briefing_fset.html?ethnicpaygap.html~main

____ (2004). 'The Unequal Academy: UK Academic Staff 1995–96 to 2002–03', from http://www.aut.org.uk/index.cfm?articleid = 916

Bagihole, B. and Goode, J. (2001). 'The Contradiction of the Myth of Individual Merit, and the Reality of a Patriarchal Support System in Academic Careers: A Feminist Investigation', *European Journal of Women's Studies*, 8(2): 161–80.

Barblan, A. (2002). 'The International Provision of Higher Education: Do Universities Need GATS?', *Higher Education Management and Policy*, 14(3): 77–92.

Bargh, C., Bocock, J., Scott, P., and Smith, D. (2000). *University Leadership: The Role of the Chief Executive*. Buckingham, UK: Open University Press.

Barnett, R. (1999). *Realizing the University in an Age of Supercomplexity*. Buckingham, UK: Society for Research into Higher Education & Open University Press 2000.

____ (2003). *Beyond all Reason: Living with Ideology in the University*. Buckingham, UK: Open University Press.

____ (2006). 'Shaping the Liquid University', Unpublished paper Given to the Institute for Advanced Studies 'Universities and Ideas' Seminar Series, Royal Fort House, University of Bristol, 27 April.

Baty, P. (2002*a*). 'Analysis: Good Teachers or Great Stage Managers?', *The Times Higher*, London, 9 August.

Baty, P. (2002*b*). 'Philosophy Scores Add to QAA Criticism', *The Times Higher*, London, 22 June.

Beasley, T. and Pembridge, K. (2000). 'The Potential for Mutual-Growth Mergers between UK Universities', *Perspectives*, 4(2): 41–7.

Becher, T. and Trowler, P. (2001). *Academic Tribes and Territories: Intellectual Enquiry and the Cultures of Disciplines*. Buckingham, UK: Society for Research into Higher Education & Open University Press.

Benninghof, M. and Sormoni, P. (2005). 'Culture in Interaction: The Practical Constitution of Academic Identities in Laboratory Work—an Ethnographic Account', Unpublished paper given to Consortium of Higher Education Researchers Conference, Jyväskyalå, Finland, 1st–3rd September.

Bensimon, E. M. (1995). 'Total Quality Management in the Academy: A Rebellious Reading', *Harvard Educational Review*, 4 (Winter): 593–611.

Bett Report (1999). *Independent Review of Higher Education, Pay and Conditions*. London: HMSO.

Blackmore, P. (2005).'Disciplinary Difference: The Missing Factor in Understanding Leadership and Management in Universities?', Unpublished paper given to the Society for Research into Higher Education Annual Conference, University of Edinburgh, 13–15 December.

Bolton, S. C. (2005). 'Making-up Managers: The Case of NHS Nurses', *Work, Employment and Society*, 19(1): 5–23.

Boreham, P. (1983). 'Indetermination: Professional Knowledge, Organization and Control', *Sociological Review*, 31: 693–718.

Boud, D. (ed.) (1988). *Developing Student Autonomy in Learning*. London: Kogan Page.

Bourdieu, P. (1988). *Homo Academicus*. Cambridge: Polity Press.

—— (1998). *Acts of Resistance*. Oxford: Polity Press.

Boxer, L. (2005). 'Discourses of Change Ownership in Higher Education', *Quality Assurance in Education*, 13(4): 344–52.

Brandes, D. and Ginnis, P. (1986). *A Guide to Student Centred Learning*. London: Basil Blackwell.

Brehony, K. J. (2001).'Using And Abusing The Past: The Use of History in the Performance Related Pay Debate', Unpublished paper presented to the American Educational Research Association, Annual Meeting, Seattle, April.

—— and Deem, R. (2003). 'Education Policy: New Labour, New Education 1997–2002', in N. Ellison and C. Pierson (eds.), *New Developments in British Social Policy*. London: Palgrave, pp. 177–93.

Brennan, J. and Shah, T. (2000). *Managing Quality in Higher Education*. Buckingham, UK: Open University Press.

Broadbent, J. and Laughlin, R. (2002). 'Public Service Professionals and the New Public Management: Control of the Professions in the Public Services', in K. McLaughlin, S. P. Osborne, and E. Ferlie (eds.), *New Public Management: Current Trends and Future Prospects*. London: Routledge, pp. 95–108.

Brooks, A. (1997). *Academic Women*. Buckingham, UK: Open University Press.

—— and Mackinnon, A. (2001). *Gender and the Restructured University*. Buckingham, UK: Open University Press.

Brown, R. (2002). 'New Labour and Higher Education', Unpublished professorial lecture given at the University of East London, 26 March 2002.

Brown, T. (2004).'Regional Collaboration: Opportunities and Challenges for Higher Education Institutions in Responding to Emerging Regional Policy Initiatives', Unpublished paper presented to the Higher Education Network (22) of the European Conference on Educational Research, Rethymnon, Crete, 22–25th September.

Butler, P. (2002). 'Public Service Ethos 'Under Threat' From Private Involvement', Retrieved September 2003 from http://www.society.guardian.co.uk/futurefor-publicservices/story /0,8150,743062,00.html

Calâs, M. B. and Smircich, L. (2001). 'Does the House of Knowledge Have a Future?', *Organization*, 8(2): 147–48.

Callender, C. (2002). *Social Policy and Society*, 1–2: 83–94.

Carter, J., Fenton, S., and Modood, T. (1999). *Ethnicity and Employment in Higher Education*. London: Policy Studies Institute.

Castells, M. (1996). *The Rise of the Network Society*. Oxford: Blackwell.

—— (1997a). *The Information Age: Economy, Society and Culture*, Vol. 1, *The Rise of the Network Society*. Malden, MA and Oxford: Blackwell.

—— (1997b). *The Information Age: Economy, Society and Culture*, Vol. 2, *The Power of Identity*. Malden, MA and Oxford: Blackwell.

—— (1997c). *The Information Age: Economy, Society and Culture*, Vol. 3, *End of Millenium*. Malden, MA and Oxford: Blackwell.

Child, J. (2005). *Organization: Contemporary Principles and Practice*. Malden, MA and Oxford: Blackwell.

Child, J. and McGrath, R. G. (2001). 'Organizations Unfettered: Organizational Form in an Information-Intensive Economy', *Academy of Management Journal*, 44(6): 1135–48.

Christiansen, L., Stombler, M., and Thaxton, L. (2004). 'A Report on Librarian-Faculty Relations from a Sociological Perspective', *Journal of Academic Librarianship*, 30(2): 116–21.

Clark, B. (1998). *Creating Entrepreneurial Universities: Organisational Pathways of Transformation*. New York and Amsterdam: Elsevier.

Clark, H., Chandler, J., and Barry, J. (1998). 'Scholarly Relations: Gender, Trust and Control in the Life of Organisations', Paper presented at the European Group for Organisational Studies, Maastricht University, The Netherlands, Jossey-Bass.

Clarke, J. (2004). *Changing Welfare, Changing States: New Directions in Social Policy*. London: Sage.

—— (2005). 'Performing for the Public: Doubt, Desire and the Evaluation of Public Services', in P. Du Gay (ed.), *The Values of Bureaucracy*. Oxford: Oxford University Press, pp. 211–32.

—— and Newman, J. (1994). 'The Managerialisation of Public Services', in J. Clarke, A. Cochrane, and E. McLaughlin (eds.), *Managing Social Policy*. London: Sage, pp. 13–31.

Clarke, J. and Newman, J. (1997). *The Managerial State: Power, Politics and Ideology in the Remaking of Social Welfare*. London: Sage.

____ Gewirtz, S., and McLaughlin, E. (eds.) (2000). *New Managerialism, New Welfare?* London: Sage.

Clegg, S. and McAuley, J. (2005). 'Conceptualising Middle Management in Professional Organisations: A Multi-Faceted Discourse', *Journal of Higher Education Policy and Management*, 27(1): 1–16.

Committee on Higher Education (1963). *Higher Education: Report of the Committee Under the Chairmanship of Lord Lionel Robbins*. London: HMSO.

Comptroller and Auditor General (2002). *Widening Participation in Higher Education in England*. London, National Audit Office: HMSO.

Cook, R. (2001). 'Worthy Project or Just a Game?', *The Times Higher Education Supplement*, London: 7.

Corbett, A. (2005). 'The Lisbon Process and Education', from http://www.e-education-europe.org/uk/rubriques /europers/1.asp

Courpasson, D. (2000). 'Managerial Strategies of Domination: Power in Soft Bureaucracies', *Organisation Studies*, 21(1): 141–62.

Cowen, R. (1996). 'Performativity, Post Modernity and the University', *Comparative Education*, 32(2): 245–58.

Crouch, C. (1970). *The Student Revolt*. London: Bodley Head.

Currie, J., Harris, P., and Thiele, B. (2000). 'Sacrifices in Greedy Universities: Are they Gendered?', *Gender and Education*, 12(3): 269–92.

Cuthbert, R. (ed.) (1996). *Working in Higher Education*. Buckingham, UK: Open University Press.

Cutler, T. and Waine, B. (2000). 'Managerialism Reformed? New Labour and Public Sector Management', *Social Policy and Administration*, 34(3): 318–32.

____ (2001). 'Report: Performance Management—the Key to Higher Standards in Schools?', *Public Money and Management*, 21(2): 69–72.

____ (2004). 'Performance Without Pay? Managing School Budgets Under Performance Related Pay: Evidence from the First Year of PRP', *Financial Accountability and Management*, 20(1): 57–75.

David, M. and Woodward, D. (eds.) (1998). *Negotiating the Glass Ceiling: Careers of Senior Women in the Academic World*. London: Falmer Press.

Davis, G. (2000). 'Policy Capacity and the Future of Governance', in G. Davis and M. Keating (eds.), *The Future of Governance*. St Leonards, New South Wales: Allen & Unwin.

de Boer, H. (2005).'Higher Education in the Netherlands', Unpublished draft country report presented to Expert Seminar on 'Changes in the Governance Regime of Public Sector Research. The Examples of Austria, Germany, the Netherlands and the UK', 21–22 January 2005, Centre for Research on Higher Education and Work, University of Kassel, Germany.

____ Enders, J., and Schimank, U. (2005). 'Orchestrating Creative Minds: The Governance of Higher Education and Research in Four Countries Combined', Paper presented at 'Verschrankung Externer and interner Governance' Workshop, University of Kassel, Germany, 17–18 February.

_____ _____ _____ (2006). 'On the Way Towards New Public Management? The Governance of University Systems in England, The Netherlands, Austria, and Germany', in D. Jansen (ed.), *New Forms of Governance in Research Organizations—Disciplinary Approaches, Interfaces and Integration*. Dordrecht, The Netherlands: Springer.

Dearlove, J. (1997). 'The Academic Labour Process: From Collegiality and Professionalism to Managerialism and Proleterianisation?', *Higher Education Review*, 30(1): 56–75.

Deem, R. (1984). 'The Case of Bucks College', *British Journal of Sociology of Education*, 4(3): 176–9.

_____ (1996). 'Border Territories: A Journey Through Sociology, Education and Women's Studies', *British Journal of Sociology of Education*, 17(1): 5–19.

_____ (1998). 'New Managerialism in Higher Education—the Management of Performances and Cultures in Universities', *International Studies in the Sociology of Education*, 8(1): 47–70.

_____ (2001a). 'Globalisation, New Managerialism, Academic Capitalism and Entrepreneurialism in Universities; Is the Local Dimension Still Important?', *Comparative Education*, 37(1): 7–20.

_____ (2001b).'New Managerialism and the UK University: The Managers and the Managed Compared', Unpublished paper presented to the British Educational Research Association Conference, University of Leeds.

_____ ((2002).'Enhancing Teaching in Higher Education; Change Agents, the UK Learning and Teaching Support Network Initiative and the Case of the UK Education Subject Centre: A Critical Analysis', Unpublished paper given to the European Conference of Educational Researchers, Lisbon, 11–14 September.

_____ (2003a). 'A Future for Higher Education?', *Public Money and Management*, (April): 78–79.

_____ (2003b). 'Managing to Exclude? Manager-Academic and Staff Communities in Contemporary UK Universities', in M. Tight (ed.), *International Perspectives on Higher Education Research: Access and Inclusion*. Amsterdam and London: Elsevier Science JAI, pp. 103–25.

_____ (2004a).'Devolution and Education Policy in the United Kingdom: An Over-view', Unpublished paper presented to Symposium on 'Devolution and UK Education policies', British Educational Research Association Conference, Manchester University, 15–18 September.

_____ (2004b). 'New Managerialism in UK Universities: Manager-Academics Accounts of Change', H. Eggins (ed.), *Globalization and Reform in Higher Education*. Buckingham, UK: Open University Press, pp. 55–67.

_____ (2004c). 'The Knowledge Worker, the Manager-Academic and the Contemporary UK University: New and Old Forms of Public Management', *Financial Accountability and Management*, 20(2 May): 107–28.

Deem, R. (2006*a*). 'Changing Research Perspectives on the Management of Higher Education: Can Research Permeate the Activities of Manager-Academics?', *Higher Education Quarterly*, 60(3): 203–28.

—— (2006*b*). 'Conceptions of Contemporary European Universities: To Do Research or not to do Research?', *European Journal of Education*, 41(2): 281–304.

—— and Brehony, K. J. (2005). 'Management as Ideology: The Case of "New Managerialism" in Higher Education', *Oxford Review of Education*, 31(2): 213–31.

—— and Hillyard, S. (2002). 'Making Time for Management—the Careers and Lives of Manager-Academics in UK Universities', in G. Crow and S. J. Heath (eds.), *Social Conceptions of Time*. Basingstoke, UK: Palgrave, pp. 126–43.

—— and Johnson, R. J. (2000). 'Managerialism and University Managers: Building new Academic Communities or Disrupting Old Ones?', in I. McNay (ed.), *Higher Education and Its Communities*. Buckingham, UK: Open University Press, pp. 65–84.

—— and Johnson, R. N. (2003). 'Risking the University? Learning to be a Manager-Academic in UK Universities', *Sociological Research on Line*, 8: 3, Retrieved August 2006 from http://www.socresonline.org.uk/8/3/contents.html

—— and Lucas, L. (2007). 'Research and Teaching Cultures in Two Contrasting UK Policy Locations: Academic Life in Education Departments in Five English and Scottish Universities', *Higher Education*.

—— and Morley, L. (2006). 'Diversity in the Academy? Staff and Senior Manager Perceptions of Equality Policies in Six Contemporary UK Higher Education Institutions', *Policy Futures*, 4(2): 185–202.

—— Fulton, O., Johnson, R., Hillyard, S., et al. (2001). 'New Managerialism and the Management of UK Universities', End of Award Report, Swindon, Economic and Social Research Council http://www.esrcsocietytoday.ac.uk/ESRCInfoCentre/ViewAwardPage.aspx?data = aysN67OSmH%2f4mKibNqyEcPaU2MSTsPt6VIWlBC%2f7QiiZy5R4Ny5FWZ5Z5Q9b7dqmcsFjyRRkdvp3Y4Qs5T20rjWvCB5OhNjQwqH5bzvzFv21RGde9Q2wasdGaAPh5%2bTZLDDuX3pxbOQ%3d&xu = &isAwardHolder = &isProfiled = &AwardHolderID = &Sector=

—— Lucas, L., and Mok, K. H. (2006).'East Meets West Meets "World Class". What Is a World Class University in the Context of Europe and Asia and Why does It Matter?', Unpublished paper given to Annual Conference of the Consortium of Higher Education Researchers, 7–9 September, Kassel, Germany.

Delamont, S., Atkinson, P., and Parry, O. (1997*a*). 'Critical Mass and Doctoral Research; Reflections on the Harris Report', *Studies in Higher Education*, 22(3): 319–32.

—— Parry, O., and Atkinson, P. (1997*b*). 'Critical Mass and Pedagogic Continuity: Studies in Academic Habitus', *British Journal of Sociology of Education*, 18(4): 533–49.

—— Atkinson, P., and Parry, O. (2000). *The Doctoral Experience: Success and Failure in Graduate School*. London: Falmer Press.

Delanty, G. (2001). *Challenging Knowledge: The University in the Knowledge Society.* Buckingham, UK: Open University Press.

Dent, M. and Whitehead, S. (eds.) (2002). *Managing Professional Identities: Knowledge, Performatives and the 'New' Professional.* London: Routledge.

Department for Education and Skills (2003). 'The Future of Higher Education: White Paper', from http://www.dfes.gov.uk/highereducation/hestrategy/

—— (2006). 'Reform of Higher Education Research Assessment and Funding', from http://www.dfes.gov.uk/consultations/conDetails.cfm?consultationId = 1404%20

Department of Education and Science (1987). *Higher Education: Meeting the Challenge.* London: HMSO.

Dewatripont, M., Thys-Clement, F., and Wilkin, L. (eds.) (2002). *European Universities: Change or Convergence?* Bruxelles: Editions de L'Universities de Bruxelles.

Dill, D. (2003). 'Degradation of the Ethics: Teaching, Research and Regulation', Plenary address presented to the Society for Research in Higher Education Annual Conference 'Research, Scholarship and Teaching: Changing Relationships', 16–18 December, Royal Holloway College, University of London.

—— and Soo, M. (2005). 'Academic Quality, League Tables, and Public Policy: A Cross-national Analysis of Universities Ranking System', *Higher Education*, 49: 495–533.

Dimaggio, P. (2001). *The Twenty First Century Firm.* Princeton, NJ: Princeton University Press.

Dobson, I. R. (2000). 'Them and Us'—General and Non-General Staff in Higher Education', *Journal of Higher Education Policy and Management*, 22(2): 203–10.

Du Gay, P. (2000). *In Praise of Bureaucracy.* London: Sage.

Edwards, M. (1998). 'Commodification and Control in Mass Higher Education: A Double-Edged Sword', in D. Jary and M. Parker (eds.), *The New Higher Education: Issues and Directions for the Post-Dearing University.* Stoke on Trent: Staffordshire University Press, pp. 253–72.

Eggins, H. (ed.) (1997). *Women as Leaders and Managers in Higher Education.* SRHE. Buckingham, UK: Open University Press.

Elkin, J. (2002). 'The UK Research Assessment Exercise 2001', *Libri*, 52(4): 204–8.

Enders, J. (2001a). 'Academic Staff in the European Union', in J. Enders (ed.), *Employment and Working Conditions of Academic Staff in Europe.* Westport, CT: Greenwood Press.

—— (ed.) (2001b). *Employment and Working Conditions of Academic Staff in Europe.* Westport, CT: Greenwood Press.

—— and Fulton, O. (eds.) (2002). *Higher Education in a Globalising World: International Trends and Mutual Observations. A Festschrift in Honour of Ulrich Teichler.* Dordrecht, The Netherlands: Kluwer.

Enteman, W. (1993). *Managerialism: The Emergence of a New Ideology.* Wisconsin, WI: University of Wisconsin Press.

Eraut, M. (1994). *Developing Professional Knowledge and Competence.* London: Falmer Press.

Eraut, M. (2000). 'Non Formal Learning, Implicit Learning and Tacit Knowledge in Professional Work', F. Coffield (ed.), *The Necessity of Informal Learning*. Bristol, UK: Policy Press.

Etzkowitz, H. and Leydesdorff, L. (1997). *Universities in the Global Knowledge Economy*. London: Pinter Press.

European Commission Representation in UK (2006). 'Report on Seminar "Delivering on the Modernisation Agenda for Universities; Education, Research and Innovation"', 'Delivering on the modernisation agenda for universities; education, research and innovation', London, 29 June.

European Higher Education Ministers (2005). 'The European Higher Education Area—Achieving the Goals: Communiqué of the Conference of European Ministers Responsible for Higher Education', from http://www.dfes.gov.uk/bologna/

European University Association (2003).'European University Association Statement on the Bologna Process', Statement to the EU Ministerial Meeting on the Bologna Process, Berlin, 18–19 September.

Evetts, J. (1994). *Becoming a Secondary Headteacher*. London: Cassell.

Exworthy, M. and Halford, S. (1999). 'Professionals and Managers in a Changing Public Sector: Conflict, Compromise and Collaboration', in M. Exworthy and S. Halford (eds.), *Professionals and the New Managerialism in the Public Sector*. Buckingham, UK: Open University Press, pp. 1–17.

—— —— (eds.) (1999). *Professionals and the New Managerialism in the Public Sector*. Buckingham, UK: Open University Press.

Fagin, C. M. (1997). 'The Leadership Role of a Dean', *New Directions for Higher Education*, 98: 95–100.

Fairclough, N. (2005). 'Discourse Analysis in Organization Studies: The Case for Critical Realism', *Organization Studies*, 26(6): 915–39.

—— Jessop, R., and Sayer, A. (2002). 'Critical Realism and Semiosis', *Journal of Critical Realism*, 5(1): 2–10.

Farnham, D. and Horton, S. (eds.) (1993). *Managing the New Public Services*. London: McMillan.

—— and J. Jones (1998). 'Who Are the Vice-Chancellors? An Analysis of Their Professional and Social Backgrounds, 1990–1997', *Higher Education Review*, 30(3): 42–58.

Farrell, C. and Morris, J. (2003). 'The 'Neo-Bureaucratic' State: Professionals, Managers and Professional Managers in Schools, General Practices and Social Work', *Organization*, 10(1): 129–56.

Fergusson, R. (2000). 'Modernizing Managerialism: The Case of Education', in J. Clarke, S. Gewirtz, and E. McLaughlin (eds.), *New Managerialism, New Welfare?*. London: Sage.

Ferlie, E. and Fitzgerald, L. (2002). 'The Sustainability of the New Public Management in the U.K.', in S. Osbourne (ed.), *Trends in New Public Management*. London: Routledge, pp. 341–53.

Ferlie, E., Ashburner, L., Fitzgerald, L., and Pettigrew, A. (1996). *The New Public Management in Action*. Oxford: Oxford University Press.

Ferlie, E., Hartley, J., and Martin, S. (2003). 'Changing Public Service Organisations: Current Perspectives and Future Prospects', *British Journal of Management*, 14 (special issue): S1–S14.

Fielden, J. and Lockwood, G. (1973). *Planning and Management in Universities*. London: Chatto & Windus.

Fischer, F. (2004). *Reframing Public Policy: Discursive Politics and Deliberative Practices*. Oxford: Oxford University Press.

Flude, M. and Hammer, M. (eds.) (1990). *The Education Reform Act 1988: Its Origins and Implications*. London: Falmer Press.

Flynn, R. (1999). 'Managerialism, Professionalism and Quasi-Markets', in M. Exworthy and S. Halford (eds.), *Professionals and the New Managerialism in the Public Sector*. Buckingham, UK: Open University Press.

—— (2000).'Soft Bureaucracy, Governmentality and Clinical Governance: Theoretical Approaches to Emergent Policy', Unpublished paper given to ESRC Seminar Series on Governing Medicine, Bradford, November.

Foucault, M. (1991). 'Governmentality', in C. Gordon and P. Miller (eds.), *The Foucault Effect: Studies in Governmentality*. London: Harvester Wheatsheaf, pp. 87–104.

Frank, T. (2000). *One Market Under God: Extreme Capitalism, Market Populism and the End of Economic Democracy*. New York: Secker & Warburg.

Freidson, E. (1988). *Professional Powers: A Study of the Institutionalization of Formal Knowledge*. Chicago, IL: University of Chicago Press.

—— (1994). *Professionalism Reborn: Theory, Prophecy and Policy*. Cambridge: Polity Press.

—— (2001). *Professionalism: The Third Logic*. Cambridge: Polity Press.

French, N. J., Massy, W. F., and Young, K. (2001). 'Research Assessment in Hong Kong', *Higher Education*, 42(1): 35–46.

Fuller, S. (2002). *Knowledge Management Foundations*. London: Butterworth Heinemann.

Fulton, O. (1996). 'Which Academic Profession Are You in?', in R. Cuthbert (ed.), *Working in Higher Education*. Buckingham, UK: Society for Research into Higher Education & Open University Press, pp. 157–69.

—— and Holland, C. (2001). 'Academic Staff in the United Kingdom', in J. Enders (ed.), *Employment and Working Conditions of Academic Staff in Europe*. Frankfurt am Main: Gewerkschaft Erziehung und Wissenschaft.

Gane, M. and Johnson, T. (eds.) (1993). *Foucault's New Domains*.

Gani, D. (2002). 'Research Assessments That Go with the Grain', Chartered Institute of Management Accountants Lecture, 26 September, University of Edinburgh Business School.

Gewirtz, S., Ball, S., and Bowe, R. (1995). *Markets, Choice and Equity in Education*. Buckingham, UK: Open University Press.

Gibbons, M. (1998). 'A Commonwealth Perspective on the Globalisation of Higher Education', in P. Scott (ed.), *The Globalisation of Higher Education*. Buckingham, UK: Open University Press, pp. 70–87.

_____ Limgoges, C., Nowotny, H., Schwartzman, S., et al. (1994). *The New Production of Knowledge: The Dynamics of Science and Research in Contemporary Societies*. London: Sage.

Gibbs, G. (1992). *Improving the Quality of Student Learning*. Bristol, UK: Technical and Education Services Ltd.

Giddens, A. (1991). *Modernity and self identity*. Cambridge: Polity Press.

_____ (1992). *The Transformation of Intimacy*. Cambridge: Polity Press.

_____ (1998). *The Third Way. The Renewal of Social Democracy*. Cambridge: Polity Press.

_____ (2000). *The Third Way and Its Critics*. Cambridge: Polity Press.

Goddard, A. (2002a). 'Justify Huge v-c Pay Rises', *The Times Higher Education Supplement*, London, 15 March.

_____ (2002b). 'Research to be Cut, Newby Says', *The Times Higher Education Supplement*, London, 28 June.

_____ (2002c). 'Union Fury as v-c Pay hits £309k', *The Times Higher Education Supplement*, London, 8 February.

_____ (2003). '£750,00 Wage Rise for Those at the Top', *The Times Higher Education Supplement*, London, 7 February: 8–9.

_____ (2004). 'Unions Cry Foul Over Hike in v-cs' Pay', *The Times Higher Education Supplement*, London, 20 February.

_____ (2005). 'Female Heads Big Winners in Pay Stakes', *The Times Higher Education Supplement*, 25 February.

Government, H. M. S. (2001). 'Special Educational Needs and Disability Act', Retrieved October 2004 from http://www.hmso.gov.uk/acts/acts2001/20010010.htm

Great Britain: Chancellor of the Duchy of Lancaster (1993). *Realising Our Potential: A Strategy for Science, Engineering and Technology: A Government White Paper*. London: HMSO.

Grey, C. (1999). 'We Are All Managers Now: We Always Were: On the Emergence and Demise of Management', *Journal of Management Studies*, 36(5).

Gronn, P. (2000). 'Distributed Properties: A New Architecture for Leadership', *Educational Management and Administration*, 28: 317–38.

Gronn, P. C. (2002). 'Distributed Leadership as a Unit of Analysis', *Leadership Quarterly*, 13(4): 423–51.

_____ and Hamilton, A. (2004). 'A Bit More Life in the Leadership: Co-Principalship as Distributed Leadership Practice', *Leadership and Policy in Schools*, 3(1): 3–35.

Habermas, J. (1989). *The Structural Transformation of the Public Sphere: An Inquiry into a Category of Bourgeois Society*. Cambridge: Polity Press.

Halsey, A. H. (1992). *Decline of Donnish Dominion: The British Academic Professions in the Twentieth Century*. Oxford: Clarendon Press.

Hammersley, M. (2000). *Taking Sides in Social Research: Essays on Partisanship and Bias*. London: Routledge.

—— (2002). *Educational Research: Policy Making and Practice*. London: Paul Chapman.

Hancock, N. and Hellawell, D. (2003). 'Academic Middle Management in Higher Education: A Game of Hide and Seek?', *Journal of Higher Education Policy and Management*, 25(1): 5–12.

Hannan, A. and Silver, H. (2000). *Innovating in Higher Education*. Buckingham, UK: Open University Press.

—— —— (2004). 'Enquiry into the Nature of External Examining', from http://www.heacademy.ac.uk/resources.asp?process=full_record&section=generic&id=376

—— —— (2006). 'On Being an External Examiner', *Studies in Higher Education*, 31(1): 57–70.

Harley, S. (2002). 'The Impact of Research Selectivity on Academic Work and Identity in UK Universities', *Studies in Higher Education*, 27(2): 187–206.

—— (2003). 'Research Selectivity and Female Academics in UK Universities: from Gentleman's Club and Barrack Yard to Smart Macho', *Gender & Education*, 15(4): 377–92.

—— and Lee, F. S. (1997). 'Research Selectivity, Managerialism and the Academic Labour Process: The Future of Non-Mainstream Economics in UK Universities', *Human Relations*, 50(11): 1427–60.

—— and Lowe, P. (1998). 'Academics Divided: The Research Assessment Exercise and the Academic Labour Process', Leicester, Occasional paper 48, Leicester Business School, De Montfort University.

Harman, G. and Harman, K. (2003). 'Institutional Mergers in Higher Education: Lessons from International Experience', *Tertiary Education and Management*, 9(1): 29–44.

Harris, P., Thiele, B., and Currie, J. (1998). 'Success, Gender and Academic Voices. Consuming Passion or Selling the Soul', *Gender and Education*, 10(2): 133–62.

Harvey, D. (1990). *The Condition of Post Modernity*. Oxford: Blackwells.

—— (2003). *The New Imperialism*. Oxford: Oxford University Press.

Harvey, L. (2005). 'A History and Critique of Quality Evaluation in the UK', *Quality Assurance in Education*, 13(4): 263–76.

Hattie, J. and Marsh, H. W. (1996). 'The Relationship between Research and Teaching: A Meta-Analysis', *Review of Educational Research*, 66: 507–42.

Henkel, M. (1997). 'Academic Values and the University as Corporate Enterprise', *Higher Education Quarterly*, 51(2): 134–43.

—— (2000). *Academic Identities and Policy Change in Higher Education*. London: Jessica Kingsley.

Her Majesty's Government (2002). 'Amendment to the Race Relations Act 2002 (Public Bodies)', Retrieved October 2002 from http://www.cre.gov.uk/duty/index.html

Her Majesty's Government (2004). 'Higher Education Act', Retrieved October 2004 from http://www.legislation.hmso.gov.uk/acts/acts2004/20040008.htm

Hey, V. (2000).'The Construction of Academic Time: Subcontracting Academic Labour in Research', Unpublished paper presented to British Sociological Association 'Making Time, Marking Time', University of York.

—— (2001). 'The Construction of Academic Time', *Journal of Education Policy*, 16(1): 67–84.

Higher Education Funding Council (2005). 'National Student Survey', from http://www.hefce.ac.uk/learning/nss/

Higher Education Funding Council for England (2005). 'Centres for Excellence in Teaching and Learning', from http://www.hefce.ac.uk/learning/tinits/cetl/final/brochure.pdf

Higher Educational Statistical Agency (2006). 'Summary of Academic Staff (Excluding Atypical) in all UK Institutions 2004/05', from http://www.hesa.ac.uk/holisdocs/pubinfo/staff/staff0405.htm

Hill, P. (2004). 'Women Crack Glass Ceiling', Retrieved September 2004 from http://www.thes.co.uk/search/story.aspx?story_id = 2014001

Hinings, C. R. and Greenwood, R. (1988). *The Dynamics of Strategic Change*. Oxford: Basil Blackwell.

Hockey, J. (2003). 'Art and Design Practice-Based Research Degree Supervision: Some Empirical Findings', *Arts and Humanities in Higher Education*, 2(2): 173–85.

Hoggett, P. (1996). 'New Modes of Control in the Public Service', *Public Administration*, 74: 9–32.

—— (2005). 'A Service to the Public: The Containment of Ethical and Moral Conflicts by Public Bureaucracies', in P. Du Gay (ed.), *The Values of Bureaucracy*. Oxford: Oxford University Press, pp. 165–90.

Hood, C. (1991). 'A Public Management for All Seasons', *Public Administration*, 69 (spring): 3–19.

—— (1995). 'Contemporary Public Management: A New Global Paradigm?', *Public Policy and Administration*, 10(2): 104–17.

—— (1998). *The Art of the State: Culture, Rhetoric, and Public Management*. Oxford: Oxford University Press.

Horlick-Jones, T. (2004). 'Experts in Risk? Do they Exist?', *Health Risk and Society*, 6 (2): 107–11.

—— and Sime, J. (2004). 'Living on the Border: Knowledge, Risk and Transdisciplinarity', *Futures*, 36: 441–56.

House of Commons Select Committee on Public Administration (2002). 'Seventh Report (on Public Service Values)', Retrieved September 2003 from http://www.parliament.the-stationery-office.co.uk/pa/cm200102/cmselect/cmpubadm/263/26302.htm

Howard, M. and Tibballs, S. (2003). 'Talking Inequality: What Men and Women Think about Equality in Britain Today', Manchester, The Future Foundation for the Equal Opportunities Commission.

Huisman, J., de Boer, H., and Goedegebuure, L. (2005). 'New Public Management at Dutch Universities. A Clash of Cultures or Peaceful Practice?', Unpublished paper presented at the Society for Research into Higher Education Annual Conference, University of Edinburgh, UK, 13–15 December.

Husbands, C. T. (1998). 'Job Flexibility and Variations in the Performance and Motivations of Longer Term Part-Time Teaching Auxiliaries at the London School of Economics and Political Science', *Work, Employment and Society*, 12(1): 121–44.

____ and Davies, A. (1997). 'Postgraduate Students Who Teach; their Employment Roles as Teaching Assistants, Demonstrators, Contract Workers, Journeypersons in British Higher Education', Society for Research in Higher Education, University of Warwick, Unpublished paper.

Jacques, M. (2002). 'The Age of Selfishness', *Guardian*, 24 October, London.

Jarrar, Y. and Mohamed, Z. (2001). *Becoming World Class Through a Culture of Measurement*. Bradford, UK: Bradford University Management Centre.

Jarratt, A. (1985). *Report of the Steering Committee for Efficiency Studies in Universities*. London: Committee of Vice Chancellors and Principals.

Jary, D. and Parker, M. (1998). *The New Higher Education: Issues and Directions for the Post-Dearing University*. Stoke on Trent: University of Staffordshire.

Jenkins, A. (2005). 'Guide to the Research Evidence on Teaching-Research Relations', Retrieved November 2005 from http://www.heacademy.ac.uk/resources.asp?process=full_record&section=generic&id=383

Jessop, B. (2002). *The Future of the Capitalist State*. Cambridge: Polity Press.

Johnson, R. (2002). 'The Meaning of Collegiality When in Tension with Managerialism: The Value Basis of University Work and Organisation', in G. Fowler (ed.), *Academic Performance*. London: Edwin Mellor Press.

____ and Deem, R. (2003). 'Talking of Students: Tensions and Contradictions for the Manager-Academic and the University in Contemporary Higher Education', *Higher Education*, 46(3): 289–314.

Joint Negotiating Committee for Higher Education Staff (2003). 'The Framework Agreement', from http://www.ucea.ac.uk/framework_agreement.html

Kean, L. and Scase, R. (1998). *Local Government Management: The Rhetoric and Reality of Change*. Buckingham, UK: Open University Press.

Keating, M. (2001). 'Devolution and Public Policy in the United Kingdom. Divergence or Convergence?', Retrieved 3 March from http://www.devolution.ac.uk/Keating_paper2.htm

Kehm, B., Lanzendorf, U., and Gerlof, K. (2005).'Changes in the Governance of Public Research in Germany', Unpublished paper presented at an Expert Workshop on 'Changes in the Governance Regime of Public Sector Research. The Examples of Austria, Germany, the Netherlands and the United Kingdom', 21–22 January, Centre for Research on Higher Education and Work, University of Kassel University, Germany.

Kekaele, J. (1999). "Preferred" Patterns of Academic Leadership in Different Disciplinary (sub)Cultures', *Higher Education*, 37(3): 217–38.

Kickert, R. (1995). 'Steering at a Distance: A New Paradigm of Public Governance in Dutch Higher Education', *Governance: An International Journal of Policy and Administration*, 8(1): 135–57.

King, R. (ed.) (2004). *Universities into the 21st Century: The University in the Global Age*. Basingstoke, UK: Palgrave.

Kirkpatrick, I. and Ackroyd, S. (2003). 'Archetype Theory and the Changing Professional Organization: A Critique and Alternative', *Organization*, 10(4): 731–50.

_____ Ackroyd, S., and Walker, R. (2005). *The New Managerialism and Public Service*. Basingstoke, UK: Palgrave.

Kitchener, M. (1999). 'All Fur Coat and No Knickers: Contemporary Organizational Change in UK Hospitals', in D. Brock, M. Powell, and C. R. Hinings (eds.), *Restructuring the Professional Organization*. London: Routledge, pp. 183–99.

_____ (2002). 'Mobilizing the Logic of Managerialism in Professional Fields: The Case of Academic Health Centre Mergers', *Organization Studies*, 23(3): 369–420.

_____ Kirkpatrick, I., and Whipp, R. (2000). 'Supervising Professional Work Under New Public Management: Evidence from an "Invisible Trade"', *British Journal of Management*, 11(3): 213–26.

Knight, P. and Trowler, P. R. (2001). *Departmental Leadership in Higher Education*. Buckingham, UK: Open University Press.

Knights, D. and Richards, W. (2003). 'Sex Discrimination in UK Academia', *Gender, Work and Organisation*, 10(2): 213–38.

Kogan, M. and Hanney, S. (2000). *Reforming Higher Education*. London: Jessica Kingsley.

Korten, D. (1995). *When Corporations Rule the World*. London: Earthscan.

Kwiek, M. (2003). 'The Social Functions of the University in the Context of the Changing State/Market Relations', in J. de Groofe and G. Lauwers (eds.), *Globalisation and Competition in Higher Education*. Antwerp: Wolf Legal.

_____ (2004). 'The Emergent Educational Policies Under Scrutiny. The Bologna Process from a Central European Perspective', *European Educational Research Journal*, 3(4).

_____ (2005). 'The University and the State in a Global Age: Renegotiating the Traditional Social Contract?', *European Educational Research Journal*, 4(4): 324–42.

_____ (2006*a*). *The University and the State*. Peter Lang.

_____ (2006*b*). 'Welfare State in Transition: Changing Public Services in a Wider Context', 'Interrogating the "Global" and the "Local" in Higher Education' Seminar in the Geographies of Knowledge, Geometries of Power: Higher Education in the 21st Century Economic and Social Research Council funded seminar series, Unpublished paper presented at Gregynog, University of Wales, 18 January.

Laffin, M. (1998). *Beyond Bureaucracy: The Professions in the Contemporary Public Sector*. Aldershot, UK: Ashgate.

Lambert Committee on Business-University Collaboration (2003). 'Lambert Review of Business-University Collaboration', Retrieved April from http://www.hm-treasury.gov.uk/consultations_and_legislation/lambert/consult_lambert_index.cfm

Lane, C. and Bachmann, R. (1998). *Trust Within and Between Organisations*. Oxford: Oxford University Press.

Lanzendorf, U. and Dellwing, M. (2005). 'Changes in Public Research Governance in Austria', Unpublished paper presented at an Expert Workshop on 'Changes in the Governance Regime of Public Sector Research. The Examples of Austria, Germany, The Netherlands and the United Kingdom' 21–22 January, Centre for Research on Higher Education and Work, University of Kassel, Germany.

Larson, M. S. (1977). *The Rise of Professionalism: A Sociological Analysis*. Berkeley, CA: University of California Press.

_____ (1990). 'In the Matter of Experts and Professionals', in M. Burrage and R. Torstendahl (eds.), *The Formation of Professions*. London: Sage, pp. 24–50.

Lauwerys, J. (2002). 'The Future of the Profession of University Administration and Management', *Perspectives*, 6(4): 93–7.

Lave, J. and Wenger, E. (1991). *Situated Learning: Legitimate Peripheral Participation*. New York: Cambridge University Press.

Layer, G. (2005). *Closing the Equity Gap: The Impact of Widening Participation Strategies in the UK and USA*. Leicester, UK: National Institute of Adult Continuing Education.

Leadbeater, C. (2003). *Personalisation through Participation*. London: Demos.

Leon, P. (2002). Is Prodigy Finally Ready to Prosper?, *The Times Higher*, 16 August, London: 7.

Levay, C. and Waks, C. (2005). 'Professions and the Pursuit of Transparency: Two Cases of Professional Response', Unpublished paper presented at the 4th International Critical Management Studies Conference, July, Cambridge.

Levidow, L. (2002). 'Marketizing Higher Education: Neoliberal Strategies and Counter-Strategies', *The Commoner*, Retrieved January from http://www.thecommoner.org

Lindsay, R., Breen, R., and Jenkins, A. (2002). 'Academic Research and Teaching Quality: The Views of Undergraduate and Postgraduate Students', *Studies in Higher Education*, 27(3): 309–28.

Liu, N. C. and Cheng, Y. (2005). 'Academic Ranking of World Universities—Methodologies and Problems', *Higher Education in Europe*, 30(2): 127–36.

Livingstone, H. (1974). *The University: An Organizational Analysis*. Glasgow, UK: Blackie.

Llewellyn, S. (2001). 'The Two-Way Windows: Clinicians as Medical Managers', *Organization Studies*, 22(4): 593–624.

_____ and Northcott, D. (2002). 'The Average Hospital', Unpublished paper presented to the European Group for Organization Studies Conference, Barcelona, July.

Lucas, L. (2001). 'The Research Game: A Sociological Study of Academic Research work in Two Universities Dept of Sociology', Unpublished Ph.D. Thesis, University of Warwick.

—— (2006). *The Research Game in Academic Life*. Maidenhead, UK: Open University Press & the Society for Research into Higher Education.

Lund University Libraries (2006). 'Directory of Open Access Journals', from http://www.doaj.org/

Lyotard, J. F. (1984). *The Postmodern Condition: A Report on Knowledge*. Manchester, UK: Manchester University Press.

MacIntyre, A. (1981). *After Virtue: A Study in Moral Theory*. London: Duckworth.

McKay, S. (2003). 'Quantifying Quality: Can Quantitative Data ("Metrics") Explain the 2001 RAE Ratings for Social Policy and Administration?' *Social Policy and Administration*, 37(5): 444–67.

McKendrick, J. (2002). 'PFI in Scottish Schools: More Questions than Answers?', Unpublished paper given to the Chartered Institute of Management Accountants Public Sector seminar, 26–27 September, University of Edinburgh Business School.

McLaughlin, I. P., Badham, R. J., and Palmer, G. (2005). 'Cultures of Ambiguity: Emergence and Ambivalence in the Introduction of Normative Control', *Work, Employment and Society*, 19(1): 67–89.

McLaughlin, K., Osborne, S., and Ferlie, E. (eds.) (2002). *New Public Management: Current Trends and Future Prospects*. London: Routledge.

McNay, I. (1995). 'From the Collegial Academy to Corporate Enterprise; The Changing Cultures of Universities', in T. Schuller (ed.), *The Changing University*. Buckingham, UK: Open University, pp. 105–15.

—— (2003). 'Assessing the Assessment: An analysis of the UK Research Assessment Exercise, 2001, and Its Outcomes, with Special Reference to Research in Education', *Science and Public Policy*, 30(1): 47–54.

McNulty, T. and Ferlie, E. (2004). 'Process Transformation: Limitations to Radical Organizational Change within Public Service Organizations', *Organization Studies*, 25(8): 1389–412.

Maddox, B. (2002). *Rosalind Franklin: The Dark lady of DNA*. London: Harper-Collins.

Marginson, S. (2004).'Global Public Space and Global Marketplace: Rethinking the Public/Private Divide in Higher Education', Plenary address to the Society for Research in Higher Education Annual Conference, University of Bristol, 14–16 December.

—— and Considine, M. (2000). *Enterprise University in Australia. Governance, Strategy and Reinvention*. Cambridge: Cambridge University Press.

—— and Sawir, E. (2005). 'Interrogating Global Flows in Higher Education', *Globalisation, Societies and Education*, 3(3): 281–310.

Marquand, D. (2004). *Decline of the Public*. Cambridge: Polity Press.

Marsden, D. and French, S. (1998). *What a Performance—Performance Related Pay in the Public Services*. London: Centre for Economic Performance, London School of Economics.

Meadow Orlans, K. P. and Wallace, R. (eds.) (1994). *Gender and the Academic Experience—Berkeley Women Sociologists*. Lincoln, USA and London: University of Nebrasksa Press.

Meijers, J. and Nutgteren, B. (1997). *The Euopean University in 2010*. Utrecht, the Netherlands: Universiteit Utrecht.

Merisotis, J. and Sadlak, J. (2005). 'Higher Education Ranking: Evolution, Acceptance, and Dialogue', *Higher Education in Europe*, 30(2): 97–101.

Metcalf, H., Rolfe, H., Stevens, P., and Weale, M. (2005). 'Recruitment and Retention of Academic Staff in Higher Education', Retrieved August 2005 from http://www.niesr.ac.uk/pubs/searchdetail.php?PublicationID=645

Middlehurst, R. (1993). *Leading Academics*. Buckingham, UK: Open University Press.

Middlemass, K. (1979). *Politics in Industrial Society: The Experience of the British System Since 1911*. London: Andre Deutsch.

Miller, D. (2003). 'What Is Best Value?: Virtualism—The Larger Context?', Unpublished conference paper given at Oxford University, March.

——— (2005). 'What Is Best 'Value'? Bureaucracy, Virtualism and Local Governance', in P. Du Gay (ed.), *The Values of Bureaucracy*. Oxford: Oxford University Press, pp. 233–54.

Mintzberg, H. (1979). *The Structuring of Organisations*. Engelwood Cliffs, NJ: Prentice-Hall.

——— (1983). *Structures in Fives*. London: Prentice-Hall.

Misztal, B. T. (1996). *Trust in Modern Societies*. Cambridge: Cambridge University Press.

Modood, T. and Acland, T. (1996). 'Race Equality Staffing Policies in Higher Education: Conclusion', Race and Higher Education Conference, Southampton, London: Policy Studies Institute.

Mok, K.-h. (2000a). 'Marketising Higher Education in Post-Mao China', *International Journal of Educational Development*, 20(1): 109–26.

——— (2000b). 'Reflecting Globalisation Effects on Local Policy: Higher Education Reform in Taiwan', *Journal of Education Policy*, 15(6): 637–60.

——— (2005a). '*Globalisation and Changing Higher Education Governance in East Asia*', Unpublished paper presented to a Culture, Learning and Identity in Organisations seminar, Graduate School of Education, University of Bristol.

——— (2005b). 'The Quest for World Class University: Quality Assurance and International Benchmarking', *Quality Assurance in Education*, 13(4): 277–304.

——— (2005c). 'Globalization and Educational Restructuring: University Merging and Changing Governance in China', *Higher Education*, 50(1): 57–88.

——— and James, R. (eds.) (2005). *Globalisation and Higher Education in East Asia*. New York and Singapore: Marshall Cavendish Academic.

217

Moodie, G. C. and Eustace, R. (1974). *Power and Authority in British Universities*. London: Allen & Unwin.

Mooney, G. and Poole, L. (2004). 'A Land of Milk and Honey? Social Policy in Scotland after Devolution', *Critical Social Policy*, 24(4): 458–83.

Morey, A. I. (2003). 'Major Trends Impacting Faculty Roles and Rewards: An International Perspective', *Society for Research in Higher Education International News*, (52): 2–5.

Morgan, L. (2001). 'Departmental Leadership in Higher Education', *Higher Education Quarterly*, 55(3): 343–8.

Morley, L. (1999). *Organising Feminisms: The Micropolitics of the Academy*. London: Macmillan.

—— (2003). *Quality and Power in Higher Education*. Buckingham, UK: Open University Press.

Moses, I. (1985). 'The Role of the Head of Department in Pursuit of Excellence', *Higher Education*, 14: 337–54.

—— (1990). 'Teaching, Research and Scholarship in Different Disciplines', *Higher Education*, 19: 351–75.

Musselin, C. and Becquet, V. (2005). 'Academic Work and Academic Identities: A Comparison of four Disciplines', Unpublished paper given to Consortium of Higher Education Researchers Conference, Jyväskyalä, Finland, 1–3 September.

Naidoo, R. (2003). 'Repositioning Higher Education as a Global Commodity: Opportunities and Challenges for Future Sociology of Education Work', *British Journal of Sociology of Education*, 24(2): 249–59.

—— and Jamieson, I. (2005). 'Empowering Participants or Corroding Learning? Towards a Research Agenda on the Impact of Student Consumerism in Higher Education', *Journal of Education Policy*, 20(3): 267–81.

National Committee of Inquiry into Higher Education (1997). 'Higher Education in the Learning Society', from http://www.leeds.ac.uk/educol/ncihe/

Newby, H. (2002). 'Developing a Strategic View of Higher Education Over the Next 10 Years', Keynote address by the Chief Executive of the Higher Education Funding Council for England, to the HEFCE Annual Conference at the University of Manchester Institute of Science and Technology', Retrieved 5 September 2002 from http://www.hefce.ac.uk/aboutus/thefuture/conf/

Newman, J. (2001). *Modernising Governance: New Labour, Policy and Society*. London: Sage.

—— (2002). 'Managerialism, Modernisation and Marginalisation', in E. Breitenbach, A. Brown, F. McKay, and W. J. Basingstoke (eds.), *The Changing Politics of Gender Equality in Britain*. Basingstoke, UK: Palgrave, pp. 102–23.

—— (2006). 'Going Public: People, Policy and Politics', from http://www.open.ac.uk/inaugural-lectures/p3_7.shtml

Newman, J. H. (1976). *The Idea of the University (Modern Edition)*. Oxford: Oxford University Press.

Newsome, C. G. (1997). 'What Does a Dean Do?: Identifying the Elements of Deanship Practice and Effectively Communicating with Different Audiences are Essential Ingredients in the Art of Successful Deaning', in M. J. Austin, F. L. Ahearn, and R. A. English (eds.), *The Professional School Dean: Meeting the Leadership Challenges*. Jossey-Bass Issue 98: 101–8.

Nunn, A. (2002). 'GATS, Higher Education and "Knowledge Based Restructuring" in the UK', *Education and Social Justice*, 4(1): 32–43.

Nyhan, R. (2000). 'Changing the Paradigm, Trust and its Role in Public Sector Organisations', *American Review of Public Administration*, 30(1): 87–109.

Ogbonna, E. and Harris, L. (2004). 'Work Intensification and Emotional Labour Among UK University Lecturers: An Exploratory Study', *Organization Studies*, 25(7): 1185–203.

Opinion (2006). 'Head for Business, Heart for Academe: What Makes a Good Vice-Chancellor?', *The Times Higher Education Supplement* (25 August): 14.

Osborne, D. and Gaebler, T. (1993). *Reinventing Government: How the Entrepreneurial Spirit is Transforming the Public Sector*. New York: Plume.

Palfreyman, D. and Warner, D. (2004). *Managing Crisis*. Maidenhead, UK: McGraw-Hill.

Pan, D. (1998). 'The Crisis of the Humanities and the End of the University', *Telos*, 111 (Spring): 69–106.

Parker, J. (2002). 'A New Disciplinarity: Communities of Knowledge, Learning and Practice', *Teaching in Higher Education*, 7(4): 373–86.

Parker, M. and Jary, D. (1994). 'The McUniversity: Organisation, Management and Academic Subjectivity', *Organization*, 2(2): 319–38.

Parry, G. (1999). 'Education Research and Policy Making in Higher Education: The Case of Dearing', *Journal of Education Policy*, 14(3): 225–41.

_____ (2001a). 'Reform of Higher Education in the United Kingdom', in B. Nolan (ed.), *Public Sector Reform: An International perspective*. Basingstoke, UK: Macmillan, pp. 117–32.

_____ (2001b). 'Academic Snakes and Vocational Ladders: The Philip Jones Memorial Lecture', Leicester', NIACE.

Patterson, G. (2000). 'Findings on Economies of Scale in Higher Education: Implications for Strategies of Merger and Alliance', *Tertiary Education and Management*, 6(4): 259–69.

Perkin, H. J. (1989). *The Rise of Professional Society: England Since 1880*. London: Routledge.

Peters, M. (2006). *Universities and Internationalization: Past, Present and Future*. Plenary address to University of Bristol Institute of Advanced Studies 'Ideas and Universities' Group One Day Conference on 'Universities and Internationalisation', Royal Fort House, University of Bristol.

Piper, D. W. (1994). *Are Professors Professional? The Organisation of University Examinations*. London: Jessica Kingsley.

Pollitt, C. (1993*a*). *Managerialism and the Public Services: Cuts or Cultural Change in the 1990s?* Oxford: Blackwell Business.

_____ (1993*b*). 'Running Hospitals', in R. Maidment and G. Thompson (eds.), *Managing the United Kingdom*. London: Sage.

_____ (2003). *The Essential Public Manager*. Buckingham, UK: Open University Press.

Pollitt, C. and Bouckaert, G. (2000). *Public Management Reform: A Comparative Analysis*. Oxford: Oxford University Press.

_____ Birchall, J., and Putman, K. (1998). *Decentralising Public Service Management*. Basingstoke, UK: London.

Pollitt, C. H. (1999). *Performance or Compliance?: Performance Audit and Public Management in Five Countries*. Oxford: Oxford University Press.

Pollock, A. M. (2004). *NHS PLC: The Privatisation of Our Health Care*. London: Verso.

_____ and Price, D. (2004). 'Public Risk for Private Gain', from http://www.ucl.ac.uk/spp/download/health_policy/B1428.pdf

_____ Shaoul, J., and Vickers, N. (2002). 'Why Public/Private Ownership Deals Are Bad for Your Health', Retrieved October 2004 from http://cpsu-spsf.asn.au/public_interest/0502/98.html

Power, M. (1997). *The Audit Society*. Oxford: Oxford University Press.

Pratt, J. (1997). *The Polytechnic Experiment 1965–1992*. Buckingham, UK: Open University.

Prichard, C. (2000). *Making Managers in Universities and Colleges*. Buckingham, UK: Open University Press.

_____ and Wilmott, H. (1997). 'Just how Managed Is the McUniversity?', *Organisation Studies*, 18(2): 287–316.

Quality Assurance Agency (2002). 'Subject Benchmarking', Retrieved October 2002 from http://www.qaa.ac.uk/crntwork/benchmark/index.htm

Quinn, J. (2004).'Working Class "Drop Out" from HE: Cultural Narratives and Local Contexts', Unpublished paper presented to the International Sociology of Education Conference Sociology and Sociology of Education: Making Connections for Future Directions, The Montague on the Gardens, London, 2–4 January.

Readings, B. (1996). *The University in Ruins*. Cambridge, MA: Harvard University Press.

Reay, D. (2000). ' "Dim Dross"; Marginalised Women both Inside and Outside the Academy', *Women's Studies International Forum*, 23(1): 13–22.

Reed, M. (1995). 'Managing Quality and Organisational Politics: TQM as a Governmental Technology', in I. Kirpatrick and M. Martinez-Lucio (eds.), *The Politics of Quality in the Public Sector*. London: Routledge, pp. 44–64.

_____ (1996). 'Expert Power and Control in Late Modernity: An Empirical Review and Theoretical Synthesis', *Organization Studies*, 17(4): 573–97.

_____ (2002*a*). 'New Managerialism and the Management of UK Universities', in M. Dewatripont, F. Thys-Clement, and L. Wilkin (eds.), *European Universities: Change or Convergence?* Bruxelles: Editions de L'Universities de Bruxelles, pp. 69–83.

_____ (2002*b*). 'New Managerialism, Professional Power and Organisational Governance In UK Universities: A Review and Assessment', in A. Amaral, G. A. Jones, and B. Karseth (eds.), *Governing Higher Education: National Perspectives on Institutional Governance*. Dordrecht, The Netherlands: Kluwer.

_____ (2004). 'Beyond the Iron Cage? Bureaucracy and Democracy in the Knowledge Economy and Society', in P. Du Gay (ed.), *Defending Bureaucracy*. Oxford: Oxford University Press.

_____ (2005). 'Reflections on the "Realist Turn" in Organization and Management Studies', *Journal of Management Studies*, 42(8): 1621–44.

Reed, M. and Anthony, P. (2003). 'Between an Ideological Rock and an Organizational Hard Place: NHS Management in the 1980's and 1990's, in T. Clarke and C. Pitelis (eds.), *The Political Economy of Privatization*. London: Routledge.

_____ and Deem, R. (2002). New Managerialism: The Manager-Academic and Technologies of Management in Universities—Looking Forward to Virtuality?, in K. Robins and F. Webster (eds.), *The Virtual University? Information, Markets and Managements*. Oxford: Oxford University Press, pp. 126–47.

Reed, M. I. (2001). 'Organization, Trust and Control: A Realist Analysis', *Organization Studies*, 22(2): 201–23.

Richards, D. and Smith, M. J. (2004). 'The Hybrid State: Labour's Response to the Challenge of Governance', in S. Ludlam and M. J. Smith (eds.), *Governing as New Labour*. Basingstoke, UK: Palgrave, pp. 106–25.

Riddell, S. and Tinklin, T. (2003). 'Disabled Students in Higher Education: Legislation, Teaching, Learning and Assessment', in M. Slowey and D. Watson (eds.), *Higher Education and the Lifecourse*. Buckingham, UK: Open University Press and Society for Research into Higher Education.

_____ _____ and Wilson, A. (2005). 'New Labour, Social Justice and Disabled Students in Higher Education', *British Educational Research Journal*, 31: 623–43.

Roberts, Sir G. (2003). 'The Roberts Report on the Future of the Research Assessment Exercise', Bristol, Higher Education Funding Council for England.

Robertson, S. L., Bonal, X., and Dale, R. (2002). 'GATS and the Education Service Industry: The Politics of Scale and Global Reterritorialization', *Comparative Education Review*, 46(4): 472–96.

Rose, N. (1999). *Powers of Freedom: Reframing Political Thought*. Cambridge: Cambridge University Press.

Rosenthal, M. M. (2002). 'Medical Professional Autonomy in an Era of Accountability and Regulation: Voices of Doctors Under Siege', in M. Dent and S. Whitehead (eds.), *Managing Professional Identities: Knowledge, Performativity and the 'New' Professional*. London: Routledge, pp. 61–80.

Rowland, S. (2000). *'Teaching and Research: A Marriage on the Rocks?'*, Paper presented at the European Conference on Educational Research, Edinburgh, 20–23rd September, http://www.leeds.ac.uk/educol/documents/00001622.htm

Rowley, G. (1997). 'Mergers in Higher Education: A Strategic Analysis', *Higher Education Quarterly*, 51(3): 251–63.

Rustin, M. (1994). 'Flexibility in Higher Education', in R. Burrows and B. Loader (eds.), *Towards a Post Fordist Welfare State*. London: Routledge.

Saint-Martin, D. (1998). 'The New Managerialism and the Policy Influence of Consultants in Government: An Historical-Institutionalist Analysis of Britain, Canada and France', *Governance: An International Journal of Policy and Administration*, 11(3): 319–56.

Sanders, C. (2006). '25% Wage Hike for v-cs', *The Times Higher Education Supplement*, 10 March, London.

Santiago, R., Carvalho, T., Amaral, A., and Meek, V. L. (2006). 'Changing Patterns in the Middle Management of Higher Education Institutions: The Case of Portugal', *Higher Education*, 52(2): 215–50.

Sastry, T. and Bekhradnia, B. (2006). Using Metrics to Allocate Research Funds. Oxford: Higher Education Policy Institute.

Sauve, P. (2002). 'Trade, Education and the GATS: What's In, What's Out, What's All the Fuss About?' *Higher Education Management and Policy*, 14(3): 47–76.

Scase, R. and Goffee, R. (1989). *Reluctant Managers: Their Work and Lifestyles*. London: Unwin Hyman.

Schuller, T. (1995). *The Changing University*. Buckingham, UK: Open University Press.

Scott, P. (1995). *The Meanings of Mass Higher Education*. Buckingham, UK: Open University Press.

—— (ed.) (1998). *The Globalisation of Higher Education*. Buckingham, UK: Open University Press.

—— (1999). 'The Post-Modern University?', in A. Smith and F. Webster (eds.), *Contested Visions of Higher Education in Society*. Buckingham, UK: Open University Press, pp. 36–47.

Scottish Executive (2003). 'A Framework for Higher Education in Scotland: Higher Education Review Phase 2', Retrieved August 2005 from http://www.scotland.gov.uk/library5/lifelong/herp2–00.asp

Scottish Executive (2004). 'The Competitiveness of HE in Scotland: phase 3', Retrieved August 2005 from http://www.scotland.gov.uk/Topics/Education/Higher-Education/16640/7807

Scottish Higher Education Funding Council & Scottish Executive Education Department (2002). 'Applied Educational Research: Joint Funding Scheme with the Scottish Executive Education Department, Circular letter HE/26/02'

Scottish Parliament (2005). 'Further and Higher Education (Scotland) Act', Retrieved August 2005 from http://www.scottish.parliament.uk/business/bills/pdfs/b26bs2.pd

Scottish Standing Committee (2007). 'National Committee of Enquiry into Higher Education (the Garrick Report)', Retrieved October 2006 from http://www.leeds.ac.uk/educol/ncihe/scottish.htm

Sennett, R. (1998). *The Corrosion of Character: The Personal Consequences of Work in the New Capitalism*. London & New York: W.W. Norton.

Sennett, R. (2002*a*). *The Fall of Public Man*. London: Penguin Press.

—— (2002*b*). 'The New Class Struggle', University of West of England Centre for Critical Theory: The Alternative Series Public Lectures, The Watershed, Harbourside, Bristol, 26 February.

—— (2006). *The Culture of the New Capitalism*. Yale, CT: Yale University Press.

Shah, S. and Brennan, J. (2000). 'Quality Assessment and Institutional Change: Experiences from 14 Countries', *Higher Education*, 40(3): 331–49.

Shanahan, P. and Gerber, R. (2004). 'Quality in University Student Administration: Stakeholder Conceptions', *Quality Assurance in Education*, 12(4): 166–74.

Shanghai Jiao Tong Institute of Higher Education (2006). 'Academic Ranking of World Universities 2006', Retrieved August 2006 from http://ed.sjtu.edu.cn/ranking.htm

Shattock, M. (1999). 'Governance and Management in Universities: The Way We Live Now', *Journal of Education Policy*, 14(3): 271–82.

—— (2003). *Managing Successful Universities*. Maidenhead, UK: Open University Press.

Shore, C. and Roberts, S. (1995). 'Higher Education and the Panopticon Paradigm: Quality Assurance as a Disciplinary Technology', *Higher Education Quarterly*, 27(3): 8–17.

—— and Wright, S. (1999). 'Audit Culture and Anthropology: Neo-Liberalism in British Higher Education', *The Journal of the Royal Anthropological Institute*, 5(4): 557–75.

Silver, H. (1996). 'External Examining in Higher Education—A Secret History', in R. Aldrich, (ed.), *In History and in Education*. London: Woburn Press, pp. 187–208.

Simmonds, J. (1976). 'Academic Leadership and Keeping Change Going: a Personal View', *Studies in Higher Education*, 1(2): 137–41.

Skodvin, O. J. (1999). 'Merger in Higher Education—Success or Failure?', *Tertiary Education and Management*, 5(1): 65–80.

Slaughter, S. and Leslie, G. (1997). *Academic Capitalism*. Baltimore, MD: Johns Hopkins University Press.

Smith, A. and Webster, F. (eds.) (1997). *The Postmodern University? Contested Visions of Higher Education in Society*. Buckingham, UK: Open University Press.

Smith, D., Scott, P., Bocock, J., and Bargh, C. (1999). 'Vice-Chancellors and Executive Leadership in UK Universities: New Roles and Relationships?', in M. Henkel and B. Little (eds.), *Changing Relationships Between Higher Education and the State*. London: Jessica Kingsley, pp. 280–306.

Smith, D. N. (1999). 'New Leaders at the Top? The Educational and Career Paths of UK University Vice-Chancellors (1960–1996)', *Higher Education Management*, 11: 113–35.

Smith, G. and May, D. (1993). 'The Artificial Debate between Rationalist and Incrementalist Models of Decision Making', in M. Hill (ed.), *The Policy Process: A Reader*. London: Harvester.

Smyth, J. (1995). *Academic Work*. Buckingham, UK: Open University Press.

Sporn, B. (1996). 'Managing University Culture: An Analysis of the Relationship between Institutional Culture and Management Approaches', *Higher Education*, 32: 41–61.

Startup, R. (1976). 'The Role of the Departmental Head', *Studies in Higher Education*, 1(2): 233–43.

Stothart, C. (2006). 'Top Cop Gets £20K More than Professor', *The Times Higher Education Supplement*, London, 12 May.

Strathern, M. (2000). *Audit Cultures: Anthropological Studies in Accountability, Ethics and the Academy*. London: Routledge.

Strebler, M. and O'Regan, S. (2005). 'Non-Disclosure and Hidden Discrimination in Higher Education', from http://www.hefce.ac.uk/pubs/rdreports/2005/rd09_05

Taggart, G. J. (2003). 'A Critical Review of the Role of the English Funding Body for Higher Education in the Relationship between the State and Higher Education in the Period 1945–2003', Unpublished EoD. Thesis, Graduate School of Education, Bristol, University of Bristol.

Tapper, T. and Salter, B. (1998). 'The Dearing Report and the Maintenance of Academic Standards: Towards a New Academic Corporatism', *Higher Education Quarterly*, 52(1): 22–34.

Taylor, P. (1999). *Making Sense of Academic Life: Academics, Universities and Change*. Buckingham, UK: Open University Press.

Teelken, C. and Braam, G. (2002). 'Guarding and Preserving the Autonomy of the Individual Professional. Performance Management in Higher Education Institutions in International Perspective,' Paper presented to the European Educational Research Association, Lisbon, Portugal, 11–14 September.

The Times Higher Education Supplement (2005). 'World University Rankings', Retrieved August from http://www.thes.co.uk/worldrankings/

Thomas, L. and Quinn, J. (2007). *First Generation Entry into Higher Education: An International Study*. Maidenhead, UK: Open University Press.

Thompson, A. and Baty, P. (2002). 'Union Fury Over PRP Push the times Higher', London, 13: 1 September.

Thompson, E. P. (1970). *Warwick University Ltd: Industry, Management and the Universities*. Harmondsworth, UK: Penguin Education.

Thompson, G. (2003). *Between Hiearchies and Markets: The Logic and Limits of Network Forms of Organization*. Oxford: Oxford University Press.

Thrift, N. (2005). *Knowing Capitalism*. London: Sage.

Tierney, W. G. (2005). 'Trust and Culture in Higher Education', Plenary Address Given to Consortium of Higher Education Researchers Annual Conference, Jyvaskala, Finland.

Times Higher Education Supplement (2004). 'Mind the Gap: Academic Salaries 2003–4 (Gender Comparison)', *The Times Higher Education Supplement* from http://www.thes.co.uk/statistics/academic_pay/salary_comparisons/mind_the_gap.aspx

Times Higher Education Supplement (2006). 'Vice Chancellor Pay 2004–5', from http://www.thes.co.uk/statistics/academic_pay/senior_academics/2004–2005.aspx?window_type = popup

Townley, B. (2002). 'Managing with Modernity', *Organisation*, 9(4): 549–73.

—— (2003). 'Foucault's Work and Weber's Rationalization Thesis, and the Relevance of these to Understanding Changes in the Management of the Public Sector', Unpublished paper presented to the ESRC Seminar Series: 'Reconfiguring the Sociology of Education: Boundaries, Themes and Theories: Seminar 3, "Sociology of Education and Management/Organisation Theory", University of Edinburgh, 9 May.

—— Cooper, D. J., and Oakes, L. (2002). 'Performance Measures and the Rationalization of Organizations', *Organization Studies*, 24(7): 1045–71.

Trow, M. (1993). *Managerialism and the Academic Profession: The Case of England*. Berkeley, CA, University of California.

—— (1994). 'Managerialism and the Academic Profession: the Case of England', *Higher Education Policy*, 7(2): 11–18.

—— (1997). 'More Trouble than it's Worth', *The Times Higher*, (24.10.97): 26.

—— (1998). 'Governance in the University of California: The Transformation of Politics into Administration', *Higher Education Policy*, 11(2/3): 201–16.

Trowler, P. (1998a). *Academics Responding to Change: New Education Frameworks and Academic Cultures*. Buckingham, UK: Open University Press.

—— (1998b). 'What Managerialists Forget: Higher Education Credit Frameworks and Managerialist Ideology', *International Studies in the Sociology of Education*, 8(1): 91–110.

—— (2001). *Higher Education Policy and Institutional Change*. Buckingham, UK: Open University Press.

Tysome, T. (2006). 'Women Find Their Way up the Ladder', *The Times Higher Educational Supplement*, London, 24 February.

UNESCO European Centre for Higher Education (1989). 'Magna Charta Universitatum Europaearum: Higher Education in Europe', *Quarterly Review of the UNESCO European Centre for Higher Education*, X1V(1).

Universities UK (2004). Patterns of Higher Education Institutions in the UK: Fourth Report. London: Universities UK.

Universities UK (2006). 'Higher Education in Facts and Figures', Retrieved October 2006 from http://bookshop.universitiesuk.ac.uk/downloads/Facts_2006.pdf

Universities UK and Standing Conference of Principals (2004). *Patterns of Higher Education Institutions in the UK: Fourth Report*. London: UUK, SCOP.

Van den Bosch, H. and Teelken, C. (2000). 'Organisation and Leadership in Higher Education. Learning from Experiences in the Netherlands', *Higher Education Policy*, 13(4): 379–97.

Veld, R. J. (1981). 'Survival During the Eighties', *International Journal of Institutional Management in Higher Education*, 5(2): 97–107.

Von Humboldt, W. (1976). 'University Reform in Germany: Reports and Documents', *Minerva*, 8: 242–50.

Von Tunzelmann, N. and Mbula, E. K. (2003). *Changes in Research Assessment Practices in other Countries Since 1999: Final Report*. Bristol, UK: Higher Education Funding Council for England.

Waine, B. (2000). 'Managing Performance Through Pay', in J. Clarke, S. Gewirtz, and E. McLaughlin (eds.), *New Managerialism, New Welfare*. London: Sage, pp. 236–49.

Walford, G. (1987). *Restructuring Universities: Politics and Power in the Management of Change*. Beckenham, UK: Croom Helm.

Walker, M. and Warhurst, C. (2000). 'In Most Classes you Sit Around Very Quietly at a Table and get Lectured at': Debates, Assessment and Student Learning', *Teaching in Higher Education*, 5(1): 33–49.

Wallace, M. and Pocklington, K. (2002). *Managing Complex Educational Change: Large-Scale Reorganisation of Schools*. London: Routledge.

Walsh, K. (1995). *Public Services and Market Mechanisms: Competition, Contracting and the New Public Management*. London: Macmillan.

Watson, D. (2000a). 'Fixed Term Staff', Retrieved March 2002 from http://www.aut.org.uk/campaigns/cascamp/hesastatistics98-9.html

Watson, D. (2000b). *Managing Strategy*. Buckingham, UK: Open University Press.

Watson, J. D. (1969). *The Double Helix: A Personal Account of the Discovery of the Structure of DNA*. New York: Mentor.

Webb, J. (1999). 'Work and the New Public Service Class', *Sociology*, 33(4): 747–66.

Weber, M. (1948). 'Science as a Vocation', in H. H. Gerth and C. W. Mills (eds.), *From Max Weber: Essays in Sociology*. London: Routledge & Kegan Paul, pp. 129–56.

Weingart, P. (2005). 'Impact of Bibliometrics Upon the Science System: Inadvertent Consequences?', *Scientometrics*, 62(1): 117–31.

Wenger, E. (1998). *Communities of Practice: Learning, Meaning and Identity*. Cambridge: Cambridge University Press.

Wenger, E., McDermott, R. A., and Snyder, W. (2002). *Cultivating Communities of Practice: A Guide to Managing Knowledge*. Boston, MA: Harvard Business School Press.

Wepner, S. B., Wilhite, S. C., and Onofrio, A. D. (2003). 'Understanding Four Dimensions of Leadership as Education Deans', *Action in Teacher Education*, 25(3): 13–23.

White, L. (1962). *Medieval Technology and Social Change*. Oxford: Clarendon Press.

Williamson, P. (1989). *Corporatism in Perspective: An Introductory Guide to Corporatist Theory*. London: Sage.

Wilson, L. (2004). *'Transformation in Higher Education: A European Perspective,'* Plenary Address to the Society for Research into Higher Education Annual Conference, University of Bristol, 14–16 December.

Winter, R. (1995). 'The University of Life plc: The "Industrialisation of Higher Education"', in J. Smyth (ed.), Academic work. Buckingham, UK: Open University Press, pp. 129–43.

Wisby, E. (2002). 'Subject Benchmarking as a New Mode of Regulating Teaching in Higher Education and its Implications for Academic Autonomy—Including a case Study of the Sociology Benchmarking Group', Unpublished Ph.D. Thesis, Division of Education, University of Sheffield, Sheffield, UK.

Wolf, A. (2002). *Does Education Matter?* London: Penguin Books.

Wolverton, M., Gmelch, W. H., Wolverton, M. L., and Sarros, J. C. (1999). 'Stress in Academic Leadership: U.S. and Australian Department Chairs/Heads', *Review of Higher Education*, 22(2). 165–86.

Wood, M. (2002). *'The Politics of Resource Allocation in UK Universities and the Case for the Introduction of Internal Markets'*, Unpublished paper presented at Chartered Institute of Management Accountants Public Sector Seminar, Edinburgh University, 26–27 September.

Woods, P. A., Bennett, N., Harvey, J., and Wise, C. (2004). 'Variabilities and Dualities in Distributed Leadership: Findings from a Systematic Literature Review', *Educational Management, Administration and Leadership*, 32: 439–57.

Index